SHELTER
FROM THE
STORM

SHELTER
FROM THE
STORM

HOW A COVID
MORTGAGE MELTDOWN
WAS AVERTED

MARK CALABRIA

Print ISBN: 978-1-952223-56-3
eBook ISBN: 978-1-952223-57-0

Cover design: Faceout Studio, Amanda Hudson
Imagery from Getty Images and Shutterstock.

Library of Congress Cataloging-in-Publication Data has been applied for.
Library of Congress Control Number: 2022950205

Printed in the United States of America.

CATO INSTITUTE
1000 Massachusetts Ave. NW
Washington, DC 20001
www.cato.org

Dedicated to
The staff of the Federal Housing Finance Agency,
America's financial first responders

And in memory of
Charlie, my ever-present furry pandemic companion

Contents

Abbreviations and Acronyms

APA	Administrative Procedure Act
CARES Act	Coronavirus Aid, Relief, and Economic Security Act
CBOE	Chicago Board Options Exchange
CDC	Centers for Disease Control and Prevention
CDS	credit default swap
CEA	Council of Economic Advisers
CEO	chief executive officer
CFPB	Consumer Financial Protection Bureau
CRT	credit risk transfer
DOJ	U.S. Department of Justice
EEOB	Eisenhower Executive Office Building
FDIC	Federal Deposit Insurance Corporation
FEMA	Federal Emergency Management Agency
FHA	Federal Housing Administration
FHFA	Federal Housing Finance Agency
FHLB	Federal Home Loan Bank System
FICO	Fair Isaac Corporation
FSOC	Financial Stability Oversight Council
GAO	U.S. Government Accountability Office
GFC	Great Financial Crisis

GSE	government-sponsored enterprise
HAMP	Home Affordable Modification Program
HARP	Home Affordable Refinance Program
HEARTH Act	Homeless Emergency Assistance and Rapid Transition to Housing Act
HUD	U.S. Department of Housing and Urban Development
LIBOR	London Interbank Offered Rate
MBA	Mortgage Bankers Association
MBS	mortgage-backed security
mREIT	mortgage real estate investment trust
MSR	mortgage servicing right
NAHB	National Association of Home Builders
NAR	National Association of Realtors
NEC	National Economic Council
NLIHC	National Low Income Housing Coalition
OCC	Office of the Comptroller of the Currency
OFHEO	Office of Federal Housing Enterprise Oversight
OGC	Office of General Counsel
OTS	Office of Thrift Supervision
P&I	principal and interest
REIT	real estate investment trust
Repo	repurchase
ROE	return on equity
SALT	state and local taxes
SEC	U.S. Securities and Exchange Commission
TARP	Troubled Assets Relief Program
TBA	to be announced
UI	unemployment insurance
VIX	volatility index
WHO	World Health Organization

Foreword

Wall Street bailouts have become de rigueur in Washington. The big bank bailouts during the 2008/2009 Great Financial Crisis (GFC) that once produced outrage are now rationalized as "saving the system" and "making money for the government," the favorite saws of the crony capitalist. Accommodative monetary policy and massive lending facilities have become standard responses to smooth market turbulence, and they protect Wall Street profits in times of stress. Regrettably, too many public officials have concluded that it's far easier to shower government money on powerful financial players than to tell them to stand on their own two feet, lest they face the wrath of industry lobbyists and their powerful friends in political and media circles. So, we should celebrate that rare public servant who is willing to take the heat and prioritize the interests of the public over the interests of richly paid financial smart guys who are supposed to be able to navigate difficult markets. One such individual is Mark Calabria, a well-regarded but little-known libertarian economist who, during the COVID-19 pandemic, headed a little-known but important financial regulator, the Federal Housing Finance Agency (FHFA).

In this book, Calabria recounts the harrowing and disruptive events inflicted on the housing market during the COVID-19 pandemic and the unseemly clamoring by some in the mortgage finance industry for help.

Early in the pandemic, it was obvious that millions of homeowners and renters would not be able to make their mortgage or rent payments given the massive loss of jobs and incomes stemming from government lockdowns. Calabria and the FHFA were at the center of the storm, responsible for oversight of mortgage giants Fannie Mae and Freddie Mac as well as the Federal Home Loan Bank system, all of which are central to the plumbing of our housing finance system. In coordination with Congress and the Department of Housing and Urban Development, they quickly put in place programs to give homeowners and tenants temporary relief from their mortgage and rental obligations. The programs they designed were standardized, broadly available, and simple to administer. This was in stark contrast to the complex, bureaucratic approach to homeowner relief during the GFC, when homeowners were overburdened with red tape and stingy relief programs that were more about protecting lenders and investors from losses than preserving home ownership. This time, the focus was on homeowners and renters, not the finance industry. And it worked.

Although the programs were hugely successful, they prompted predictable complaints from those parts of the mortgage industry that were going to lose revenue as a result of forbearance. Particularly vocal were firms called "mortgage servicers," whose job was to collect mortgage payments from homeowners and forward them to investors who had purchased security interests in those mortgages. Many of those servicers had knowingly undertaken legal commitments to advance payments out of their own pockets when homeowners stopped making them, a risk for which they had been compensated. Nonetheless, their industry trade groups brought relentless pressure on Calabria to support a government-backed lending facility to help them, arguing that Armageddon would ensue if he didn't. After thoughtfully assessing the data, Calabria said no, resisting substantial pressure from politicians, media, and even the Federal Reserve. He rightly judged that the industry was overestimating take-up rates for mortgage forbearance and felt the mortgage servicers had the cash resources to meet their obligations. He thought their real concern was that using their own money would be less profitable to them than using low-cost financing from the government. He called their bluff. There were no bailouts, and the system continued functioning just fine.

Calabria recounts many other instances in which he was pilloried for trying to protect the public and taxpayers. His proposal to dramatically strengthen capital requirements for Fannie Mae and Freddie Mac was met with fierce resistance, even though these multitrillion-dollar enterprises were basically insolvent when he assumed office, posing substantial risk for taxpayers. He was viciously attacked for trying to increase the fees Fannie and Freddie charge for guaranteeing mortgages to cover pandemic-related losses, even though the companies were in desperate need of capital and the fee was limited to refinances of higher-balance loans. He also provides important insights on the current state of housing finance and the unintended consequences of well-intentioned monetary policies that have grossly inflated housing values. With frightening clarity, he describes fragilities in the system that persist because of low capitalization levels at Fannie and Freddie and the lenders and servicers who generate the mortgages that Fannie and Freddie guarantee.

Calabria also discusses the virtues of government service and his successful efforts to revive morale at the FHFA when scandal forced its previous leader out of office. He credits many of the fine career staff members at the FHFA, as well as government-sponsored enterprise leadership, for their roles in protecting homeowners and tenants during the pandemic. Throughout the book, he shows himself to be a dedicated, thoughtful public servant, in defiance of those who typecast conservatives and libertarians as anti-government.

Unlike the many "bailout glorification" books published after the GFC that topped bestseller lists, Calabria's book will probably have a more limited audience. Too bad—it should be required reading for any aspiring public servant who wants to buck what Calabria calls the "rescue first, ask questions later" trend. As he writes in concluding this excellent book, "Bailouts-or-nothing is a false choice. We have compassionate, effective, and efficient options. . . . Let's hope these lessons are not forgotten next time."

—Sheila Bair
Former chair of the Board of Directors for
Fannie Mae and former chair of the
U.S. Federal Deposit Insurance Corporation

Introduction

COVID-19 was not only an unprecedented shock to our health care system, but also an unprecedented threat to our economic well-being, including our mortgage and housing markets. While the primary focus of the federal response was appropriately on the health care aspects of the pandemic, including efforts such as vaccine development under Operation Warp Speed, a critical aspect of the response to reduce the spread of COVID-19 was helping keep families in their homes.

Economists at Duke University have estimated that limiting evictions and foreclosures by facilitating "shelter in place" reduced COVID-19 infections by almost 4 percent and deaths by 11 percent.[1] And researchers at the Federal Reserve Bank of St. Louis have estimated that each percentage point increase in forbearance prevented a 3.5 percentage point increase in unemployment.[2] While one can and should always debate the accuracy of statistical estimates, the forbearance programs implemented in response to COVID-19 saved lives and jobs.

As then director of the Federal Housing Finance Agency (FHFA), which oversees Fannie Mae, Freddie Mac, and the Federal Home Loan Banks, I was responsible for leading a large portion of that response. This is the story of how millions of families were provided mortgage and rental assistance, both to keep them safe and to keep our financial

markets functioning, and it offers a peek behind the curtain of government decisionmaking in a crisis. It is also the story of how we did so
at little to no cost to the taxpayer and resisted regular calls for industry
bailouts and subsidies. The lesson here is that you can help Main Street
directly without having to bail out Wall Street.

The year 2020 began promisingly for our nation's housing market and
for families seeking to achieve the dream of homeownership. After peaking in 2005 at 69 percent, the percentage of families in America owning
their own home hit bottom in 2016 and then began a strong upward trend.
In fact, 2019 turned out to be one of the best years for housing in decades,
seeing the addition of over 2 million new homeowners. Of course, 2020
ended up being full of surprises, not just for the housing market.

While the benefits of homeownership—especially financial ones—are
often oversold and exaggerated, there is something special about owning
your own roof, something deep and central to the very notion of America.
While Napoleon might have seen the English as a "nation of shopkeepers,"
he might well have called America a "nation of homeowners." That was
the case heading into COVID-19. Prices, sales volume, and homeowner
equity were all increasing when COVID-19 hit. Much of this strength,
of course, was due to the strong underlying economy, particularly the job
market. Had COVID-19 struck in, say, 2008 or 2011, the impact on our
housing and financial markets would have been significantly worse.

———

What turned a housing slump into a financial crisis in 2008 was the
long march toward greater financialization of our mortgage market. It
was far from the first housing slump in American history. The Savings
and Loan Crisis of the 1980s was driven partly by declines in the housing
markets of New England and Texas. But there also had been housing
busts in the 1970s, 1950s, and of course during the Great Depression of
the 1930s. Most of these, however, did not result in large shocks to our
financial markets.

What made 2008, and a few precious days in 2020, especially fragile
were the deep connections between our housing markets and Wall Street.
Unfortunately, those interconnections had strengthened by 2020, with the

result being unprecedented interventions in the mortgage market by both the FHFA and the Federal Reserve.

———

As a front-row observer of the 2008 mortgage crisis, I am strongly convinced that much of the federal response was poorly structured, especially the mortgage assistance initiatives, the Home Affordable Modification Program (HAMP) and the Home Affordable Refinance Program (HARP). As will soon be evident, my decisionmaking was driven largely by the intention to not repeat the design flaws of HAMP and HARP. We would do it right, or at least better, this time.

One of the problems of the 2008 mortgage crisis, and one I hoped to avoid, was the "paper chase" associated with programs such as HAMP and HARP. Generally, for borrowers to be eligible for forbearance or other mortgage assistance, a substantial amount of paperwork was required. There were countless stories of documents being lost or rejected. In some instances, applications with false information were even being submitted by either the lender or the borrower. We also did not want to create disincentives for work in the design of our forbearance programs. Our relief efforts had to support a recovering job market, not hamper it.

The job market data also made it crystal clear that this was going to be mainly a renters' crisis. While we were able to modify existing homeowner forbearance programs quickly and cleanly, as the FHFA had considerable experience in this area from responding to natural disasters, we needed to create something for renters—and to do it fast.

Like other federal agencies, we spent most of the pandemic engaged in mandatory telework, operating from our kitchens, spare bedrooms, and patios. In fact, being an independent agency at the time, we were able to conduct an agency-wide telework exercise before the bulk of the federal government did. That allowed us to gauge our effectiveness and support needs.

I believe that one of the first things any leader must recognize is that it is others in the organization who implement the directives and orders that come down from above. Or, as I regularly quipped, "I don't do anything. I just direct others to." For me to be effective as a leader and for the FHFA to have an effective COVID-19 response, the agency's staff needed to be and feel supported. Not only were they working around the clock, but they were dealing with the same issues that families across the country and the world were facing: How to deal with children at home. How to share space with a spouse or roommates who are now also working from home. How to process grief and loss.

Leading a large organization during a pandemic would have been a challenge for anyone. Unfortunately, when I arrived, 11 months before COVID-19, the FHFA lacked direction and had deep-seated morale problems. While part of this resulted from the former permanent director's sexual harassment charges, which I had to address and settle immediately, there had also been questions as to whether the agency would even continue to exist. Various reform proposals for Fannie Mae and Freddie Mac contained different roles for its regulator. And despite clear statutory direction, the agency seemed in limbo from the decade-long conservatorships of Fannie Mae and Freddie Mac. When I walked through the doors of the FHFA, most of the staff neither respected nor trusted senior agency leadership, as various employee surveys illustrated. To fulfill the mission to protect the mortgage market, that needed to change. Before the FHFA could demonstrate its support for borrowers and renters, it first had to demonstrate its support for its own employees.

History is likely to record the federal COVID-19 response to the mortgage market as the Coronavirus Aid, Relief, and Economic Security (CARES) Act. The CARES Act put into statute basically what we at the FHFA had already established a few weeks earlier. Congress clearly believed that we were on the right track.

Perhaps as the result of implementing an honor system for borrowers, coupled with uncertainty surrounding the job market, a few commentators warned that mortgage forbearance rates could get as high as 40 or 50 percent. That could threaten the financial viability of many nonbank mortgage servicers. It was for this reason that many in the field, including the trade associations representing the mortgage industry, were calling for a government-backed lending facility to fund the liquidity needs of mortgage servicers.

Our foremost priority was to protect the safety of existing borrowers and renters. We always started from that premise. I had fully accepted that there might be instances where focusing on the health of families might pose significant problems for the functioning of the mortgage market. I also recognized that in a pandemic accompanied by massive job losses, many families might need to sell their homes while others would want to buy new ones that better accommodated remote work. COVID-19 was also a stark reminder that so much of the real estate and mortgage process has traditionally been face-to-face. Obviously, we would have to find a way to make the mortgage process a bit less personal.

———

As if responding to a pandemic was not enough, our mortgage finance system was deeply broken coming into COVID-19. When I started at the FHFA in April 2019, Fannie Mae and Freddie Mac were leveraged 1,000 to 1. The two companies had about $6 billion in equity behind about $6 trillion in risk. Any companies so highly leveraged would be certain to fail in a crisis. All it would take would be a strong wind to blow them over. Luckily, Treasury Secretary Steven Mnuchin and I reached an agreement in September 2019 that would allow the two companies to start building capital. Given the costs associated with COVID-19, had that agreement not been reached, Fannie and Freddie would have failed from their losses. Sadly, one does not get much credit in Washington for avoiding problems.

Having worked on getting the FHFA created while I was on the staff of the Senate Banking Committee, I was committed to seeing the agency become, as Sen. Richard Shelby of Alabama used to say, a "world-class regulator." Little did I know before taking the job how much further we had to go. Despite the FHFA being operational since 2008, several congressional directives, such as a risk-based capital rule, had not been completed at the time that I assumed leadership. Nor was the agency adequately and appropriately staffed. Getting Fannie and Freddie ready to leave conservatorship was our main task in fulfilling our congressional mandate. But to do so, we also needed to get the FHFA ready.

———

The universe, perhaps sensing that responding to a pandemic and turning around a troubled agency were not enough, decided to make the job even more interesting by having a group of Fannie and Freddie shareholders sue to end the independence of the FHFA. More specifically, they sought to make the director (me) of the FHFA removable by the president of the United States. In the summer of 2020, the Supreme Court agreed to hear what was then *Collins v. Mnuchin* (later to become *Collins v. Yellen*). Oral arguments would be heard on December 9, 2020, with a final decision released on June 23, 2021. With that, my time leading the FHFA would come to an end.

The refrain loudly heard during every crisis is that one must abandon one's principles. That message comes most prominently from industries seeking a bailout. I hope to demonstrate here that people can maintain their principles in a crisis—and that the outcomes can be the better for it. We could focus the rescue efforts on families and not simply hope that a Wall Street bailout would trickle down to Main Street. We could also structure the system in a manner that targeted assistance to those who needed it most. I hope here to lay out some lessons that can be applied to future financial crises. Fingers crossed.

Chapter 1
An American Dream

Las Vegas, Nevada, Thursday, January 23, 2020.

Something about the Philips smart lightstrips just fascinated me—the flexibility, maybe, of lights that bend. I would need that kind of flexibility in the days ahead. Or perhaps I am just easily distracted by shiny objects.

There are few experiences that so vividly display the uniqueness of America as the annual International Builders Show, organized by the National Association of Home Builders (NAHB). As director of the Federal Housing Finance Agency (FHFA), I was there that day at the Las Vegas Convention Center to deliver remarks on the state of our housing finance system. But first, I simply had to take a tour of the one million square feet of exhibits.

We Americans tend to like our homes big and equipped with the latest gadgets. As my own home in Washington was built in 1917, I can get a little envious of the amenities found in today's new homes—the temperature control systems, the latest lighting, the newest kitchen options. Just how many ways is it possible to, say, cook a chicken?

If the Kitchen Debate between Vice President Richard Nixon and Soviet First Secretary Nikita Khrushchev were held today, after walking through the builders' show I am convinced that America would still win hands down. Little did I know then that a pandemic would again test our economic system.

As I stared intently at a display smart lightstrip, meant to go underneath the overhang of kitchen counters, my chief of staff, John Roscoe, tapped my shoulder. As I turned, John leaned forward to say, "China has locked down Wuhan."

Only four days earlier, the World Health Organization (WHO) had announced that COVID-19 can be transmitted from person to person. And only two days after that announcement, the first U.S. case of COVID-19 had been confirmed in Washington State. Would a lockdown work? Could we avoid a global spread? It would be another week before the White House would announce travel restrictions between the United States and China

I had once been a China dove, hopeful that international engagement would reinforce and encourage a freer and more open society in China. While that optimism had already started to fade, two years of working on China issues for Vice President Mike Pence had made me even more skeptical of anything coming out of that country. Although I had long come to view reports from our intelligence agencies as tilted toward alarmism, what I had heard during those two years at the White House dramatically changed my views. Would China contain COVID-19? Would this be a repeat of SARS? And, most relevant for me, would our mortgage system be ready to withstand any stress?

China's heavy-handed, centralized government control approach would initially be widely applauded.[1] Ultimately, America's more decentralized approach, with states such as Florida forging their own path, would prove the better response. A similar debate would occur in response to the financial distress that resulted from lockdowns and the associated decline in our economy.

———

Behind every effective leader stands a great chief of staff. Or at least I attribute much of the FHFA's success in responding to COVID-19 to John Roscoe. I met John in February 2017. I had just started as chief economist for Vice President Pence. Roscoe worked in the White House Office of Presidential Personnel. He would supervise the vetting of nominations for independent regulators, including the financial regulators.

Having served in the George W. Bush administration and having handled nominations for the Senate Banking Committee, I deeply believed that personnel choices mattered. With Vice President Pence's blessing and direction, I threw myself into the work of recruiting and screening nominees for the Trump administration. Where Roscoe brought a great sense of people and politics, I brought some very strong thoughts on policy. Together, often with Andrew Olmem, who was deputy director of the White House National Economic Council (NEC), we worked to get the right people into the right positions.

How someone would respond to a crisis was at the top of my list of criteria. Vice President Pence had opposed the bank bailouts of 2008, as had I. We wanted competent, credible nominees. We also wanted financial regulators who would not default to rescuing Wall Street every time the markets hit a bump. That vetting process would ultimately determine how our financial regulatory system responded to COVID-19.

In the process of evaluating so many other individuals, John and I had managed to appraise each other. By the time I became FHFA director, both John and I instinctively knew that he would be coming to the FHFA as well.

———

Andrew Olmem was with us in spirit at the builders' show in Las Vegas. In the flesh, he was back in his West Wing office at the White House, where he was number two to director Larry Kudlow of the NEC. Andrew would serve as the daily point of contact for the FHFA and the other financial regulators, along with his primary deputy, Francis Brooke.

We had first met almost 20 years earlier, when Andrew joined the staff of the Senate Banking Committee. I had joined the Committee staff a few years earlier and had already begun working on our legislative efforts to fix the mortgage finance system. Unfortunately, those efforts were too late to avoid the 2008 financial crisis.

Andrew and I immediately bonded during those days on the committee. He had worked in the economics division of the Richmond Federal Reserve before law school as an assistant to economist Jeff Lacker, later to become president of the Richmond Fed. There were times when Andrew acted like a lawyer who thought he was an economist, and I acted like an economist who thought he was a lawyer. Fortunately, those efforts were complementary.

Since Andrew joined the NEC staff just a couple of weeks after I joined the vice president's office, he and I immediately had partners in the White House whom we knew and trusted. Washington, particularly the White House, can be an intimidating place if you do not have a trusted network. As importantly, Andrew's pragmatism was a helpful balance to my general push for purity. Having been through the 2008 crisis together, we had a common vision of the mistakes and missteps of that year. That history allowed the FHFA, even as an independent regulator, to work seamlessly with the White House.

———

Also joining me that day in Las Vegas was Dr. Ben Carson, then the secretary of the Department of Housing and Urban Development (HUD). I would be speaking after Dr. Carson. Considering his fame, I knew he would be a tough act to follow. Not only had he run for president, but he'd also had a groundbreaking career in neurosurgery, dramatized by his autobiography *Gifted Hands* (which was later made into a movie with Dr. Carson portrayed by Cuba Gooding Jr.).

It was a pleasure spending time with Dr. Carson, who was still celebrating the birth of a grandson the previous week. Despite his many honors and degrees, I have always sensed that the most important titles for Dr. Carson are "dad" and "granddad."

Having served as Vice President Pence's liaison to HUD, I had gotten to know Dr. Carson. The days ahead would bring us even closer together. When the White House would assemble a COVID-19 task force, Dr. Carson's presence would provide me with a source of regular updates to complement those from my existing contacts in the vice president's office.

One might not normally choose a physician for HUD secretary. Given the circumstances, it ended up being an inspired choice. Secretary Carson had begun his tenure focused on the adverse impact of lead paint on brain development in children living in public and assisted housing, a pressing issue because of the age of much of our nation's public housing.

With the uncertainties surrounding COVID-19, I found it reassuring to regularly hear the views of a physician. Dr. Carson's involvement also helped reinforce that we were responding primarily to a public health crisis and only secondarily to a financial one.

———

Our mortgage market tends to run in the background, like the operating system on your phone, drawing attention only when something goes wrong. It usually works so well that few ever notice, even when you might be in the market for a new mortgage. But the American mortgage market is one of the most critical, and largest, of our financial markets. It would also play a central role in the economic response to COVID-19, particularly during the financial stresses of March 2020.

In 2020, over $12 trillion in fixed-income securities—that is, debt with a set payment amount and schedule—was issued.[2] Normally, the largest portion of that is the U.S. Treasury market. And indeed, 2020 was a record year for Treasuries, with $3.89 trillion issued. Just edging that out, however, was the distribution of $3.99 trillion in mortgage-backed securities (MBS). Add another $1 trillion of unsecured debt supplied by Fannie and Freddie, and you get about 40 percent of all fixed-income debt issuance in 2020 being related directly to the mortgage market.

Usually the stock, or equities, markets tend to grab the financial headlines. But in 2020, total equity issuance amounted to $390 billion, or about 3 percent of the total fixed-income securities issued. Most of that issuance is also secondary offerings. Even though 2020 was the strongest year for initial public offerings since 2014, at $85 billion it was still small compared with the issuance of MBS.

In fairness, the amount of corporate equity distributed is usually quite small next to the total outstanding, which in the United States is about $65 trillion. About a third of that is traded on the New York Stock Exchange (NYSE), another third on the NASDAQ, and the remaining third on smaller exchanges or over the counter.

Whereas equity is perpetual, the $11 trillion MBS market in the United States is constantly maturing, paying off, or otherwise turning over. That can make it a greater financial stability concern than equities, which never need to be repaid.

In addition to a significant volume of new issuance relative to outstanding issues, the MBS market is subject to high levels of trading. On a typical day in 2020, almost $300 billion in MBS traded hands. Only the amount of daily trading in U.S. Treasuries is larger.

By comparison, in 2020 just under $180 billion in NYSE-listed shares traded hands on the average day. Another $200 billion in NASDAQ-listed shares traded hands on the average day in 2020.

Mortgage-backed securities are also foundational to the functioning of the repurchase (repo) market, which provides about $4 trillion in short-term funding to our financial markets.[3] Typically, repos are collateralized loans—that is, the loan is secured by the pledging of specific assets. While most repos are backed by U.S. Treasuries as collateral, about 10 percent are collateralized by MBS.[4] Accordingly, disruptions to the MBS market can lead to disruptions in the repo market.

American mortgage markets are unique in many ways. Foremost is the size of those markets. Few other countries have home lending levels approaching the size of the U.S. market. Most importantly, few other countries have so closely integrated their mortgage and capital markets. While it's an open question whether this interconnectedness might reduce funding costs in normal times, it leaves our financial markets, and hence our economy, extremely vulnerable to changes in our mortgage and housing markets.

Housing is not only a major part of our overall economy, but also a significant portion of a family's typical expenses, with shelter costs, such as a mortgage or rent, consuming about 15 percent of the average family's income.[5] For workers making less than $30,000, shelter costs, on average, consume over a third of their income.[6] These individuals often worked in retail and restaurants, the sectors that would be most affected by the COVID-19 shutdowns.

———

Economist Ed Leamer of UCLA once quipped, the "housing market is the business cycle."[7] On some level, that is certainly true. It had been a slow, often painful recovery for the housing market from the depths of the 2008 financial crisis.

After peaking in the second quarter of 2004 at 69 percent, America's homeownership rate continued a steep decline before hitting bottom in the summer of 2016 at 63 percent.[8] COVID-19 hit just as home-ownership had been improving, increasing to 65 percent by March 2020, on par with our long-run average. America had also managed to work off its excess inventory of empty homes, with the percentage of vacant single-family homes returning to its long-run average of just over 1 percent by March 2020. Housing had really started to stabilize after a difficult decade.

As with many social trends, the housing recovery from the Great Recession was felt differently across racial groups. After having peaked in the middle of 2004 at 49.7 percent, the black homeownership rate had been on a steady decline. By the time my predecessor was confirmed in 2014, it had declined to 43.5 percent. The black home-ownership rate would continue to slide despite an aggressive push to weaken mortgage underwriting standards in hopes of expanding mort-gage access.

By the time I walked in the door at the FHFA, the black homeown-ership rate had plunged to 40.6 percent. I knew the attempts to expand homeownership by weakening mortgage standards would only set families up for failure. I immediately reversed those misguided efforts. Hard experience had proven that sustainable homeownership depended on strong, sensible underwriting. Homeownership might also not be the right choice at any given time. During my White House service, I worked regularly to prevent the administration from setting a target homeownership rate, since such a strategy had led previous administra-tions badly astray.

After almost a year of strengthening mortgage quality—the FHFA had in fact cut in half the share of mortgages with three or more high-risk factors—the black homeownership rate had actually increased to 44 percent by March 2020. By summer 2020, it would hit 47 percent. We had massively reduced risk in the mortgage system, while seeing the largest annual increase in black homeownership ever recorded.

Less dramatic but similar patterns were witnessed in the Hispanic homeownership rate. After peaking in 2007 at 50 percent, the rate began a steady decline, until hitting bottom in 2015 at 44 percent. It stood at just over 46 percent when my tenure at the FHFA began. While exhibiting considerable jumps during COVID-19, the Hispanic homeownership rate settled at a percentage point higher when I left the FHFA in June 2021 than it had been when I had started a little more than two years earlier.

While our changes in mortgage policies were helping, a strong job market, particularly for low-income and minority workers, was turning around the housing market. Between January 2017 and September 2019, the black unemployment rate fell from 7.5 to 5.5 percent, the lowest on record. Similar declines in the Hispanic unemployment rate occurred, also setting a record low in September 2019.

Housing affordability was modestly helped by declining mortgage rates. Upon my arrival at the FHFA, the 30-year fixed rate stood at 4.12 percent. By September 2019, it had dropped to 3.49. It hovered around 3.6 percent until late January 2020.

A strong job market and sensible mortgage policies were finally delivering positive results for the U.S. housing market. By any standard, 2019 was the best year for housing in over a decade. And it was not accomplished with gimmicks or a policy-driven sugar high, but in a sustainable and careful manner.

Yes, my remarks in Las Vegas that day reflected a celebration of America's housing market. The progress was undeniable. But I also warned, "Today's strong economy is a reminder that the best housing policy is a jobs policy. But if you look under the hood of our housing and mortgage markets, there are reasons to believe the foundation is vulnerable."[9]

After describing our efforts to strengthen the mortgage system, I ended with what had become one of my favorite quotes: "As President Kennedy said, 'the time to repair the roof is when the sun is shining.' Now is the time for bold reforms because our economy and housing market are strong. This will not always be the case."[10]

Little did I know that as I was uttering those words before an audience of home builders, a virus was spreading and had reached America's shores.

———

During my second year of graduate school, I took a course in public finance, mostly because I was a fan of the professor. One of the assignments involved writing a paper on off-budget mechanisms to finance government. For some reason lost to a fading memory, I chose to write about government-sponsored enterprises (GSEs), such as Fannie Mae and Freddie Mac. I don't know where the paper is anymore—probably on a lost three-inch floppy disk. Oddly enough, the current deputy chief economist for Fannie Mae, Mark Palim, was sitting just a few seats away from me in that graduate course.

Whether destiny or not, my path since graduate school led me deeper and deeper into the world of mortgage finance and housing. Eventually it led me to the top of a federal agency overseeing a $7 trillion footprint. For a farm kid from the foothills of Appalachia in rural Virginia to rise to working in the White House and then leading the federal response to mortgage and housing disruptions during a pandemic is truly an American Dream.

Chapter 2

Nonbanked

Citibank, Wells Fargo, Bank of America, JPMorgan Chase—these are all household names. If you are like most Americans, you hold an account, if only a checking account, with one of these companies. You may even have a decades-long relationship with one of them. Despite their continued dominance of our financial markets, these banks have become increasingly less relevant in the mortgage market. More and more, the making (originating) and maintaining (servicing) of mortgages are being conducted by nonbank financial service companies with less familiar names, like Lakeview, PennyMac, Carrington, LoanDepot, or NewRez.

Perhaps you went to your bank to get a mortgage. Or maybe a fancy Super Bowl ad enticed you to get your mortgage with a nonbank lender. In the former case, the bank or credit union might keep the mortgage on its books. In the latter case, the nonbank lender almost always sells your mortgage to someone else, often Fannie Mae or Freddie Mac. But it does not always sell *all* of your mortgage. Many lenders retain the right to service your mortgage.

The company from which you received your mortgage is the originator. The originator can be a traditional lender, such as a bank or credit union. The originator can be a mortgage banker, who relies on short-term ("warehouse") money to fund your loan until it sells the loan to another entity, which may or may not be the ultimate investor.

Your originator can also be a mortgage broker, which arranges the terms of your loan, but the short-term funding, as well as the ultimate funding, of your mortgage will be performed by someone else.

Even if you have a mortgage, you may be forgiven for not knowing what exactly a servicer is or does. Most simply, the servicer is the entity that receives your monthly mortgage payments. In the old days, it was to whom you mailed your check. But now that is done mostly electronically. Once the servicer receives your payment, it forwards most of the payment to the ultimate investor while retaining some portion to pay your property taxes and make insurance payments.

The servicer also plays a critical role when something goes wrong with the loan, such as when a borrower can no longer pay. The servicer interfaces with the borrower, offering mitigation options such as forbearance or an arrangement of a short sale if the mortgage is no longer sustainable. In the unfortunate instance of a foreclosure, the servicer is also responsible for maintaining the property in good condition. Servicers perform a variety of recordkeeping and reporting obligations related to the mortgage as well. In a general way, the servicer is the entity that administers or manages your mortgage.

The Conference of State Bank Supervisors, a trade association representing the state bank regulators, estimated that within the United States there were 19,655 active nonbank mortgage companies, as of April 1, 2021.[1] About 80 percent of these are mortgage brokers, who do not make or fund the loans themselves. Most of the 4,978 federally insured banks, of which the Federal Deposit Insurance Corporation (FDIC) considers only 270 as specializing in mortgage lending, also originate mortgages.[2] The 5,068 federally insured credit unions also make mortgages, although only to their eligible members.[3]

———

To make the topic even more complex, originators can be servicers, and servicers can also be originators. But they do not have to be.[4]

Before the Savings and Loan Crisis of the 1980s, it was most common for the originator, servicer, and investor in mortgages to all be the same institution. While there has long been an active mortgage banking

industry—going back to at least the 1870s—in which loans were originated and then sold to investors such as life insurance companies, even
those mortgage bankers were both originator and servicer. They also did
not dominate the overall market, except in then frontier areas lacking
established deposit-taking banks.[5]

The 1980s collapse of the savings and loan industry is still being felt
in the mortgage market today. The disappearance of thousands of thrifts
opened the door for mortgage bankers to gain considerable market share.
This expansion of mortgage companies would not have been possible
had it not been for the willingness of Fannie Mae to massively increase
its buying of mortgages, taking the credit risk once borne by the savings
and loans. At the time, Fannie Mae operated mainly as a giant thrift,
taking mortgage risk directly onto its balance sheet. Unfortunately, this
tendency also resulted in the effective failure of Fannie Mae in 1981,
resulting in a government rescue. Some things never change.

The growth of nonbank mortgage lenders was also facilitated by the
development of automated underwriting, which was made easier by the
maturation of the three dominant credit bureaus, Equifax, Experian, and
TransUnion, as well as the introduction of the Fair Isaac Corporation
(FICO) score. Before these technology developments, the norm in mortgage lending was a by-hand underwriting, often requiring considerable
time and expertise. To some extent, the massive growth in the market
share of nonbank lenders was a result of the 1980s and 1990s revolution in
personal desktop computing. The technological and process limitations
of manual underwriting often meant that only the loans we would today
call "prime" credit were being made before the 1980s. Today, prime is
generally defined as a FICO or equivalent score of 680 or more (on a
scale of 300 to 850). Before the 1980s, borrowers who would now be
labeled "subprime" often did not get mortgages at all. Even government
programs, such as the Federal Housing Administration (FHA) mortgage insurance of the Department of Housing and Urban Development
(HUD), were limited to prime borrowers until the 1970s.

Some of the soon-to-be-removed constraints were legal. Without
the ability to price mortgages according to borrower risk, to maintain
profitability and hence a sustainable mortgage business, lenders limited

credit to the middle-to-upper band of borrowers. While this resulted in some cross-subsidies, they were believed to be minor and difficult to evaluate before the growth of automated underwriting.

A big change came in 1982 with the passage of the Alternative Mortgage Transaction Parity Act. This legislation helped introduce risk-based mortgage pricing, contributing to the later development of the subprime mortgage market.

Whereas the savings and loan crisis opened the door for nonbank mortgage lenders, the proliferation of subprime and Alt-A lending opened the floodgates.[6] The model during the early days of subprime, the late 1980s and 1990s, was one in which nonbank lenders, such as Household Financial, Beneficial, The Money Store, and Long Beach Mortgage, would originate and service loans that were packaged into private-label mortgage-backed securities (MBS), generally assembled (sponsored) by investment banks.

Whether it was concerns about reputation or regulatory scrutiny or just plain old risk management, commercial banks largely avoided subprime mortgages, except for FHA lending. The Russian default crisis in August 1998, along with the Federal Reserve–assisted rescue of hedge fund Long-Term Capital Management, resulted in temporary disruptions in the U.S. capital markets that caused several nonbank mortgage lenders to fail, as those lenders were highly dependent on the short-term money markets.

Of course, failure among nonbank mortgage companies can mean little more than declaring bankruptcy, walking away from your creditors, and then starting business all over again under a new name.

Our economy barely registered the failure of numerous nonbank mortgage lenders that resulted from Russia's default. The nonbank lenders that survived grew and expanded as the mortgage markets reached new heights in the early 2000s.

While mortgage servicing continued to be dominated by depositories in the 2000s, nonbanks made almost a third of mortgage originations, by dollar volume, in the boom year of 2006. According to a paper by Marshall Lux and Robert Greene for Harvard's Kennedy School, 15 of the 25 subprime mortgage lenders in 2006 were nonbanks, a significant shift from previous years.[7]

The dramatic increase in nonbank mortgage origination in the 2000s was facilitated by both investment banks, which would often pool the loans into securities, and Fannie Mae and Freddie Mac, which would end up as the largest purchasers of subprime MBS as well as significant buyers of individual subprime mortgages. Without the support of Wall Street, along with Fannie and Freddie, nonbanks would have remained a marginal player in the years leading up to the 2008 crisis.

Although nonbank lenders were a sizable minority of the market going into 2007, they constituted a large share of institutional failures. Their heavy dependence on short-term funding, particularly lines of credit from banks, left them vulnerable. The mismatch between the maturity of their assets and their overnight funding sources also left nonbanks highly exposed to interest rate movements. Starting in the summer of 2006, the yield curve inverted, leaving short-term rates often higher than long-term rates. The yield curve remained inverted for almost a year, resulting in significant losses to nonbanks.

According to FDIC estimates, the number of nonbank mortgage lenders declined by almost a third between 2005 and 2009, whereas the number of depository mortgage lenders decreased by only about 4 percent.[8] The market share of nonbanks in mortgage origination plunged. By 2008, nonbanks had almost completely left the business of servicing residential mortgages. Despite the dramatic shakeout of nonbanks during the 2008 financial crisis, their demise was short-lived. By 2012, the mortgage market began shifting away from banks and again toward their nonbank competitors.

———

Ironically, the widely touted National Mortgage Settlement in 2012 had the long-term effect of pushing banks away from mortgage servicing, leaving borrowers to be more likely serviced by nonbank servicers, who are subject to less oversight. In February 2012, the U.S. Department of Justice (DOJ) and HUD, along with 49 state attorneys general, announced a global agreement on mortgage servicing issues with Bank of America, Citibank, Wells Fargo, JPMorgan Chase, and Ally Bank.

The deal has been seen by some as the launching pad for then California attorney general Kamala Harris.[9] At the time, Harris claimed that as a result of the settlement, "California families will finally see substantial relief after experiencing so much pain from the mortgage crisis."[10] She further claimed that California families would receive $18 billion in relief.[11] The settlement also brought to national attention New York's aggressive state attorney general, Eric Schneiderman.[12]

The agreement included over 300 individual changes to servicing standards, intended to both improve the quality of mortgage servicing and bring greater uniformity.[13] The settlement also incorporated consumer relief and payments to state governments. While some, including me at the time,[14] questioned just how much real incremental assistance was being provided to borrowers, the more onerous servicing standards would remain.[15]

President Barack Obama called the settlement "landmark" and discussed the role that "robo-signing" played. As President Obama observed, "In many cases, they didn't even verify that these foreclosures were actually legitimate. Some of the people they hired to process foreclosures used fake signatures too—on fake documents to speed up the foreclosure process. Some of them didn't read what they were signing at all."[16]

President Obama was correct to point out these fraudulent practices, but both banks and nonbanks engaged in them.[17] By working with only the largest banks and excluding nonbanks from coverage, the settlement created a regulatory playing field now tilted further toward nonbanks.

In addition to increased compliance costs from the arrangement, the largest banks also took a major blow to their corporate reputations, and rightly so. It might not always seem this way, but the biggest U.S. banks spend a lot of time and resources worried about how they are perceived by the public. I can personally attest to that, having seen the results of a handful of focus groups and surveys regarding the banks' public reputations.

Since having a checking or savings account at, say, Bank of America provides almost the same benefits as having an account at Wells Fargo, a bank can take a sizable hit to its market share because of reputational concerns. For instance, in the letter to shareholders in its 2015 annual report, JPMorgan Chase cited reputational concerns for its plans to reduce its participation in FHA lending and to exit its servicing of delinquent Fannie and Freddie mortgages.[18]

Because nonbank mortgage lenders are not household names and have few relationships with consumers other than mortgages, they are less vulnerable to concerns about their image. There are also close to zero reputational penalties attached to individual bad actors in the mortgage industry. Of course, not everyone at Countrywide, one of 2008's largest subprime lenders, was responsible for the company's misdeeds and failure, but the degree to which the nonbank mortgage industry is still staffed with Countrywide alumni is simply shocking.

One of the more appalling examples of missing accountability is Freddie Mac's hiring of David Lowman to run its single-family mortgage business after Lowman was ousted from JPMorgan Chase because of Chase having illegally foreclosed on active-duty military personnel.[19] To his credit, David Brickman, upon becoming chief executive officer, fired Lowman from Freddie. However, the mortgage industry being what it is, Lowman had no problem getting another executive position within the business.[20]

I have nothing against Mr. Lowman personally and use his case as an example only since it is so well documented by the press and known within the industry. I know of at least a dozen other examples that are just as bad but simply not as well documented or public. As the Center for Public Integrity has noted, top executives from numerous failed subprime mortgage lenders found themselves back at work within the field soon after the crisis.[21] The point is that one individual is not at fault; it is a systemic problem facing the nonbank mortgage sector that a reputation for misconduct counts for virtually nothing as long as one can bring in business.[22]

Although one cannot attribute all the change in the market to the 2012 National Mortgage Settlement, it is stunning that the overall nonbank share of servicing in the year before the settlement was 7 percent, whereas it rose to 24 percent the following year.[23] In 2013, banks sold the servicing rights to more than $500 billion in mortgages to nonbanks.[24]

I experienced an adverse impact directly. As a likely result of the settlement, Bank of America sold the servicing of my mortgage to a little-known nonbank servicer that later failed.

I do not doubt that Obama and Harris, along with 48 other state attorneys general, believed that the settlement would be a long-run positive for borrowers and perhaps even for financial stability. But whatever its intentions, the agreement accelerated a move of servicing from banks to nonbanks, with a resulting decline in both financial stability and consumer protection.

———

The Obama administration also drove both mortgage origination and servicing from banks to nonbanks through its use of the federal False Claims Act. This legislation was passed during the Civil War as a result of fears that suppliers to the Union army were engaged in fraudulent behavior, such as providing the army with defective materials or spoiled foods. The False Claims Act has always included penalties in addition to actual damages. In 1986, those penalties were increased to triple the amount of harm. Having penalties that are multiples of actual damages is not a novel concept and is standard in circumstances in which the government has been defrauded, especially where such fraud is hard to detect. And of course, there must be actual damages for there to be penalties.

The DOJ under Obama took the view that the False Claims Act covered lenders doing business with the FHA, located within HUD. There's nothing particularly novel in this interpretation. The FHA is part of the federal government, and some lenders have defrauded the FHA.

What made this a significant issue was the large wave of delinquencies within the FHA and the degree to which the DOJ would pursue minor defects in the mortgage process. If there isn't a delinquency resulting in a loss to the FHA, then there's no damage to treble. But the FHA, which the Obama administration inherited, was witnessing record delinquencies, with some crisis-era loan cohorts showing past-due rates of over 30 percent. Clearly, the FHA was bleeding. Obama's DOJ was looking for lenders to cover some of those losses. I have considerable sympathy for that view.

I once heard Obama's first FHA head, Dave Stevens, say that "all mortgages have some defects." Stevens's point was not that all mortgages were faulty, but rather that the DOJ was going after mistakes that he and the industry viewed as immaterial. The lenders did have a point. The FHA's standards of very low down payments, poor borrower credit, and extremely high debt burdens will, in a stressed environment, result in a lot of delinquencies. The high level of FHA delinquencies witnessed in the Great Recession was mostly the result of the FHA's own weak underwriting standards, not widespread fraud. Yet lenders were being held responsible for insignificant errors that would have been ignored in a strong housing market. In a very real sense, lenders were making shoddy loans for the FHA because that's what the FHA wanted or at least allowed.

There were cases of lenders setting out to cheat the FHA. The most infamous example was that of mortgage lender Taylor, Bean & Whitaker.[25] Sadly, in that instance, Fannie was aware of some of the bad behavior and did not feel any obligation to tell the FHA or Freddie, the latter of which was cheated by the same lender.[26] I'm known to be tough on the mortgage industry, but even I do not see evidence to suggest that the behavior of Taylor, Bean & Whitaker is anything near the industry's norm.

To some degree, the Obama DOJ was making up for a weak enforcement culture at the FHA.[27] Punishment of lenders by the FHA has historically been quite rare. And there has long been a revolving door between the FHA and the mortgage business. For instance, Stevens went directly from being head of the FHA to being head of the Mortgage Bankers Association, the primary lobbying arm of the industry.[28]

After several years of effort as a Senate staffer, in 2008 I was able to help get additional powers for the FHA to fight fraud signed into law.[29] Those authorities had also been requested by HUD's then inspector general Ken Donohue. But those authorities were still discretionary. The FHA had to choose to use them.

Although the mortgage industry considered the DOJ's use of the False Claims Act problematic, it was actually a poorly crafted substitute for enforcement that the FHA should have been doing for itself.

The real problem was that, like the 2012 National Mortgage Settlement, it was aimed mostly at banks. As Willie Sutton might have said, that's where the money is. Unfortunately, such an enforcement regime creates incentives for institutions without much to lose to enter FHA lending. Nonbanks do not suffer the same sort of reputation losses that a False Claims Act carries. They also can more easily "go out of business" to avoid penalties in a manner that is not really an option for banks. The ease of entry and ability to move seamlessly across companies may make the nonbank mortgage business more competitive, but it also reduces the penalties for misconduct.

————

There were undoubtedly bad actors in the mortgage industry before the 2008 financial crisis. Some of them are still in the business. That, of course, does not minimize the role that destructive government policies played in the crisis. The biggest driver of the financial crisis was normal, relatively decent people rationally responding to the perverse incentives they faced.

Ironically and hopefully unintentionally, many of the commercial banks that pulled back from directly originating and servicing mortgages now serve as warehouse lenders to the very nonbank lenders that have taken their former mortgage business. A warehouse lender provides direct short-term facilities or lines of credit to nonbank mortgage lenders. As this lending is not tied directly to any specific mortgage, the warehouse lender avoids the reputational and regulatory risk associated with the mortgage but still generates a profit from the mortgage business. Because warehouse lending is usually short-term, for the time between closing of the loan and delivery to the next player in the chain, the warehouse lender also avoids the interest rate risk inherent in mortgage lending. The time from closing to delivery normally runs from 30 to 90 days.

Because of these policy changes and shifts in the marketplace, nonbank mortgage lenders were back in force. By 2016, nonbank mortgage origination for the first time surpassed that of banks. The phoenix-like rise of the nonbank mortgage lenders could have been possible only with the assistance of federal subsidies. In the decade from 2010 to 2020, nonbanks effectively doubled their market share of Fannie, Freddie, and FHA lending. In market segments not dominated by government lenders, such as the jumbo mortgage market, banks continued their dominance.

———

Unbundling in consumer markets is usually driven by economic efficiencies. Producers of turntables are unlikely to have any economic advantage in the production of vinyl records, for instance. So, for those of you who still get your music on vinyl records, you probably are not buying the records and the turntable to play them on as a single package. In the mortgage industry, however, the decades-long unbundling of originating, servicing, funding, and investing of mortgages has been driven largely by regulatory arbitrage. In layman's terms, that has been just one big gaming of the rules.

The 2012 National Mortgage Settlement and the DOJ's aggressive use of the False Claims Act in relation to FHA lending were imperfect and flawed responses to very real abuses and problems. Both set in motion forces in the mortgage market that would leave the system, including borrowers, more vulnerable than ever. As the saying goes, the road to hell is paved with good intentions.

Chapter 3
March Madness

Ten a.m., Sunday, March 15, 2020. I awake to a rhythmic tapping on my back—a poking, really. A certain tabby cat, Charlie, is reminding me that his breakfast is late. Weighing in at 17 pounds, this is one Washington Fat Cat I cannot afford to ignore. At least I got to sleep in some. I would need it.

Before the feeding begins, I open the Relisten app on my phone. Listening to a Grateful Dead show from the same date in history always gets my morning off to a strong start. Today's date brings back a particularly fond memory, seeing a hometown show celebrating Grateful Dead bassist Phil Lesh's birthday in 1990. "My old buddy, you're moving much too slow. . . ."[1]

———

Following the initial lockdowns that began in northern Italy in February 2020, financial markets witnessed a measured move to safer assets. Higher-risk assets, such as corporate bonds, were being sold and exchanged for U.S. Treasuries. At first, this shift benefited the mortgage market, with the 30-year fixed rate dropping by 20 basis points between February 21 and March 5. All that decline, and more, were about to be reversed.

On March 3, the Federal Reserve announced a 50-basis-point reduction in its target federal funds rate. Despite this action, unease was building over the weekend of March 6. Only the safest of the safe was of interest to investors. The uncertainty even led to moves away from the mortgage-backed securities (MBS) issued by Fannie Mae and Freddie Mac.

This change is well illustrated by looking at Fannie and Freddie debt holdings in the offshore financial center of the Cayman Islands (a wonderful place to scuba dive, I might mention). Over the course of January 2020, Cayman Island holdings of government-sponsored enterprise (GSE) debt slightly increased as part of the global move to security. But as the pandemic worsened, Cayman holdings of GSE debt dropped considerably, falling 15 percent over the course of February 2020. A similar decline was witnessed concurrently in Bermuda, another important offshore financial center. Eurozone holdings of GSE debt also dropped significantly during the February 2020 flight to safety.

On Monday, March 9, Italy instituted a stronger lockdown and extended it to the entire country—not just the north, where lockdowns were already in place. That day also witnessed the first equity market circuit breaker, a mandatory trading halt, since 1997. More importantly for the Federal Housing Finance Agency (FHFA), March 9 began a selloff in agency MBS, with the price of these securities dropping rapidly over the next few days. Recall that as with bonds, the price of MBS moves in the direction opposite to the yield or interest rate. Falling prices translate into an increase in mortgage rates, not to mention that rapid price changes can have disruptive effects on financial stability.

Two days later, the World Health Organization (WHO) officially declared COVID-19 a global pandemic. President Donald Trump declared a national emergency. Broad travel bans were instituted, including in most of Europe. Americans traveling abroad were unsure whether they could even get home.

Despite being GSEs, the financial markets began to question the health of Fannie and Freddie, as they had done in the summer of 2008. The 30-year mortgage rate climbed by about 10 basis points during the week of March 9. It would climb almost another 30 basis points before the week of March 16 was over.

The *Wall Street Journal* reported on March 13 that the difference between the yield on MBS and the 10-year Treasury had tripled from 50 basis points at the beginning of March to about 150 basis points.

In a market crunch, investors are looking not for implied guarantees, but rather for the real thing. What buying there was in GSE debt appeared to be made in the expectation that the Federal Reserve would soon be a large purchaser.[2]

After rising in February and the beginning of March, the Bloomberg Barclays U.S. MBS Index fell more than 2 percent in the wake of Italy's March 9 extended lockdown. Liquidity in the GSE MBS market significantly declined, as the effective bid-ask spread in the agency to-be-announced (TBA) market jumped from 2 basis points in February to over 20 basis points by the middle of March.[3]

In addition to regulating Fannie and Freddie, the FHFA also supervises the Federal Home Loan Bank System (FHLB). The FHLB was created during the Great Depression to serve as a lender of last resort to savings and loans. Over the years, its membership has expanded to include commercial banks, insurance companies, and community development financial institutions.

One reason we knew the financial system needed liquidity was the massive expansion in FHLB funding activity. Generally, the FHLB lends via an "advance" on mortgage collateral, which can include MBS. From late February to the middle of March, FHLB advances increased by over $200 billion outstanding, a third more than normal activity.

———

The FHFA was still working onsite on Monday, March 9, 2020. We would switch to telework before the end of that week and not come back for over two years. We had just had an in-person board meeting at Freddie Mac. I was scheduled to speak at a financial services conference in New York on March 11. That was canceled, of course. Initially I was disappointed, as I had hoped to catch some live music while I was there. Little did I know it would be almost two years before I experienced live music again.

We continued to monitor the mortgage and financial markets throughout that week, looking for signs of stress. We had our fingers crossed, hoping for an orderly derisking.

Part of our monitoring efforts included regular communications with other financial regulators, particularly the Federal Reserve, as

well as the Treasury Department. We had been briefed that the Federal
Reserve was working on several measures to be announced the weekend of March 14. Of particular interest to me was the plan for a large
increase in purchases of Fannie and Freddie MBS. Federal Reserve purchases began on March 16 with about $5 billion in daily purchases. This
quickly ramped up to over $40 billion in daily purchases by March 27.
By the end of April, daily Federal Reserve purchases of agency MBS
were back to about $5 billion.[4]

I had mixed feelings at best about the Federal Reserve's plan,
especially the size of it. I was all for increasing liquidity. But given the
proposed amount of the purchase, I was also concerned that it could
result in a substantial move in the price of both MBS and mortgage servicing rights (MSRs). My aim was price stability in that market. That
meant avoiding not only significant price declines but also significant
price increases.

As a general matter, it is one thing for the Federal Reserve to provide short-term general liquidity to the financial markets during times
of stress. It is quite another to allocate credit on a large scale to a select
segment of the economy, in this case the mortgage market. The outsize
purchases of MBS would contribute to record levels of housing price
inflation, while also drawing capital from more productive segments of
the economy. The Federal Reserve was engineering another cycle of
crazed bidding wars in the housing market. Perhaps worse, its interventions greatly reduced the likelihood of real structural reform occurring
in our mortgage finance system. Why fix a deeply broken system when
it could just be papered over repeatedly?

To understand why I felt the Federal Reserve needed to be surgical
in its move requires us to revisit mortgage market changes that have
occurred since 2008.

———

Since the mortgage market was at the center of the 2008 crisis, you
might think that Washington had helped stabilize it in the decade since.
Unfortunately, you would be wrong. If anything, Washington had made
our mortgage market more fragile.

To a great extent, although not exclusively, the 2008 crisis was driven by mortgage credit risk. In plain English, credit risk is the possibility of loss if the borrower does not repay the mortgage. Subprime mortgages, for instance, generally have higher credit risk because the borrower has demonstrated a higher risk of not paying. This is not a moral judgment. There can be many reasons for not paying one's mortgage, some within one's control and some not.

The big difference between 2008 and 2020 in terms of the mortgage market was the role of interest rate risk. Assets with a long life, or duration, such as mortgages, see wide swings in their value when there are big changes in interest rates. This occurs because those assets must compete with newly issued assets that reflect the changed interest rate environment.

Say you hold a 10-year bond that pays 3 percent. If rates go up to 5 percent, the value of that bond declines. The decline must be sufficient that investors buying your 3 percent bond would see the same return as if they had purchased a new 5 percent bond.

Mortgages, however, are more complicated than bonds, since in the United States most of them are prepayable—that is, the borrower can pay off the mortgage at any time with little or no penalty. So, whereas a bond's value would increase with declines in interest rates, a mortgage might not. If you, as an investor, own a mortgage at 5 percent and mortgages rates decline to 3 percent, there is a good chance the borrower will refinance. Yes, you get your money back, but now you can get only a 3 percent return rather than 5 percent. Since market participants expect this outcome, sharp declines in mortgages rates can quickly show up in mortgage values.

To be clear, both credit and interest risk played roles in 2008 and 2020. To some degree, Bear Stearns was sunk because it did not manage its interest rate risk. At the time of Bear's failure, its funding costs exceeded what it was earning on its assets. But yes, credit risk was the more important of the two in 2008. In early 2020, the consensus view was that job losses related to the pandemic would result in a lot of borrowers not paying their mortgages. This increased risk was reflected in the declining value of mortgages. And, of course, what happens to the value of mortgages also happens to the value of MBS.

What made March 2020 uniquely stressful for the mortgage market is that changes since 2008 have resulted in a system that is more vulnerable to swings in interest rates. The primary cause is the greater degree to which MSRs have been traded and invested in separately from the actual mortgage.

MSRs are inherently more sensitive to interest rate swings than are the underlying mortgages. The price of a mortgage, or a mortgage-backed security, is driven by both credit and interest rate risks. The values of MSRs, however, are influenced mainly by the continued probability of receiving interest payments on the loan.

Researchers at the Urban Institute have estimated that between 2011 and 2015, the value of Fannie Mae MSRs was six times as volatile as the value of Fannie Mae MBS.[5] In certain periods, such as September 2011 and September 2012, estimated prices swung some 20 percentage points over just a few days. Such swings are massive and can be profoundly disruptive.

———

Since the Great Recession, a new player had come to critical importance in the U.S. mortgage market. Or, more accurately, an old player took on a new, larger role. This player was the real estate investment trust (REIT).

The modern REIT is basically a creation of our tax code.[6] Yes, REITs have been around in one form or another for decades—for instance, they played a minor role in the Great Depression of the 1930s. Because of a 1935 Supreme Court decision subjecting REITs to corporate taxation,[7] they fell out of favor until Congress created a special tax regime for REITs in 1960.

The important things to remember about REITs are that they have to invest most of their assets in real estate and they have to pay out most of their income as dividends to their shareholders. These obligations leave them both vulnerable to changes in the real estate markets and unable to build up significant capital in the form of retained earnings.

A subset of REITs is called mortgage REITs (mREITs). This subset derives income from the origination and purchasing of mortgages as well as from the purchasing and holding of MBS, MSRs, and mortgage credit risk transfers (CRTs). From 2009 to 2019, mREITs grew from $168 billion in assets to about $700 billion.

———

Friday the 13th of March 2020 did feel a little unlucky. In conversations with both my fellow financial regulators and market participants, there was a strong sense that something needed to be done before the markets opened on Monday. The Dow had dropped almost 22 percent between March 4 and 12. The Chicago Board Options Exchange (CBOE) Volatility Index (VIX), a widely followed measure of market instability, had been shooting straight up since Valentine's Day. On March 13, it reached levels of volatility not seen since October 2008.

Prime money market mutual funds were witnessing significant withdrawals. Over the course of March, investors would pull out over $120 billion, more than a tenth of net assets, from the prime funds. Most of this drain, almost $90 billion, would occur in the third week of March. Mutual funds would not be the only source of stress in our capital markets.

Heading into the weekend, it was clear that REITs were under stress. One of the leading mREITs, TPG RE Finance Trust, experienced almost a 30 percent decline in value in little more than the week before March 13. Trading volumes had increased almost 400 percent on TPG's REIT. Investors were running for the doors. They were not alone—similar declines were witnessed with other mREITs, such as Invesco Mortgage Capital and AG Mortgage Investment Trust.

In many ways, it was a repeat of Bear Stearns—the age-old temptation to fund long and borrow short. The business model of these mREITs was to hold long-term assets, such as MBS and MSRs, and then to use them, particularly the MBS, to borrow overnight in the repurchase, or repo, market. The MBS would be pledged as collateral for the overnight loan.

It is common practice in the overnight lending markets for some amount of margin to be posted with the lender. The margin requirement is often a function of the credit strength of the borrower and the value of the posted collateral. The margin is meant to protect the lender in case the borrower defaults and the collateral is insufficient to cover the loan. As mortgage prepayments increased, driven by declining interest rates, along with the fear that defaults would rise due to COVID-19 job losses, the values of MSRs, MBS, and CRTs all declined. Accordingly, the margins went up on mortgage-related collateral. The problem facing a handful of mREITs was that they lacked the cash to cover their margin calls without selling off assets.

For some, there was little choice but to dump agency MBS in a mad dash to raise cash. In the first three months of 2020, mREITs sold off about $120 billion in agency MBS, representing almost 40 percent of their agency MBS holdings.[8]

To support both the mortgage markets and those trading in MBS, on the evening of Sunday, March 15, the Federal Reserve announced a package of financial support. In addition to a 100-basis-point reduction in the target federal funds rate, it also announced a plan to purchase $500 billion in Treasuries and $200 billion in MBS.

Despite the Federal Reserve's efforts, on Monday, March 16, the financial markets took a beating. The Standard & Poor's 500 (S&P) dropped 12 percent just on that day. This was its largest decline since 1987. Another equity market circuit breaker was instituted, again bringing trading to a halt. The VIX spiked to levels that matched the worst of 2008. Even the REITs we were monitoring at the FHFA dropped like stones. TPG lost another quarter of its value before the markets closed that Monday. By Wednesday, March 18, TPG would lose almost three-fourths of its March 4 value. Whatever the Federal Reserve was doing with the MBS market, it clearly was not keeping the mREITs afloat.

The week would see the rollout of additional Federal Reserve facilities. On Tuesday, March 17, the Federal Reserve launched facilities for both primary dealers and the commercial paper markets. The next day, it rolled out a liquidity facility for money market mutual funds.

———

In retrospect, Sunday, March 22, marked the height of the COVID-19 financial stress. Whereas the response to the 2008 crisis was hatched in conference rooms at the Federal Reserve and the Treasury

Department, this Sunday would be spent at kitchen tables and living rooms, jumping from one phone call to another. Where a person had meetings in 2008 stretching into hours, 2020 would be one 10- to 15-minute call after another. The problems were discussed, solutions debated, and agreements reached. I do not recall the entire financial response team ever being in the same room at the same time.

I had three broad objectives that day: to review what the FHFA had established to assist homeowners and renters; to provide feedback and analysis on the drafting of the Coronavirus Aid, Relief, and Economic Security (CARES) Act; and to ensure that Monday, March 23, would not be a financial market repeat of Monday, March 16.

The morning began with check-ins with the FHFA staff. Good thing I got those out of the way early, as the rest of the day would be rather spontaneous. Around 2:30 p.m., Treasury Secretary Steven Mnuchin rang. He'd just gotten off the phone with Sen. Mike Crapo, chair of the Banking Committee.

Senator Crapo was part of the congressional leadership team negotiating the CARES Act. Mnuchin was the primary representative of the administration. Although the FHFA was an independent agency, Mnuchin called for my take on the mortgage and housing provisions being discussed for the CARES Act. What was workable? What should the White House accept? How was any of it different from what the FHFA was already doing?

Mnuchin also mentioned that he had been on the phone an hour or so earlier with Federal Reserve Chair Jay Powell. He was seeing what we were seeing: stress among the mREITs, particularly those that concentrated their holdings in Fannie and Freddie securities. Steven was giving me a heads-up that Jay would be calling me that afternoon to share his concerns.

I had dealt with the Federal Reserve long enough to expect their "rescue first, ask questions later" approach to financial markets, so I was not surprised at Jay's worry about the agency REITs. I had gotten to know Jay after he had joined the Federal Reserve Board, having been nominated by President Barack Obama. Janet Yellen, chair of the Federal Reserve Board, had deputized him to conduct outreach to Republicans on behalf of the Federal Reserve. Under Yellen, the organization was seen as contemptuous toward congressional Republicans. In my experience, that was a perception that was accurate and had been earned. While I felt that Yellen should have conducted her own outreach to Republicans, I was glad to get to know Jay and share my observations and apprehensions.

These occasional visits continued during my time at the White House. It did not hurt that Jay was a member of the Metropolitan Club, which is located a couple blocks north of the White House. In this period, never did I see him lobby to succeed Yellen, whose term as chair was coming to an end. In fact, in all my conversations with Jay, from' my time at the Cato Institute to the White House and the FHFA, every word he uttered about Yellen was friendly and supportive. He was, and still is, among her staunchest supporters.

I would spend more time with Jay as Yellen's term was about to close. While he was eventually nominated to succeed Yellen, he was not initially among the finalists. At one point, it came down to a competition between Yellen, Stanford professor John Taylor, and former Federal Reserve Board governor Kevin Warsh. The Wall Street lobbyists, and to a degree the Treasury Department, were all firmly behind Yellen. She was generally viewed as someone who would always make sure there was a floor under asset prices, protecting Wall Street from the downside risk of its leveraged bets.

Wall Street considered Taylor and, to a lesser degree, Warsh, with some doubts. Would they always make sure the Federal Reserve was there to bail them out? Of course, Vice President Mike Pence and I wanted a chair who would resist bailouts. I viewed Yellen as a nonstarter. Senate Republicans also told the White House that a renomination of Yellen would not be welcomed. On the Hill, she was generally seen as having politicized the Federal Reserve to an unprecedented degree, at least in the modern era. You would have to go back to Arthur Burns to find a more political chair.

My preference was Taylor, one of the greatest living macroeconomists and someone who had decades of experience. There are few economists I respect more. He had pushed back against Wall Street demands for an Argentine bailout during his service at the Treasury Department. Wall Street had not forgotten that sin. They would fight any Taylor nomination.

He never expressed it directly, but I felt that Pence preferred Warsh. I had known Kevin from both his earlier time at the Federal Reserve and his service in the Bush White House. I felt he would be a great choice, but I placed more weight on Taylor's experience and stature.

We also felt it was critical that whoever was Federal Reserve chair understand the nature of our economic policies, especially tax reform. The Tax Cut and Jobs Act of 2017 was structured to increase business investment and work incentives, ultimately with the intent to increase productivity, which would have a deflationary impact. Some of us at the White House worried that Yellen, stuck in a Phillips curve–Keynesian worldview, would see the 2017 tax reforms as inflationary. Both Taylor and Warsh displayed a clear grasp of what we were trying to achieve with tax and regulatory reform. Both expressed an understanding that our efforts would not be inflationary, as I believe the evidence of low inflation during the Trump years has borne out. The inflation surge that started in 2021 was the result of monetary and fiscal policies that started in 2020, not with the tax reforms of 2017.

Ultimately, none of that would matter. Once the Wall Street lobbyists gleaned that Yellen's star was setting, they scrambled for an alternative to Taylor and Warsh. That alternative turned out to be Jay Powell.

There had even been a brief discussion among some senior White House staff about approaching Harvard economics professor Jeremy Stein, who had served in the Obama White House. While I had a lot of respect for Stein and thought he would do an admirable job at the Federal Reserve, there was no way he would survive vetting by the White House's political process. To the best of my knowledge, no one reached out to him as the internal concerns about Powell faded.

I liked and respected Jay. The vice president felt the same. We saw Jay as a reasonable compromise. It might be fair to say he was not anyone's first choice at the White House, but he was widely liked and acceptable to everyone involved—most importantly the president, who would make the final decision.

———

As I was only about two weeks into working from home, I was still managing calls and emails from my kitchen table. Unfortunately, that meant bad posture and uncomfortable seating. On top of everything else, my back started to bother me because of the lack of a supportive chair. It would be another week before I'd arrange a more comfortable chair and finally accept that working from home would last a while. Not yet having heard from Powell, I thought I would take the next couple of calls from my bathtub.

In the middle of a call with John Roscoe, Powell rang on the other line. It must have been around 4:30 p.m. Jay didn't waste any time. He was concerned about the state of mREITs. More importantly, he requested that I leverage Fannie and Freddie to help.

In addition to our calls with market participants, I exchanged market intelligence with Securities and Exchange Commission (SEC) chair Jay Clayton on the afternoon of Saturday, March 21. One of the issues we discussed was the health of mREITs. Clayton's extensive financial market contacts were invaluable. He had been in the very center of the 2008 response. He also seemed to know everyone on Wall Street. Most importantly, I trusted him. We had worked on several issues together, particularly on reform of our mortgage finance system, hoping to improve the disclosure requirements for private-label mortgage securities. We both wanted to see private-label mortgage securitization play a greater role. Clayton was also seeing tension among the mREITs. Now if I could only keep the two Jays straight.

Historically, the Federal Reserve has conducted its purchases of agency MBS in the to-be-announced (TBA) market. The TBA is essentially a forward market, with settlement occurring once a month on a set schedule for each class of agency MBS. Because the Federal Reserve wanted to move quickly, it could not wait for these settlement dates. Instead, it started to purchase agency MBS directly from primary dealers, the 24 large banks that are the usual conduit for open-market operations. These are companies such as Goldman Sachs, Morgan Stanley, Wells Fargo, and Citibank.

The problem was that mREITs were not among the primary dealers. The Federal Reserve had no direct relationship with the mREITs. Although most of them were engaged in repo transactions with the primary dealers, the Federal Reserve wanted to avoid another Bear Stearns situation. Recall that the federal assistance to Bear Stearns in 2008 was routed through JPMorgan Chase, as the Federal Reserve did not have a direct relationship with Bear Stearns.

However, Fannie and Freddie did have a relationship with many of the mREITs. The mREITs not only invested in Fannie and Freddie securities, but also often originated mortgages for the companies. Some were also counterparties to Fannie and Freddie on their CRTs. Finally, any assistance to the REITs would be secured with Fannie and Freddie securities.

Jay Powell's question to me was, would we allow Fannie and Freddie to provide overnight secured funding to help the mREITs, if only to allow them to meet margin calls that week? While I felt that the financial system would survive the failure of a few mREITs, Jay was clearly troubled. I made no firm commitment but indicated that we would see what we could get set up, implying that we should organize something that would be operational before the financial markets opened the next morning.

Over the next few hours, we worked with Fannie and Freddie to establish a lending facility. It was broadly structured, but we knew that only mREITs would truly be interested. Fannie and Freddie would provide overnight financing, collateralized by agency MBS. As the business model of mREITs was essentially overnight financing of their agency MBS book, we would be stepping into the shoes of the investment banks that normally provide such financing. We were very conscious that such a move would be as much a rescue of the investment banks as it would be of the mREITs, since having Fannie and Freddie provide financing would allow the investment banks to reduce their exposure to the mREITs.

I agreed to provide the assistance, but I had no intention of providing it on overly generous terms. The lending would be provided at a penalty rate—not enough to sink anyone, but also unattractive enough that it would not be anyone's first choice. We expected market participants to look to each other first and come to us only out of genuine necessity.

Just after 7:00 p.m., Mnuchin called again to compare notes. I shared the details of my understanding with Powell. As Mnuchin had just talked to Powell, he was mostly up to speed. By that point in the evening, we had worked out the most important details, which I also shared with Steven. Soon we were both on to our next call.

I could say that Sunday, March 22, felt like a marathon, but it really felt like a repeated series of sprints. I lost track of the number of calls, but they rarely lasted more than 15 minutes each.

By 11 p.m., the pieces were in place. Monday morning would start with an offer from Fannie and Freddie to provide overnight financing of agency MBS. Even with everything in place, it was still hard to shake the unease. Oddly enough, I was fairly calm about it all. But everyone else in government was worried that Monday, March 23, would be a repeat of the previous Monday, something few had the stomach for.

For a few moments, it made me glad we were all working at a distance. I recall the panic that developed in 2001 when anthrax was found in the Senate office buildings, not to mention the feeling on 9/11 when we were told that a plane was headed in the direction of the Capitol. I believe many of the decisions during the 2008 financial crisis were impelled by a similar group psychology. Physical separation in the evolving pandemic allowed some measure of insulation from groupthink.

———

If only the same urgency could have been mustered in the years leading up to 2020. The financial strain among mREITs and other non-bank mortgage lenders did not come as a surprise. In fact, as early as 2013, the Financial Stability Oversight Council (FSOC) recognized this potential: "A shock to agency REITs could induce repo lenders to raise margins or pull back funding, which in turn could compel agency REITs to sell into a declining market, potentially impacting MBS valuations significantly."[9]

Going into 2020, the FSOC, of which I was a member, also recognized these risks. As the 2019 FSOC annual report, released in December 2019, noted, "Nonbanks also have relatively few resources to absorb adverse economic shocks. Their largest assets, mortgages held for investment or sale and mortgage servicing rights (MSRs), are often pledged as collateral or partially monetized for upfront cash. The value of MSRs can move dramatically with changes in interest rates, and MSRs can be particularly illiquid and difficult to price when default rates are high or uncertain."[10]

The annual report specifically called out potential problems among agency mREITs, warnings that turned out to be all too accurate, noting that "use of repos makes agency REITs particularly vulnerable to disruptions in the repo market, which could pose a risk to refinancing activities."[11] That, of course, is exactly what happened.

This may be the FSOC's real strength, pointing out problems in our financial system for which none of its members bear any authority or responsibility. There were no federal regulators for REITS or other nonbanks. The FHFA certainly did not have any authority in the area. We did not even have the power to inspect the nonbanks that did business with Fannie and Freddie. And of course, we did not have a statutory mandate to protect the nonbanks. What we did have a mandate to do was protect Fannie and Freddie from any problems that could arise among the nonbanks.

Until about 2019, the FSOC had mainly ignored the risks at Fannie and Freddie as well. Sadly, that is par for the course. The FSOC tries to work by consensus. No member really wants to see their agency, and hence themselves, criticized. I, however, inherited a mess with Fannie and Freddie. It would strain credibility to argue otherwise. With the continued risk regarding nonbank mortgage lenders, servicers, and investors identified, our mission at the FHFA would be to better protect Fannie and Freddie.

On March 26, 2020, just after 2:30 p.m., the FSOC met by conference call to review the last few weeks of distress and discuss the path forward. Just three days earlier, the Federal Reserve had announced that it would purchase agency MBS "in the amounts needed"—that is, without limit. After a brief discussion by members on the overall state of financial markets, the council turned to an in-depth discussion of nonbank mortgage servicers and originators. The general feeling among the council was that the worst of the market distress was behind us. The Federal Reserve had once again come riding to the rescue. Our attention would turn to those outside its safety net.

Kevin Silva, at the FHFA, would provide the group with an overview of the FHFA's data and analysis on nonbank servicers. I had come to appreciate Kevin's work. Before his long service at the FHFA, he had worked at the SEC and brought much-needed capital markets experience to the FHFA. I felt strongly that the FHFA had to present its best to our fellow financial regulators and was happy to see Kevin provide the FSOC with a data-rich picture of nonbank servicers. Karen Pence, from the Federal Reserve, who obviously shares a name with our then second lady, offered additional analysis. Karen served as the point person on these issues. I had learned a lot from reading her work over the years, as she remains one of the most insightful economists on mortgage finance issues. I could sense even then from Karen's words that the Federal Reserve would prefer to provide nonbank mortgage lenders with more support. She had coauthored an important paper on the topic in 2018.[12] Her analysis would certainly carry weight with me and others on the council.

Stephen Ledbetter, the FSOC's executive director at Treasury, shared with the council several options for addressing stress among nonbanks. While Ledbetter did not directly advocate for a nonbank rescue, he came pretty close. Sensing the division on the council and the possibility of his own staff getting too far in front of him, Mnuchin announced the creation of a task force on nonbank mortgage liquidity, which would meet the next week. Whatever the fate of nonbank mortgage lenders would be, it would not be decided in March.

The meeting did have its lighter moments. Mnuchin had a little fun contrasting for the group my long-held free-market views with all the assistance the FHFA had provided homeowners and renters over the previous weeks. I did not consider forbearance at all inconsistent with my principles, but since this was Mnuchin's way of complimenting me, I happily indulged the point. The closed executive session concluded about a quarter after three. We then called back in for a public open session. The objective was chiefly to give the public a statement on what the various council members had done to respond to March's financial market distress.

———

A contributor to the March 2020 tension is the underlying structure of how mortgage-backed securities are traded. Investors do not simply go to Fannie or Freddie and buy mortgage-backed securities, foremost because the companies usually create MBS via a swap transaction with mortgage originators. A lender, whether Wells Fargo or a nonbank like PennyMac, brings mortgages to Fannie or Freddie. The mortgages are pooled into an MBS, Fannie or Freddie guarantees the MBS, and the MBS is then swapped back to the original lender. In effect, the lender is getting back the same mortgages it originated with a GSE guarantee behind the pool. Most lenders, especially the nonbank lenders, subsequently sell that MBS to a dealer who specializes in buying and selling MBS.

These dealers, often called primary dealers, sell the MBS to investors, such as asset managers like PIMCO or BlackRock; sell the MBS to other dealers; or hold the MBS in inventory until an ultimate investor is found. Normally the primary dealers hold around $30 billion to $40 billion in agency MBS pass-through inventory.[13] These dealers entered 2020 with closer to $50 billion in inventory, but as the initial flight to quality took hold in January 2020, dealer inventories dropped by almost half. As noted above, the markets would not continue to view MBS as risk-free. Over the course of February 2020, dealer inventories doubled, entering March with over $50 billion held. In just two weeks, by March 18, 2020, those inventories would surge to $80 billion.

MBS dealers were now coming under pressure. They had to hold capital against their growing positions—capital they did not have. As one bond trader put it, "we can't bid on anything that adds to the balance sheet right now."[14] Buyer interest was disappearing, at least until the Federal Reserve swung into action. It did not help that one of the largest dealers in agency MBS, Wells Fargo, was under a regulatory asset cap, which limited its ability to provide liquidity to the MBS market.

The primary dealers who intermediate the MBS market also intermediate the Treasury market. To some degree, the ability of dealers to hold MBS inventory has been limited by the massive expansion of outstanding Treasury debt, some of which has ended up on dealer balance sheets. This is a direct example of our federal government's fiscal imbalance undermining financial stability. Post-2008 reforms, such as the Liquidity Coverage Ratio, encouraged banks to hold more Treasuries and MBS. Such holdings left dealers closer to their internal risk concentration limits when COVID-19 struck, reducing their ability to serve as MBS market makers.

The primary dealer market for MBS is also highly concentrated, with the 10 biggest dealers handling almost 90 percent of the trading volume.[15] While highly regulated, these institutions also tended to be highly leveraged. Difficulties among just a few of these could result in major disruptions to the MBS market and accordingly to the mortgage market itself. Instead of a robust, efficient mortgage finance system, we have one characterized by a handful of fragile chokepoints.

———

Financial crises are rarely caused by securities or lending that we know to be riskier ex ante. For instance, credit card and small business lending have long been known to display high losses relative to those of other types of lending, yet I can think of no financial crisis that resulted from either. It is the stuff we believe to be safe but that turns out not to be that causes crises.[16] Academics and some regulators refer to certain assets as "risk-free" or "safe." Of course, we know that nothing is risk-free. Financial institutions have even failed from losses on U.S. Treasuries.

Financial market participants and some regulators have treated agency MBS as risk-free.[17] Some have referred to supposed government guarantees behind Fannie and Freddie, which of course do not exist in statute. Bank regulators have allowed banks to hold little capital against agency MBS and have in some circumstances even encouraged banks to hold more agency MBS. These actions have reduced the soundness of our financial system, leaving us more vulnerable to crises, such as those experienced in 2008 and 2020.

Bank regulators were not the only source of regulatory distortions in the mortgage market. The SEC, in its efforts to reform money market mutual funds, inadvertently created a massive incentive for those funds to shift their assets toward the debt of the FHLB.[18] The SEC's efforts have also greatly reduced market discipline around the FHLB.[19] Given the exposure of the system to the volatile mortgage and housing markets, the treatment of system debt as a safe asset poses significant financial stability risks.[20]

My concern regarding these weaknesses led me to push for an inter-agency working group on mortgage finance in 2019, a few months into my tenure. This was not a problem I could fix on my own. Progress could be made only with the efforts of the Federal Reserve and the SEC. Fortunately, both Jay Clayton and Federal Reserve vice chair for supervision Randall Quarles pledged to support the effort. Unfortunately, we were not able to make progress on these efforts when COVID-19 hit.

———

The financial market disruptions of March 2020 were in direct response to the uncertainties arising from COVID-19. The inability of our financial markets to weather that response without a massive injection of support from the Federal Reserve, however, was a direct result of the policy response to 2008. The failures and conservatorships of Fannie Mae and Freddie Mac limited their ability to serve as dealers or market makers in the MBS market. Capital and liquidity regulations implemented in response to 2008 limited the ability of Wall Street broker-dealers to fully respond to the market pressures on MBS. The massive growth of nonbanks, particularly mREITs, that resulted from the 2008 response has created an entire mortgage origination, servicing, and investment infrastructure built on sand. Some may see the Federal Reserve, or the federal government writ large, as the hero here, but the fact remains that the Federal Reserve has become the buyer-, dealer-, and lender-of-last-resort in the mortgage market because policymakers, in response to 2008, hobbled the ability of the rest of the market to effectively respond.

As the Financial Stability Board has so correctly observed, "the exceptional measures taken . . . were not aimed at addressing the underlying vulnerabilities that amplified the stress. The financial system remains vulnerable . . . as the underlying structures and mechanisms that gave rise to the turmoil are still in place."[21] To translate, buckle up: we still have some mortgage market bailouts in our future.

Chapter 4

A Renter Recession

April 27, 2020. I'm working from my kitchen table, going over my remarks for an afternoon call with housing advocates organized by the National Low Income Housing Coalition (NLIHC). The external affairs coordinator of the Federal Housing Finance Agency (FHFA), Danielle Walton, gives me a rundown of who will be on the call.

Reaching distressed renters was a unique challenge. For mortgages guaranteed by Fannie Mae or Freddie Mac, we knew who those families were; in conjunction with mortgage servicers, the enterprises had a contractual relationship with borrowers. We had no such relationship with renters. The mortgage contract was with the property owner. We had no information for the renters.

Fannie and Freddie operate in the secondary mortgage market. They are not consumer-facing companies. Neither they nor the FHFA had in place a mechanism to directly reach borrowers or renters.

I had also learned during the 2008 crisis that borrowers and renters do not always want to engage with their lenders or landlords. Sometimes they are overwhelmed with their situation. Some choose to ignore it. Others prefer to work with a trusted third party in their community, such as a nonprofit or their place of worship.

If we could not reach renters directly, maybe we could reach those who could. The NLIHC is an umbrella organization—an organization of organizations—with many members and affiliates working at the local level. If we could get our message to these local organizations, hopefully they could get the message to families in need.

———

Recessions usually hit renters harder than homeowners. That is not too surprising, as renters are, on average, much younger and poorer and are less attached to the labor market than homeowners. Renters also tend to work in segments of the economy that are discretionary. For instance, even in non-pandemic times, going out to eat at a restaurant is a discretionary choice.

Job losses in March and April 2020 were disproportionately concentrated in industries whose workers were more likely to be renters than homeowners. In March 2020, just over 32 percent of workers were renters. Among employees at bars and restaurants, however, the proportion of renters was close to half: 48 percent for restaurants and 56 percent for bars. Nursing and residential care facility workers are also much more likely to be renters than the overall workforce is. Retail establishments, too, such as clothing stores, have workers that are more likely to be renters than most other professions do.

By some estimates, about half of renters suffered a drop in pay early in the pandemic.[1] While many of them were back at work by July 2020, we still needed a financial bridge of a few months. Unfortunately, many renters would experience joblessness well into 2021. Renter and landlord surveys suggest that between 10 and 20 percent of renters were paying late by the end of 2020, about twice the typical rate of delinquency.

Renters, just like homeowners, rely on unemployment insurance (UI) to cover necessities such as shelter costs when they lose their jobs. Even in the best of times, however, the state-based unemployment systems are slow to process claims. Researchers have estimated that only about 6 percent of the unemployed in March 2020 were receiving UI payments. While that number jumped to just over 50 percent in April 2020, it took until May 2020 for 85 percent of the unemployed to be receiving payments.[2] Even a couple of months of rent or mortgage flexibility could make all the difference until UI payments kicked in.

One reason for the delay was the outdated nature of many state UI systems. Perhaps the most infamous example was the request by the state of New Jersey for COBOL programmers.[3] It so happened that New Jersey's UI system runs on a 40-year-old mainframe. While the remote work status of state employees likely added to the delay in processing UI claims, these systems have been plagued by various problems for decades. It is truly a tragedy that policymakers, at both the federal and the state levels, are not prioritizing an overhaul of the UI system.

A majority of black households are renters. For that reason alone, the economic impact of COVID-19 would fall heavily on minority communities. We were still a month away from the death of George Floyd, which would bring criminal justice and racial justice issues to the top of the national agenda. From the very beginning of the pandemic, I would check Washington's COVID-19 numbers daily. As a resident of Ward 2, I could not fail to notice that parts of the city—such as Wards 6 and 8, with their concentrations of black seniors—were getting hit particularly hard. While I am concerned about the recent tendency in public policy to view everything through a racial lens, COVID-19 was a stark reminder that where you live greatly determines the quality of health care, education, and public safety you receive. That is one reason I have long been a big advocate of both educational and housing choice. After all, it is poorer and minority families that suffer most from dysfunctional, inefficient, and sometimes corrupt local governments. So, while minority borrowers would benefit from mortgage forbearance, without a rental response minority families faced a greater chance of falling through the cracks.

I felt strongly that we could not repeat one of the worst injustices of the 2008 response—namely, focusing most of the federal assistance on the households that needed it the least while ignoring those who needed it the most. The typical response in Washington is to shower benefits on the college-educated upper and upper-middle classes. Witness the regular calls for student debt relief or federal tax offsets for state and local taxes (SALT). I had not forgotten that in the process of creating the FHFA, the provisions for which many members of Congress fought the hardest were the expansion of Fannie and Freddie mortgage purchases to higher-income households. There was literally nothing in the negotiations that Rep. Barney Frank and House Speaker Nancy Pelosi wanted more than to have greater mortgage subsidies for the upper class.

Mortgage refinance programs also were established for those who were current on their mortgage and not experiencing any trouble paying, while borrowers who had lost their jobs and did have trouble paying were pushed into complex programs, often with no end in sight. Reverse triage. This time we would focus our efforts on those most in need.

———

I was probably a bit of an odd fit for the NLIHC's weekly COVID-19 call. In addition to me, the callers would hear from former Obama Department of Housing and Urban Development (HUD) Secretary Julián Castro and Democratic attorneys general from Minnesota and the District of Columbia. The intent was not to be partisan; it was more the result of existing relationships than anything else.

Despite the fact that the NLIHC is a left-leaning organization, I had developed a good working relationship with them over my 20-some years in Washington. I had even coauthored an op-ed with their head, Diane Yentel, just before I joined the White House in 2017.

One of the first people I got to know in Washington housing policy circles was the NLIHC's founder, Cushing Dolbeare. By the time she passed away in 2005 at age 78, Cushing was widely recognized as "the dean of housing advocates," as the *New York Times* called her.[4] Perhaps befitting the daughter of management consultants, Cushing was a data person, regaling us younger analysts with stories of the days of punch cards and magnetic tapes. In addition to being a vocal advocate, Cushing was also a Quaker to the core, practicing an art of persuasion and consensus building long lost in Washington. Her data-driven, consensus-building focus on the truly needy has been a constant influence on my own approach to public policy.

Diane Yentel does an admirable job carrying on that mission. While other voices would urge the FHFA to keep the refinance market for wealthier homeowners going, Diane would regularly remind us of the needs of low-income renters. In Washington, the squeaky wheel gets the grease. Had it not been for Diane's efforts, I suspect our attentions would have been further diverted to the needs of Wall Street rather than Main Street or, more importantly, renters in need of help.

Despite that shared focus, I suspect there were plenty of times that left Diane and other advocates frustrated with our unwillingness to get creative with our authority. I have long criticized government agencies for going beyond their legal authorities, as I believe such actions are a direct assault on the democratic legitimacy of our government. I had not been elected, but rather, as they say, selected. I do appreciate that Diane and most housing advocates understood our situation. Indeed, I found it somewhat refreshing how often the fact that we had legal limits within which to operate was accepted and respected. All that said, we were more than willing to use the authority we did have.

———

The FHFA had both the 2008 experience and the response to natural disasters, such as hurricanes, on which to model our homeowner response. We did not have that experience for apartment buildings. We would need to create a renter response from the ground up.

The single-family rental piece would be an extension of our single-family homeowner forbearance program. In fact, there was no difference in treatment between single-family homes occupied by owners or renters. The two would have the same options.

A similar framework was created for the apartment market, with the added requirement that in exchange for forbearance, apartment owners would agree not to evict any tenants for not being able to pay rent during the forbearance period. One could still evict for other reasons, such as destruction of property or being a nuisance. And the landlord would have every right to expect any back rent missed to be repaid. How to help landlords stay afloat while not being paid rent was outside our powers at the FHFA; that issue would have to wait for Congress.

Getting the message out to homeowners and letting them know where to go were relatively easy. Many of the largest mortgage lenders added user-friendly interfaces on their websites and phone applications. As a regular user of my Wells Fargo app, I noticed early in the pandemic that the bank had created a generally consumer-friendly and visible process for requesting COVID-19 forbearance.

Renters, however, almost never know if their landlord even has a mortgage, much less who owns or services that mortgage. We did not know who the renters were, and they did not know who we were. This inability to directly reach renters was a challenge.

If we could not target outreach to individual renters, maybe we could help renters target the enterprises. One solution we stumbled on was the creation of an online lookup tool. Renters would be directed to a Fannie or Freddie website, enter their address, and learn whether one of the enterprises guaranteed the mortgage on their property.[5]

The lookup tools were not without their problems and limitations. Foremost, the FHFA lacked the ability to create a combined Fannie and Freddie database in a timely manner. We had only recently established a multifamily analytics group at the FHFA and were still staffing up. We had a great leader, Siobhan Kelly, but her team was significantly under-resourced. Renters would have to go to both the Fannie and the Freddie websites to check on the eligibility of their properties.

Not surprisingly, both Fannie and Freddie were initially hostile to having publicly available lookup tools. It is not that they did not want to help renters; I believe they did. Both were fearful that if competitors in the apartment lending space could figure out which properties had Fannie- or Freddie-owned mortgages, then those competitors could pitch the landlords on a new mortgage or change their business strategy to better compete with Fannie and Freddie. This is, of course, the primary flaw in the Fannie and Freddie model: they were chartered to be backstops to the mortgage market, but both obsess about their market share. If someone else can come along and provide a better loan for the property, that is a great thing for the public, just not for Fannie and Freddie executives, who believe that their career advancement and compensation depend on cranking out high mortgage volumes. Fortunately, a little shaming and invoking of the public good brought the companies' executives around.

Perhaps more frustrating was that it took some time to improve the matching algorithms. If the renter entered "Main Street" and the actual address was "Main Avenue," they would likely not get a match. We never achieved perfection, as the initial lookup tools appeared to generate a lot of false negatives, but we continued to make progress. Something that is 80 percent workable is better than not trying at all.

———

COVID-19's stress on renters was also not just an abstraction to me. I think of myself as an "accidental landlord," in that I owned a rental property, which had been my first home. My plan had always been to sell into a strong market, which I finally did in spring 2022. Like so many renters, one of my tenants suffered a job loss due to COVID-19. Ultimately, that tenant decided to move out, given the uncertainty of their job prospects. Moving out did not cure the problem of late rent payment. Over the course of 2020–2021, I lost about 50 percent of my rental income. Fortunately for me, being a landlord was not my primary source of income. I could absorb that loss and did so.

Many landlords depend on the rent being paid to make their own expenses, such as providing for their retirement income. Unlike most homeowners, who have equity and an incentive to repay any arrears, after a few months of missed payments, renters have a strong incentive to just leave and stick the landlord with the outstanding rent. Yes, a landlord could sue, but that could easily end up costing more in time and effort than one would recover in rent. COVID-19 and the associated policy response were a hard blow to small landlords.

The topic of renting often recalls visions of apartment living.[6] But a significant portion of renters—about a third—live not in apartments but in single-family homes. While corporate ownership of single-family rentals has gotten some public (including congressional) attention, the fact is that over 70 percent of single-family rentals are owned by individual investors.[7] Even the vast majority (almost 75 percent) of smaller multiunit rental properties, those with two to four rental units, are owned by individual investors. A third of rental properties with 5 to 24 units are also owned by individuals.

The FHFA's ability to reach renters was also limited by the surprisingly large number of rental units without a mortgage, as our only leverage (no pun intended) was via the mortgage. Almost 60 percent of single-family rentals were owned free and clear—that is, without any loan. Even about 40 percent of smaller multiunit rental properties are owned outright. Overall, about 40 percent of the rental units in the United States are free of mortgages, making it impossible for the FHFA to assist those landlords or their tenants.

Our reach was even more limited than that. Rental units without a mortgage were likely to be older and to have more affordable market rents. Those are the very units likely to be occupied by workers experiencing a decline in earnings or job loss.

Of course, not having a mortgage reduces a landlord's costs, enabling the landlord to better absorb lost rental income. That was certainly my case. I did not like losing the rental income, but it was bearable since I owned my rental property mortgage-free. That said, I, as well as other landlords, still had to pay property taxes and other expenses.

Rental properties with mortgages, especially those guaranteed by Fannie or Freddie, were likely to be larger, newer properties. Many of these owners would rather take the hit of a few units not paying than risk open forbearance for all their tenants. Forbearance was an automatic option for homeowners, but landlords could choose not to offer forbearance to renters. Of course, the various eviction moratoriums, both federal and local, might change a landlord's calculus.

These larger properties were also more likely to have tenants already receiving government rental assistance, such as Section 8. For instance, renters living in properties with at least 150 units were six times as likely to have a Section 8 voucher as tenants in single-family rental properties.[8] These subsidies would continue to be paid regardless of the job market or the path of the pandemic. Job loss could mean that even Section 8 tenants might have difficulty paying their portion of the rent, but since the tenant's portion was based on his or her income, over time the government share would offset that loss.

Within the Fannie and Freddie apartment business, it was the smaller properties that were more likely to take forbearance. For example, once the apartment forbearance programs were fully up and running, by late May 2020, Freddie Mac reported that the typical loan size was

$6.4 million. The average Freddie Mac apartment mortgage, by comparison, was $12.5 million in 2020. By late May 2020, just over 4 percent of Freddie Mac apartment mortgages were in forbearance.

Not surprisingly, the performance of student (usually college) housing and senior housing was slightly worse, approaching 5 percent of Freddie Mac multifamily loans. One in five Freddie Mac apartment loans in forbearance in May 2020 was in New York City. Yes, New York City was the area most affected early in COVID-19, but Freddie also had a disproportionate presence there. New York landlords have also been far more likely to participate in federal mortgage programs than landlords elsewhere.

The process of trying to assist renters via their landlord's mortgage was convoluted at best, but those were the only tools we had at the FHFA. In addition to providing mortgage relief to landlords with Federal Housing Administration (FHA) loans, Secretary Ben Carson and his team at HUD also suspended evictions for tenants in public housing and other HUD-assisted properties. Our combined efforts with HUD—as well as those with the Department of Agriculture, which administers a large portfolio of rural housing loans—would never cover even half of the rental market. Some estimates suggested that the combined FHFA and HUD efforts were reaching only about a third of renters.[9] Since I believe our rental markets should be less dependent on government, this is not necessarily a bad thing. That said, it did limit the reach of any federal solution.

A broader rental solution would have to come from somewhere else. It is for that reason that discussions turned to an eviction moratorium. As the FHFA was then an independent regulator, we were not part of the discussions over whether the Centers for Disease Control and Prevention (CDC) should or could implement a moratorium on evictions. We were made aware of the discussions by our contacts in the White House.

I quickly got the sense that the idea for an eviction moratorium came directly from President Donald Trump. If anything, the CDC and the White House staff were uncomfortable with that proposal, if not outright opposed to it. But as I always reminded myself during my

White House service, the president is the one who got elected, not me. The role of advisers is to advise. If you do not like it when your advice is not taken, your option is to accept it or leave.

There is some irony in an eviction moratorium being pushed by Trump, as he had spent so much of his business career as a landlord, the profession most adversely impacted by the moratorium. It certainly cuts against the constant media refrain that he managed the presidency for his own benefit.

I thought it best for the FHFA to remain somewhat distanced from the issue. It was not a position I wanted to be associated with or forced into defending. On policy grounds, I am never a fan of rewriting contracts. Not only does that usually end badly, but I also believe it erodes the critical expectation in our society that promises are meant to be honored. Besides the fact that the FHFA was then an independent agency, it was not our place to opine on White House policies.

Landlords ultimately adjusted their behavior. A direct result of the moratorium was the offsetting actions of landlords. Higher security deposits were demanded. Tighter standards for new tenants, such as higher credit scores, were required. And of course, rents went up. All of this was predictable.

I have never liked eminent domain. Yes, it's mentioned in the Constitution. But it is often abused and misused, with its victims being primarily the poor. All that said, the basic principle that if the government takes property, it should pay for it is a sound one. Temporary taking of a property via an eviction moratorium should be similarly compensated. If the government wants tenants to be able to stay rent-free, then the government should at least cover the rent.

This was somewhat the position taken by many congressional Democrats, to their credit. During my regular calls with individual Democrats on both the Senate Banking Committee and the House Financial Services Committee, I would be asked about the impact of COVID-19 on renters. I would consistently reply that the pandemic was indeed a renter crisis, far more so than for homeowners. Several congressional Democrats wanted me to publicly endorse funding for renter relief. I am flattered that those members believed my voice would have any influence on the process.

On two occasions, Democrats in the House of Representatives did pass legislation providing COVID-19 rental assistance of $100 billion.[10] This was multiples of what any analyst was projecting as needed and was viewed more as a "messaging bill" than as a serious piece of legislation. I have always appreciated the ability of Rep. Al Green, a Democrat from Texas, one of the sponsors of these bills, to craft a catchy phrase. In this case, his saying "the rent must be paid, not delayed" failed to move the Senate.

A somewhat frustrating issue was that as an independent regulator, the FHFA really was not part of the legislative process. Negotiations were made between the administration, generally represented by Treasury Secretary Steven Mnuchin, and Congress. As I had no veto power over anything, I believed it best to make no public requests or suggestions and to simply share my observations and data with Congress and the administration in private.

Despite its public posture, the Trump White House appeared open to some sort of rental assistance. I never got the impression that they believed it was necessary, despite the moratorium, but I did get the sense that rental assistance was not some sort of red line never to be crossed. Despite the occasional public appearance of hard lines, almost everything in Washington is to some degree negotiable.

The important question was, "How much?"

Democrats were throwing out numbers that seemed wildly excessive, such as the aforementioned $100 billion. Some excess is to be expected. I have always approached public policy by trying to start with the "right" number, to the extent that there is one. Standard Washington practice, however, is to begin with a grossly inflated number, with the expectation that after endless rounds of negotiation, one ends up near the right number. I cannot say I relish this standard.

An additional aspect was the degree to which any assistance should be limited directly to distress from COVID-19. I firmly believe that a crisis response should deal only with the crisis at hand and not be cover for addressing issues that predate the crisis. My rationale is that the normal due diligence process, which is already inadequate, is weakened during a crisis. The probability of harmful and half-baked ideas getting into law increases in a crisis environment. If a proposal is truly thought-ful and consensus based, it should be able to pass into law under regular order. Crisis legislation rarely results in good long-term policy.

To better ground the question in data, the White House requested my participation in a call with the Treasury Department, the National Economic Council, and the Council of Economic Advisers (CEA). Tyler Goodspeed, acting CEA chair, offered CEA's analysis. Tyler's numbers were close to mine. It felt as if Mnuchin wanted me on the call mostly as a reality check on whatever numbers the White House offered. By this point, I had already become Mnuchin's go-to for quick housing and mortgage statistics. It seemed that decades of working with such data was finally becoming useful.

———

I never really understood the administration's public objections to rental assistance, when internally there appeared to be some openness to negotiation. Of course, there is always the unfortunate reality in Washington that once you agree that something is a problem, you can lose control of the solution. I agreed that the overall spending levels in the Coronavirus Aid, Relief, and Economic Security (CARES) Act and subsequent COVID-19 relief were far beyond what was needed and would eventually add to inflationary pressures. So, sure, I am strongly against wasting trillions on issues barely related to the pandemic, such as the massive bailout of state and local governments. But if you *are* going to spend trillions, a few billion for rental assistance seems justifiable, especially if you are going to impose an eviction moratorium on land-lords. In the end, Congress did decide to provide emergency rental assistance. The omnibus appropriations bill that was passed in 2020 allo-cated $25 billion, later followed by another $21.55 billion in March 2021 under the American Rescue Plan Act.

This $46.55 billion in rental assistance was far beyond any reasonable measure of need related to the pandemic. Even the liberal-leaning Urban Institute gauged the need at half that amount. The Urban Institute esti-mated that almost 80 percent of lost income for renters would be covered by a combination of UI and pandemic relief payments. Consistent with my own figures at the time, an upper bound of needed rental assistance was $15 billion. Even $10 billion, had it been means-tested and targeted, would have largely addressed the need. This is an amount that could even have been covered by a small fee on Fannie and Freddie activities.

———

The CARES Act created a moratorium on evictions from properties receiving some sort of federal subsidy. The moratorium was short-lived by design, lasting only four months. In addition, the CARES Act moratorium covered only about a third of renters. There were many state and local eviction moratoriums as well. In part, the state and local moratoriums resulted from an initial closing of courtrooms that could process eviction cases. As the end of the federal moratorium approached in late July 2020, many advocates warned of an "eviction tsunami." The left-leaning Aspen Institute predicted that "30 to 40 million" people would be at risk of eviction.[11]

Then came August 2020. The federal moratorium lapsed. And yet, no tsunami ensued. However, the predicted wave of evictions did result in the Trump administration's having the CDC impose a federal eviction moratorium on September 4, 2020. When the CDC moratorium was finally struck down by the Supreme Court because of the CDC's lack of legal authority, warnings of an eviction deluge again surfaced but also again proved false.

Yuliya Panfil, of the left-leaning think tank New America, and David Spievack, a research and strategy consultant, argue that the dire warnings "helped our country's machinery creak into gear, and likely ended up saving many Americans from eviction."[12] Since federal rental assistance did not actually reach most renters until much later, that is a questionable claim. To some extent, the issue is what "at risk" means. For instance, every single person on Earth is "at risk" from dying should a meteor hit the planet. Yet that banal observation provides little assistance in making policy choices.

Some researchers would undoubtedly be led astray by the Census Bureau's experimental Pulse Survey.[13] While it is commendable that the Census Bureau attempted to provide a real-time measurement of COVID-19's impact, several long-running census surveys, such as the Current Population Survey, displayed bizarre behavior during COVID-19. One example was the dramatic shifts in homeownership reported throughout 2020. Most housing economists take these numbers with a grain of salt. Having much of the population at home during a pandemic clearly changed the characteristics of who responded to government surveys. Combine that with the pre-COVID-19 sampling weights and you get some odd results. With so much uncertainty, advocates and researchers can perhaps be given some slack here.

The problem is that without a theory, one cannot interpret the data in a meaningful way. Despite the uncertainty of COVID-19, the FHFA was able to make surprisingly accurate forecasts of mortgage forbearance. Similar success was possible for the rental market.

As Salim Furth, at George Mason University's Mercatus Center, explained to *Reason* magazine, "Landlords have an incentive to work out deals with tenants who have trouble paying their bills. The alternative is to go through the expense of evicting a tenant only to have a vacancy that might be hard to fill in tough economic times."[14] Now that is a theory that makes a lot of sense.

Just as the FHFA looked at past recessions, such as 1990–1991, 2001, and 2007–2009, and used those to model the relationship between the job market and mortgage delinquency, one could have gone back and done the same for evictions. As Furth noted in 2020, evictions did not increase in the Great Recession.[15] There was little reason to expect 2020 to be worse. In light of the difficulty landlords would have screening and getting new tenants, the COVID-19 pandemic should have caused fewer evictions per job lost than in other recessions.

It is hard not to suspect that many simply saw COVID-19 as an opportunity to argue for rental assistance to help households suffering from hardships that predated COVID-19. The American Rescue Plan Act passed in 2021 appears to have little to do with COVID-19 and simply uses the cover of a crisis to pursue other ends. Obviously, that is not the first time this has been done, and it almost certainly will not be the last.

The debate over COVID-19 rental assistance touches on a tension that I have seen repeated in crisis environments: should assistance be broad, like UI, or be tied to a specific need, such as housing or food? Washington tends to take both approaches but rarely in a comprehensive, holistic manner. There has often been an implied assumption, both in the 2008 mortgage crisis and during COVID-19, that unemployed households should not be expected to use UI to cover housing costs, despite that being one of the core reasons for the provision of UI. To its credit, the Urban Institute, the primary go-to source of housing data for Democrats in Washington, did include UI in its analysis. Politicians, however, tended to ignore that important element of the debate.

———

Worse than getting the overall number wrong was the way rental assistance was distributed. Perhaps because of HUD's long and admittedly checkered history of distributing rental assistance, Congress chose to have the Treasury Department oversee the program, in partnership with state housing finance agencies. Not surprisingly, that arrangement turned out to be a disaster. The choice of Treasury had more to do with Congressional respect for Mnuchin than with any greater competency at Treasury in relation to housing programs.

By the end of June 2021, as I was leaving the FHFA, only 14 percent of the original funding had been spent. Even by the end of 2021, only 44 percent of the overall rental assistance had been spent, almost two years after the beginning of the pandemic. By this point, the labor market had largely recovered from COVID-19. To the degree that rental assistance was needed because of COVID-19, it was needed in 2020, not 2022.

It was crystal clear from the beginning that the Treasury Department had neither the expertise nor the interest in creating an effective rental assistance program. I do not blame Treasury, at least not fully. While Treasury Secretary Janet Yellen showed little commitment to the program, preferring to spend her time jetting off to Europe to rub elbows with foreign finance ministers, Congress is to blame for placing this responsibility with an agency so clearly missuited for the job. Regardless, it is critical that if a national rental assistance emergency program is ever created again, Treasury not be its administrator. If not HUD, perhaps the Federal Emergency Management Agency? I accept that none of the choices are particularly reassuring.

———

Renters suffer disproportionately in any recession. COVID-19 and the response to it struck particularly hard at those sectors, such as restaurants and retail, that rely heavily on renters as workers. Given this uneven impact and the numerous problems in getting UI out quickly, we needed a rental component to our housing response. Fannie and Freddie were an imperfect and narrow lever to aid. But you use the tools you have, not the ones you wish for. Our response at the FHFA helped keep about 200,000 rental households in their homes during the worst of COVID-19. As importantly, we did it cooperatively with the real estate industry. No one was forced into it. And we managed to mostly cover its costs via pricing changes imposed elsewhere in the mortgage market. As we experience recessions in the future with renters again being hit the hardest, the apartment mortgage forbearance programs established during my watch can serve as an effective and efficient model.

Chapter 5

Washington CARES

Lockdowns, fear of exposure, and uncertainty surrounding both the economy and the government's evolving response resulted in the sharpest labor market decline in American history, with total nonfarm employment dropping by 22 million jobs from February to April 2020.[1] In comparison, just under 9 million jobs were lost in the Great Recession, and that occurred over two years, from 2008 to 2010, not two months.[2]

With job loss often comes housing distress. Whether the job market would recover in three months or three years, we needed to create a financial bridge to stabilize families' financial health, at least until the unemployment benefits kicked in.

We could have chosen to do nothing, to let the chips fall where they may. That would have been devastating not just to the families affected but also to the financial health of Fannie Mae and Freddie Mac, whose oversight was the primary responsibility of the Federal Housing Finance Agency (FHFA). Attempting to foreclose and resell millions of homes amid a pandemic would have bankrupted Fannie and Freddie. Not only that, but it would also have served a massive blow to their corporate brands and reputation, which despite their failures would still have had some value.

The solution would be to provide borrowers with forbearance. Not forgiveness. Forbearance would offer borrowers a "time-out." They would be able to "press pause" on their monthly mortgage payments.

The missed payments would be added to the loan balance, so they would eventually have to be repaid. The hope, of course, was that the borrowers would be back on their feet within a few months, or that they would have started to receive unemployment insurance (UI), the very purpose of which was to help workers meet their expenses, including for housing.

Ultimately, about 8 million borrowers, roughly 1 in 10 homeowners, entered mortgage forbearance during COVID-19. By 2022, over 90 percent would exit forbearance, getting back on their feet, at least in relation to their mortgage.[3] In fact, more than half would be in forbearance for three months or less. Fifteen percent would take forbearance for only a single month.[4]

About a fifth of those borrowers would continue to make their monthly payments, despite having entered forbearance. Another fifth would repay their missed payments in one lump sum. I must admit I was surprised at how often Fannie and Freddie borrowers would send in a check for three or four months of missed payments. Over a fourth paid off their entire mortgage, usually by taking advantage of the record low rates to refinance.

Unfortunately, more than two years later, just under half a million borrowers who entered COVID-19 forbearance remain behind on their mortgages. Over 70,000 of those have entered foreclosure. However, the vast majority of those were delinquent before the pandemic. Others have been unable to recover lost jobs or income.

To some extent, we were lucky at the FHFA. Forbearance rates for Fannie and Freddie loans would peak around 6 percent in May 2020, as I had predicted in March 2020. The Federal Housing Administration (FHA), however, would see forbearance rates spike to almost 15 percent and remain in double digits well into 2021. While not quite as bad as the FHA mortgages, loans guaranteed by the Department of Agriculture's Rural Housing Service would display similarly high rates of forbearance.

———

Economists often focus on output, the stuff we buy, when gauging the strength or weakness of the economy, yet most of us are laser focused on jobs, especially our own. The usual process for helping workers weather a period of unemployment is our UI system, a convoluted and often complex partnership between states and the federal government.

The UI system typically covers about half of lost earnings and about half of all workers. There are a variety of reasons some workers are not covered, but the most common are self-employment and part-time employment. The duration of coverage is within the discretion of each state government but is generally less than six months.

During severe economic downturns, Congress will typically both increase the percentage of earnings lost and extend the duration of coverage. Congress repeated this pattern during COVID-19 and also extended coverage to some workers normally outside the UI system.

For both renters and homeowners, UI coverage is generally sufficient for monthly housing expenses. Since UI benefits are capped, those with particularly high housing costs may have trouble fully covering housing costs with UI benefits. There is also no requirement that those receiving UI spend it on housing, although most appear to do so. Without UI, it is likely that foreclosures and eviction rates would be two to three times higher during an economic downturn.

As discussed in the previous chapter, however, UI payments are often slow to reach the unemployed, leaving those with little savings struggling to cover their housing costs, at least temporarily.

———

If it is just a matter of time until UI payments show up, why not just prohibit lenders and landlords from foreclosing and evicting during that time, as many states and cities were considering? Perhaps it's not the most popular thing to say, but a world that prohibited evictions and foreclosures would be one where housing was in short supply and more expensive—hence one with more homelessness and even more families with high housing cost burdens.[5] While every individual eviction or foreclosure is a tragedy for the family involved, as well as the landlord or the lender, making such actions harder would cause even more harm.[6] Prohibition of evictions would absolutely lead to landlords taking offsetting actions, such as demanding larger security deposits, higher rents, and tighter credit background checks on potential tenants. Life is composed of tradeoffs, after all. Of course, prohibition of foreclosures and evictions would also involve rewriting of contracts and government seizure of private property, with all the accompanying problems such actions create.

In the end, however, those tradeoffs are empirical questions. And when the data change, the balance of costs to benefits may well change too. To state the obvious, COVID-19 dramatically changed those trade-offs. I was a vocal critic of the endless delays to foreclosure that characterized the 2008 crisis, as well as the ill-founded bank bailouts. It became typical in the Great Recession for foreclosures to take as long as two years to complete, especially in states where the courts ran the process. Much of the 2008 response can be characterized only as kicking the can down the road. I believed, and still do, that there were much better alternatives in the 2008 crisis. In 2020, we pursued some of them. Other policies that would not have made sense in 2008 did make sense in 2020.

As important as it is to recognize the existence of tradeoffs, who gets to make them is also critical. My decision to provide forbearance to borrowers with loans guaranteed by Fannie and Freddie was not an act of charity; it was an act of self-interest. Those loans were predominantly mortgages that would eventually begin to be repaid as COVID-19 receded and the economy recovered. Any purely private business would have behaved similarly. In fact, most lenders chose to follow the model the FHFA established for their own loans, when they had no legal obligation to do so.

The biggest difference, of course, was that 2020 was a public health crisis.[7] This is not to dismiss or downplay the very real health risks that accompany evictions and foreclosures even in normal, nonpandemic times. For instance, when eviction or foreclosure results in homelessness, studies have found an increased risk of substance abuse and sexually transmitted diseases.[8] But prohibiting eviction and foreclosure even in normal times would increase the risks because of the increase in homelessness resulting from the reduction in housing access.

During my time on Capitol Hill, I served as one of the drafters and negotiators of the HEARTH Act (Homeless Emergency Assistance and Rapid Transition to Housing Act) signed by President Barack Obama in 2009, which reauthorized and modernized our homelessness assistance laws. My legislative partner in that effort and good friend Kara Stein later went on to serve as a commissioner at the Securities and

Exchange Commission. The health dangers of homelessness during a pandemic were not some fuzzy, theoretical concern to me, as I had spent earlier parts of my career studying and legislating on the issue of homelessness.

———

In March 2020, we were still learning about COVID-19's transmission mechanism. We did know that evictions and foreclosures often rely heavily on personal interactions. For the households that go through a judicial process, a cramped courtroom could easily become a super-spreader event. That is why many courthouses closed their doors early in the pandemic. Evictions and foreclosures entail other interactions as well, such as having a sheriff's deputy oversee the process onsite or spending hours at a legal aid clinic or homeless shelter. All of these were considered possible transmission risks in spring 2020.

We were in no way public health experts at the FHFA. How bad COVID-19 would be and how long it would last were questions far beyond our expertise. What we did suspect, as knowledge of COVID-19's transmission mechanism was still evolving in March 2020, was that close human interaction was the most likely avenue for the virus to spread. We also suspected that individuals or families displaced from their homes by eviction or foreclosure would likely increase the spread of the virus. It was all about reducing the transmission of COVID-19. While perhaps not as directly critical as the health care interventions, keeping families in their homes would reduce spread while also giving the health care community additional time to develop a vaccine and other mitigation tools.

Where we did have some expertise was in housing and mortgage markets. I, for starters, had led the staff work for the Senate Banking Committee in its response to Hurricane Katrina in 2005 and had handled the committee's housing and mortgage work in the years leading up to the 2008 financial crisis. While we were not able to implement reforms in time, the Senate Banking Committee made multiple efforts to strengthen our mortgage markets between 2003 and 2008. Handling the committee's response to Hurricane Katrina carried additional responsibilities when one worked for the senior senator from Alabama, one of the states most affected. The FHFA was also full of veterans of both the financial crisis and several natural disasters.

As a front-row observer of the 2008 mortgage crisis, I am strongly convinced that much of the federal response was poorly structured, especially the mortgage assistance programs, the Home Affordable Modification Program (HAMP) and the Home Affordable Refinance Program (HARP). As will soon be evident, a major influence on my decisionmaking was the intention to not repeat the design flaws of HAMP and HARP. We would do it right, or at least better, this time.

I am a big believer that decisions should be based on data as much as possible. Of course, there are always unknowns, even unknown unknowns (à la Donald Rumsfeld), and it never feels like you have sufficient data to have 100 percent confidence. But then, the markets (and families) are not going to wait. Fortunately for the FHFA, we had established a new division of research and statistics in January 2020. I recruited a well-respected industry researcher and academic, Dr. Lynn Fisher, to organize and manage the division. Lynn had done stints at the Mortgage Bankers Association, the American Enterprise Institute, and the University of North Carolina at Chapel Hill. Lynn and I quickly realized that the big driver here was going to be the job market. Loss of one's job is historically the main reason a borrower might have trouble paying their mortgage.

Lynn's team was quickly able to establish two facts. First, only about 40 percent of the immediate job losses expected from COVID-19 would involve families with mortgages—that is, this was going to be mainly a renter's crisis. And second, looking at the historical relationship between job loss and mortgage delinquency, these were likely to be costs that the mortgage industry, including Fannie Mae and Freddie Mac, would be able to bear.

———

I also wished to avoid one of the biggest mistakes of the Great Recession: structuring assistance in a way that would discourage work. The Great Recession witnessed the weakest job growth of any post–World War II recession.

As an economist, one of the issues that puzzled me most during the early years of the Great Recession was the seeming disconnect between overall consumer spending and the job market. While the economy was of course weak in the immediate aftermath of the 2008 crisis, consumer spending actually recovered relatively quickly. Normally, one would expect such an increase in spending to translate into a similar-size recovery in jobs. Economists refer to this relationship between spending and unemployment as Okun's law, named after economist Arthur Okun. But that didn't happen.

Also indicative of structural problems in the labor market was the breakdown in the Beveridge curve—that is, the relationship between unemployment and job vacancies. Job postings steadily increased once the economy hit bottom in summer 2009 but with little impact on the unemployment rate.

Many in the economics profession, at least the professional forecasters, continued to see the weak job market as a function of weak demand in the overall economy. Keep in mind that these forecasters overwhelmingly use models of the economy that are demand focused and that generally downplay, if not outright ignore, the supply side of the economy. So of course a modeling exercise built around demand factors is going to point in the direction of demand factors. For this reason, among others, forecasters consistently overprojected growth from 2009 to 2016 and systematically underprojected growth from 2016 to 2019. But that is another story.

I was among the minority of economists around 2009 and 2010 to whom it increasingly appeared that we were facing structural changes in the labor market. During a Senate hearing at the time, I had suggested that mortgage assistance programs were locking workers in place, perhaps discouraging moves from weak job markets to stronger job markets.[9] The Great Recession, for instance, was one of the few recessions in which mobility—that is, moving—decreased. It is common to perceive a recession affecting all parts of the country equally, but such is rarely the case. In 2010, for instance, focusing on the almost 15 percent unemployment rate in Nevada misses the 2010 unemployment rate of 3.9 percent experienced in North Dakota.[10] There were likely unemployed construction workers in Nevada who stayed in Nevada because of the structure of mortgage assistance programs, rather than taking work in the energy boom occurring in North Dakota.

It was not until I had started to read the work of University of Chicago professor Casey Mulligan that the pieces started to fall into place. Professor Mulligan's thesis is a simple one, even if he uses a lot of complex math to demonstrate it.[11] The idea is that a massive expansion of means-tested programs, starting in 2008 but ramping up in 2009 and 2010, resulted in very large increases in work disincentives in terms of government benefits lost because of income increases. At the center of this expansion were the mortgage assistance programs established in the Great Recession.

The admirable objective of these assistance programs was to keep families in their homes by making the mortgage payments affordable. The somewhat arbitrary target was to cap monthly mortgage payments at 31 percent of income. That number was pulled out of a hat. To illustrate just how arbitrary 31 percent is, borrowers could spend well over 50 of their income on mortgage payments when first applying for a loan insured by the FHA. So, under the federal government's guidelines, one could get a loan backed by the FHA and be eligible for assistance immediately after leaving the closing table. So much for safe, or sane, underwriting standards on the front end of the mortgage.

But the real problem was that this number effectively created an additional tax of 31 percent for each additional dollar one earned, since one's monthly mortgage payment would increase by 31 cents for every new dollar. Above a certain income threshold, borrowers lost program eligibility, so in some circumstances people could see an implied tax rate of 100 percent or more. Mulligan estimates that in some unusual instances, borrowers could face an implied tax rate of almost 400 percent. That is, for every dollar you earned, you lost $4 in mortgage relief. For most borrowers, this loss was closer to 31 percent. But combined with other expanded means-tested assistance programs, such as unemployment assistance, the total loss of government benefits for each additional dollar earned could be staggering. Mulligan's calculation indicated that these program expansions and their very strong work disincentives were the primary reasons for the weak job recovery of the Great Recession.

The public debates over work disincentives in assistance programs can quickly degenerate into emotional, and often contrived, discussions over whether recipients are "lazy." Usually, such debates serve to confuse rather than illuminate. The question of whether to help is a different one from how such assistance is to be structured. I believe the empirical evidence that incentives matter is overwhelming. But that simply raises questions about the structure of assistance, not its merits.

Since the research strongly suggested that the structure of the Great Recession mortgage assistance programs effectively punished work, a solution that would both assist families and not discourage work was needed.

Accepting that any program is going to have costs and benefits, the immediate objective was to buy time, or "flatten the curve." Since time was the objective, we decided to base mortgage forbearance not on current income but on time. While a loss of income was the immediate qualification, you would not lose your forbearance when you went back to work or earned more income. The length of assistance would be limited to our best guess as to how long the pandemic would adversely affect the job market. In March 2020, our best estimate was a three- to six-month downturn in the job market. Accordingly, we initially offered forbearance with the requirement that every three months the lender would check in on the financial status of the borrower. When Congress later codified our plan into statute, through the Coronavirus Aid, Relief, and Economic Security (CARES) Act, the maximum assistance period was fixed at 12 months.

———

Another problem of the 2008 mortgage crisis, and one I hoped to avoid, was the paper chase associated with the various mortgage assistance programs, such as HAMP and HARP. Generally, for borrowers to be eligible for forbearance or other mortgage assistance, a substantial amount of paperwork was required. There were countless stories of such papers being lost or rejected. In some instances, forms were being submitted with false information by either the lender or the borrower. As law professors Kathleen Engel and Patricia McCoy describe in their book, *The Subprime Virus: Reckless Credit, Regulatory Failure, and Next Steps*, "Servicers were inundated with paperwork. Loan files got lost or were incomplete. Borrowers would repeatedly submit the needed information only to have servicers repeatedly lose the documents in the frenzy."[12]

Such paperwork requirements were not without reason. If anyone could just apply for mortgage forgiveness or have their payments paused, a lot of borrowers who did not need help would take it, potentially overwhelming the system and adding billions of dollars to costs that might ultimately be borne by the taxpayer. In addition to the direct monetary costs, borrowers unnecessarily taking assistance would also pull human resources away from those who needed them. But in a financial crisis, you must triage. So yes, those programs were poorly executed, but there was no getting around the tradeoffs.

Another reason for such a stringent application process for mortgage assistance during the Great Recession was to determine how much assistance to grant. The Great Recession programs were generally means-tested, with benefits being reduced as one's income grew. Of course, there is a logic to such a requirement. I am the first to believe we should limit, or at least target, government resources to those most in need. That said, there was a big issue to address: any income information would be stale. With the rapid rate of job loss due to COVID-19, the use of last year's tax return would likely not offer an accurate picture of a borrower's current need.

As researchers within the Federal Reserve System later recognized, "Forbearance was especially effective due to its timeliness and the ease with which borrowers were able to take advantage of it."[13] Those, of course, were two of our main objectives in designing the programs.

———

That experience left me with a tough decision, one that could not be avoided: What would be required of borrowers? At the time, the FHFA was an independent regulator, so the decision about what would be asked of millions of borrowers seeking COVID-19 mortgage relief rested on my shoulders. The White House had yet to decide about the government-backed mortgage programs, such as those managed by the Department of Housing and Urban Development (HUD), the Department of Agriculture, and the Department of Veterans Affairs. I have worked in the White House. The deliberative process within any administration is not designed to move quickly. Most of the time, that is for the best so that various stakeholders can be heard and decisions can be made purposefully. Facing a pandemic, though, I decided to move quickly and alone, if necessary.

I made the decision to take borrowers at their word. We would direct mortgage servicers to orally inquire whether a borrower requiring assistance had suffered a financial hardship as a direct result of COVID-19, such as a job loss. I recognized from the very beginning that this was a big gamble. It could easily have been taken advantage of by borrowers not needing assistance, which had the potential to quickly overwhelm the mortgage market.

In my media appearances, I made sure not only to inform homeowners that assistance was available and how to get it, but also to discourage those who did not need assistance from applying—perhaps a first among policymakers. We had limited resources. For starters, the FHFA, Fannie, Freddie, and the mortgage servicing industry had only so many employees. Attention paid to borrowers who did not need help would pull attention away from those who did.

———

While we could do more for homeowners, we could not forget that this was a renter's crisis. We were fortunate to have a great multifamily group at the FHFA, led by Siobhan Kelly, working under Deputy Director for Mission and Goals Sandra Thompson. When you add in Maria Fernandez, who led the single-family homeowner efforts, you have the leadership team that kept families in place and kept the mortgage market going during COVID-19. This team worked long hours and brought forth solutions and resolutions to issue after issue. As my primary objective as director was to see that the FHFA truly became a world-class financial regulator, I was constantly impressed with the drive and skill of the staff. What they had lacked in past years was supportive leadership and direction.

I had been director for only 11 months when we switched to mandatory telework. Fortunately, I had known many members of our senior team for years. Others I would get to know better over multiple Skype and Zoom calls. I feel for anyone who had to take over an organization during COVID-19. Much of the functioning of any organization depends on the hard-learned experience of figuring out on whom you can rely and on whom you cannot. Such is rarely apparent from first impressions.

After all, it is others in the organization who implement the directives and orders that come down from above. For the FHFA to have an effective COVID-19 response, agency staff needed to feel, and be, supported. The FHFA staff were dealing with the same issues that families across the world were facing: How to deal with children at home. How to share space others working from home. How to process grief and loss. While the FHFA was fortunate in that we did not lose any staff to COVID-19 during my tenure, several staff members lost relatives—especially parents—and friends. Their ability to mourn was of course hindered by restrictions on funerals and other gatherings. Although not because of COVID-19, my stepfather passed away in June 2020. And I lost my uncle Rick in the summer of 2021. I have long considered myself, deservedly or not, a modestly talented writer. But crafting notes or emails to staff who lost relatives was one of the hardest, but most essential, responsibilities. Keeping employee morale high was deemed critical from the very beginning of the pandemic. A crucial part of that task included keeping employees informed.

Leading a large organization during a pandemic is a challenge. Unfortunately, the FHFA lacked direction and had deep-seated morale problems. There had been questions about whether the agency would even continue to exist. The decade-long conservatorships of Fannie Mae and Freddie Mac had left the agency in limbo. When I walked through the doors of the FHFA, most of the staff neither respected nor trusted senior agency leadership. For the FHFA to demonstrate its support for borrowers and renters, it first had to demonstrate its support for its own employees.

———

History is likely to record the federal COVID-19 response to the housing market as the CARES Act. Since the CARES Act put into statute largely what we at the FHFA had already established a few weeks earlier, Congress clearly believed the FHFA was on the right track.

I did not like Congress putting into statute what we were already doing. I had expressed that to Sen. Sherrod Brown, the senior Democrat on the Senate Banking Committee, and to his staff, who were the primary drafters of the forbearance provisions of the CARES Act. I had also told both Sen. Mike Crapo, the chairman of the Senate Banking Committee, and Sen. Pat Toomey, the next most senior Republican member of the committee. Although different sections of the CARES Act came from the House and the Senate, the mortgage provisions were drafted predominantly by the Senate.

I never doubted Senator Brown's commitment to families. While I have my policy disagreements with him, we generally got along and, I believe, respected one another. Much to his credit, I can also attest that Senator Brown never once asked me for anything on behalf of the financial services industry. I cannot say the same about other members of Congress. I also appreciated the work of his housing staff, Beth Cooper and Megan Cheney, as well as his chief of staff, Laura Swanson. Perhaps the fact that I had known Beth for many years helped smooth my relationship with Senator Brown. Back when Beth and I were both young enough to be regulars at Washington's 9:30 Club, we had even attended a few concerts together. There's nothing like a shared appreciation of music to bring people together. Yes, our politics were different, but our commitment was not. And it was not that I did not support the goals of the CARES Act since we were already pursuing them.

It was my concern that putting numerous restrictions into statute could limit our flexibility going forward. It is much easier to change guidance or even regulations than it is to change statutes. There was even one instance in which Senator Brown later requested that we do something we could not do because of the way the CARES Act was drafted. In our multifamily rental forbearance programs, for the borrowers—that is, the landlords—to be in forbearance, they had to agree not to evict any tenants for nonpayment of rent. Put simply, we would press "pause" for the landlords if they did the same for their tenants. We also made it voluntary for the landlords. They did not have to participate, but if they did, they had to share the benefit with the tenants.

The issue with the CARES Act, however, was that landlords of single-family residences, which account for about a third of renters, were not required to pass along that break to their tenants. When we initially established forbearance, the FHFA treated single-family rentals as if they were owner occupied. That is because of the similar nature in which those loans are serviced. It is also because Fannie and Freddie often do not know if the property is renter occupied. A lot of single-family rentals start out as owner occupied, and there is no requirement to inform the lender of a change in status. The result was that the apartment landlords had to pass along the benefits of their assistance, while single-family home landlords did not. At least in both cases, participation by the landlord was voluntary under the programs created by the FHFA.

As we had no direct relationship with renters, it would be left up to the landlords to figure out how to recoup any late rent. We understood that for many of them, this would essentially mean lost, or never collected, rent. But as we had no leverage with renters, we could not require late rent to be paid. Not only did we not have a relationship with renters, we did not even know who they were, as the leases were the property not of Fannie and Freddie, but of the landlords. With the weak financial health of Fannie and Freddie, we also did not have the resources to forgive landlord mortgage payments in exchange for forgiven rent, not that we had the legal authority to do so.

Yes, this problem is somewhat on me and the FHFA, as we had not fully fleshed out the renter assistance programs when the CARES Act was being drafted, but it is also due to such unforeseen circumstances that I requested that our programs not be included in the CARES Act. Unfortunately, Congress's desire to get credit for the FHFA's work ended up being more important than maintaining the flexibility to respond to changing circumstances. Since I am generally one who favors Congress's making as many of the decisions as possible (after all, its members are elected and I was not), I have been supportive of its addressing mortgage forbearance issues, as was done in the CARES Act.

———

Establishing assistance programs was just the beginning. Perhaps to be expected, there was some confusion about these programs on the parts of borrowers, renters, lenders, and the general public. With a handful of commentators calling for mortgage and rent forgiveness rather than forbearance, some families approached their lenders with the hope that any paused mortgage payments would be forgiven.[14]

Whether it would have been better to just forgive rent and mortgage payments was a question far outside our scope at the FHFA. Most importantly, we did not have the legal authority to do so. It would have to be the decision of Congress, not us. Furthermore, we simply did not have the resources. Even a targeted modest forgiveness program would have bankrupted Fannie Mae and Freddie Mac. They were already massively leveraged and on the verge of failure *without* adding tens of billions of dollars of additional losses. What's more, the FHFA's first responsibility was to oversee the safety and soundness of Fannie Mae, Freddie Mac, and the Federal Home Loan Banks. Forcing any of these entities into massive losses would have been the exact opposite of our legal responsibilities. The FHFA is not HUD or the Federal Emergency Management Agency. The FHFA is a safety and soundness regulator, not a grantmaking or household assistance agency.

Perhaps as importantly, broad mortgage forgiveness was also not needed. Job losses were concentrated predominantly among renters. Fannie and Freddie do not have relationships with renters. Their exposure was directly to homeowners and only indirectly to renters via the landlords. As for the homeowners, our internal data clearly showed that the overwhelming majority of Fannie and Freddie borrowers had significant equity in their homes. Less than 1 percent of Fannie and Freddie forbearance borrowers had loan-to-value ratios over 97 percent. The typical mortgage holders in forbearance had 20 to 30 percent equity in their homes. That is, they had the ability to pay back any paused mortgage payments. They also had extremely strong incentives to pay them back. For borrowers without that ability, we did have other options.

Requiring borrowers to pay back any forbearance also reduced the incentive of anyone who did not need the assistance to take advantage of it. While politicians might prefer giveaways to all, we did not have that option, not that we would have pursued it if we had. Fannie and Freddie were also still private companies, even if chartered by Congress and in conservatorship. Appropriately, there was no broader public expectation that private companies should voluntarily suffer losses or give away their products for free because of COVID-19. Fannie and Freddie operated under the same set of rules.

———

One issue that we wanted to avoid was any payment shock when the borrowers exited forbearance. It had been asserted that the 2008 crisis was caused by millions of borrowers being pushed into default when the interest rates on their mortgages were reset. Various mortgage products—such as so-called 5/1s and 2/28s—would function by having low fixed rates, such as for the first five years in the case of a 5/1, and then adjust to a market-driven rate, often some spread over the London Interbank Offered Rate (LIBOR). If the market rate at the time of reset was above the introductory rate, the borrower's monthly payment would increase. Depending on the rates, this rise could be quite dramatic and in theory could be sufficient to push a borrower into default.

It was common during the early days of the 2008 crisis to hear rate resets cast as the chief cause of the predicament. I believe that once mortgage rates dramatically declined and defaults continued to mount, it became clear that resets were at worst a modest contributor to the crisis. However, even with that in mind, we wished to avoid a situation in which borrowers exiting forbearance would see large rises in their monthly payments. We hoped to keep any increase modest and manageable for the borrower.

At the same time, we were trying to conserve capacity on the balance sheets of Fannie and Freddie for future workout loans. It is standard practice that if a mortgage becomes delinquent and must be modified in some manner to achieve sustainability, usually in the form of a rate reduction or extension of the term, then said loan is removed from the pool of loans that serve as collateral for agency-issued mortgage-backed securities. When that happens, the loan is generally moved onto the balance sheet.

An additional concern was to minimize any disruption to the mortgage-backed securities market, which had already experienced a rough ride in March 2020. We did not need further surprises. If we modified loans on a massive scale, we would have to remove them from the mortgage pools and replace them mostly with lower-rate loans. The result could be a sudden and significant decline in the value of mortgage-backed securities. Some of this declining value was likely unavoidable, given the rate environment, but we could at least slow that decline, bringing a little more price stability to that market, which finally determines the price that households pay for their mortgages.

The solution we settled on was to add any missed payments to the end of the loan, what we called "payment deferral." These payments would essentially be a balloon. They would be paid back once the home was sold, coming out of the proceeds like any normal mortgage. A more likely outcome, due to the low-rate environment, would be that payments would be rolled into the loan amount when the loan was next refinanced. In such cases, most borrowers would still see a substantial reduction in their monthly payments, even with the higher loan balance.

———

Mortgage forbearance offered during COVID-19 was a success, especially compared with the efforts of 2008. That outcome was not guaranteed. Almost by coincidence, my obsession with the 2008 response became an asset. There would be an opportunity to do it right this time.

The parameters of the COVID-19 mortgage response, however appropriate for a pandemic, might not be the best response for next time. And there will be a next time. Most likely, it will match the historical trend of a monetary-induced increase in mortgage rates leading to a decline in housing demand, followed by weakness in housing prices, which when mixed with a spike in unemployment leads to mortgage distress.

The precedents set during COVID-19 that are likely to be useful next time include the following: basing duration of forbearance on a fixed window in time, not on changes in income or employment; allowing borrowers to attest to hardship first, with servicers verifying eligibility later; and requiring that missed payments be paid back but not all at once. Be quick and clean and directly address the issue at hand.

One concern about forbearance design for next time is the possibility that borrowers who do not need assistance take it.[15] In 2008, many borrowers blamed their lenders for their situation.[16] Occasionally there was good reason to do so. That said, such feelings made the problem harder to solve. Forbearance and certainly foreclosure are expensive, even when successful. Fortunately, borrowers did not abuse the forbearance option during COVID-19, at least not Fannie and Freddie borrowers.[17] Next time, however, if there is again widespread borrower anger directed at lenders, we might see the return of strategic forbearance.

The success of forbearance during the COVID-19 epidemic might suggest that Fannie and Freddie should be kept in permanent conservatorship, since conservatorship was the legal vehicle for implementing forbearance. Such a conclusion is unwarranted. The problematic mortgage mitigation programs of the Great Recession were conducted during the conservatorship. They did not appear to improve the agencies' performance. We have also witnessed similar forbearance options offered on mortgages not covered by the CARES Act. Even more telling is that similar levels and flexibility of forbearance were offered in the auto loan market, where there are no government-sponsored enterprises. Now that the FHFA has lost some of its independence, the agency's ability to move quickly may well be compromised in the future. If anything, our mortgage market will be better prepared for the next crisis with Fannie and Freddie fully capitalized and operating outside conservatorship.

More importantly, I fear we will lack the leadership to make unpopular choices. My telling borrowers not to take assistance if they did not need it was not popular. I could not imagine an elected official disseminating that message. Requiring missed payments to be repaid was not popular, especially when it appeared that trillions of dollars were just being given away by Congress. And making sure it was *all* paid for, by creating a mortgage fee to recoup the cost of COVID-19 assistance, was definitely not popular. While not as obvious at the time, paying for the assistance provided by Fannie and Freddie also meant that the aid was not adding to the inflationary pressures witnessed later in the pandemic.

Chapter 6
Servicer Snags and Snarls

"The housing finance industry is about to collapse."
—April 8, 2020, Odeon Capital analyst Dick Bove[1]

As if setting up assistance for homeowners and renters were not enough, a tremendous amount of time, attention, and energy was expended from March to July 2020 to address real and imagined funding pressures on mortgage servicers.

The mortgage forbearance measures, instituted by the Federal Housing Finance Agency (FHFA) and later codified by the Coronavirus Aid, Relief, and Economic Security (CARES) Act, placed considerable liquidity demands on mortgage servicers, as they were required to temporarily fund a certain number of skipped payments. Some in the mortgage industry felt that these demands entitled them to government assistance. I read the evidence otherwise. The debate over a servicer bailout brought back echoes of 2008.

———

Perhaps as the result of implementing the honor system for borrowers, coupled with uncertainty surrounding the job market, several commentators warned that mortgage forbearance rates could get as high as 40 or 50 percent. Regularly cited forecaster Mark Zandi claimed that 30 percent of homeowners would request forbearance.[2]

Such high levels of forbearance could threaten the financial viability of many nonbank mortgage servicers. For this reason, many in the industry—including the trade associations representing the mortgage industry, such as the Mortgage Bankers Association (MBA)—were calling for a government-backed lending facility to fund the liquidity needs of mortgage servicers.

Of course, the Wall Street–paid forecasters were not the only ones yelling "fire." One anonymous industry insider cried to *Politico* that I had "torched" my credibility by not rescuing Wall Street.[3] Another Wall Street lobbyist, Michael Bright, head of the Structured Finance Association, claimed that "FHFA's stance makes little sense, either from the taxpayer's perspective or from their role as conservator. Providing short-term, collateral-backed liquidity to servicers would avoid the operational and financial challenges [of transferring those rights]."[4] This is the same argument Wall Street rolls out every time, that using bankruptcy or enforcing contracts is too complicated. I heard it repeatedly in 2008. I certainly expected it in 2020. And, sadly, we will hear it next time Wall Street is asked to honor its obligations.

Difficulties in transferring servicing were a concern before COVID-19. As the 2019 annual report of the Financial Stability Oversight Council (FSOC), of which I was a member at the time, stated, "the Enterprises and Ginnie Mae may have difficulty transferring servicing from failed nonbank servicers to healthy servicers if multiple large nonbank servicers simultaneously face distress—which may be a risk given the similarities in their business models—and if other firms are unwilling or unable to assume the servicing responsibilities."[5]

The big "if" there is having "multiple large nonbank servicers simultaneously fac[ing] distress." The truth is that it is not "too complicated" to transfer servicing for a handful of servicers and certainly not for smaller servicers. The FHFA, working with Fannie Mae and Freddie Mac, had just done a large transfer in September 2019 when Ditech failed and was acquired by New Residential Investment. Just a few months before

COVID-19 hit, we already had a trial run for addressing servicer stress. The Ditech transfer was not a one-off, since both Fannie and Freddie had significant experience transferring servicing.

This is not to minimize the effect of mortgage servicing transfers on consumers. I had experienced such an impact myself. During the Great Recession, Bank of America transferred the servicing of my mortgage to a nonbank servicer. Unfortunately, the new servicer did not make the next scheduled property tax payment on my mortgage. The District of Columbia did not express much sympathy and hit me with a penalty for the new servicer's mistake. If I had not noticed it and eventually fixed the situation with the city government, I could have lost my home to a tax lien.

What makes it even more enraging is that I am a long-time customer of Bank of America. They even hold the checking account I opened when I was 15, which they gained during one of their acquisition sprees. So much for customer loyalty.

In the case of my mortgage, the servicing was transferred from a bank to a nonbank, which does explain some of the decline in quality. The FHFA, however, was preparing to transfer mortgages from weaker companies to stronger ones. Given the shortsightedness of companies when they are at risk of failure—after all, their focus is on their survival, not their customers'—transferring from weak companies to stronger ones would likely improve, on average, the experience of mortgage customers.

———

Policymakers best serve the public, and more specifically financial markets, by being as transparent as they can, clarifying as much as possible what will occur under certain circumstances. The approach of "constructive ambiguity" adopted so often by Federal Reserve chair Alan Greenspan or the "maximum optionality" approach of Treasury Secretary Robert Rubin might suit policymakers, but it leaves the public guessing and encourages industry lobbying for exceptions and preferences. So, in the beginning of April 2020, I conducted a few press interviews, as well as Capitol Hill and industry conversations, spelling out exactly what would happen were a servicer to fail.

Apparently, some lenders recognized themselves in my public remarks about "weaker" companies and took offense. Responding on behalf of such lenders, the president of the MBA called my plan to transfer servicing "a troubling message to borrowers, lenders, and the mortgage market."[6] Oddly, the MBA wasn't troubled when we transferred the servicing of Ditech in September 2019. Rather, the opposite. I believe that certainty as to how failures would be handled is critical for financial markets—and consumers. But then, the last thing Wall Street lobbyists want to hear is that there are alternatives to bailouts. And, of course, there's always the Wall Street claim that bailouts are really to benefit borrowers, not lenders.

The transfer of servicing from weak to stronger companies was also well tested. Upon its failure, Taylor, Bean & Whitaker saw its servicing business transferred in 2009. In 2012, the servicing portfolios of both Aurora Bank (better known as being a subsidiary of Lehman Brothers) and Residential Capital were successfully transferred.[7] The same was done with Doral Bank's servicing portfolio in 2015 upon its demise.[8] These are just a few examples of servicing transfers in the case of unsuccessful companies. Even more telling is the regular selling of servicing portfolios in the normal course of business.

The preceding transfers were conducted under fairly typical market conditions, so one argument is that COVID-19 presented circumstances that would make it difficult or unfair to transfer servicing. Such logic did not deter the Federal Deposit Insurance Corporation (FDIC) from closing the First State Bank in Barboursville, West Virginia, in April 2020; the First City Bank of Florida in Fort Walton Beach, Florida, in October 2020; or the Almena State Bank in Almena, Kansas, also in October 2020.[9] These failures all likely had some adverse impact on their communities and customers. However, there is an established procedure for bank failures. The FDIC did not depart from that process during COVID-19. There was also no compelling reason for the FHFA to deviate from our established process in the case of any collapses among mortgage servicers.

———

The claim that it's too complicated to transfer servicing was not the only argument we heard. Some commentators were predicting a full

financial meltdown if the federal government did not rescue the mortgage industry. Former New York Federal Reserve staffer Chris Whalen
went as far as to declare that not rescuing mortgage servicers would
destroy the U.S. Treasury market. In Whalen's words, "Without immediate action to provide liquidity to servicers of both conventional and
government loans, the U.S. mortgage market is going to seize up.
When the servicers cannot fund their operations, then the new issue
market will come to a halt. . . . Anybody who thinks that the market
for U.S. Treasury securities can survive the collapse of the agency and
government-insured mortgage markets should think again."[10]

Apparently, the hyperbole was not enough for Whalen, as he repeatedly called for me to be "fired by President Trump" for my unwillingness
to rescue lenders. Unfortunately for Whalen, the White House did not
support rescuing mortgage servicers either. In fact, the message from the
White House was continually "stay strong and follow the facts." More
than once, I received a message from them cheering on my willingness to
stick to the data and not be rolled over by industry demands for bailouts.

The FHFA's estimates—based on the historical relationship between
job losses and mortgage delinquency, with a special dive into both the
1990s and the early 2000s—suggested that forbearances for loans purchased by Fannie and Freddie would be much lower, in the mid- to high
single digits, which turned out to be extremely accurate.

Since public commentators who were forecasting much higher numbers never publicly put forth any real analysis to support their claims or
provided their analysis when requested by the FHFA, we quite frankly
were puzzled as to how such large numbers were derived. Of course,
we accepted that our estimates could be wrong. They were based on
the past, after all, and this was indeed a novel environment. We assured
ourselves and our stakeholders that we would continue to monitor the
forbearance data as they came in. If the data suggested that different
policies were needed, we would be ready to change course.

Unfortunately, a commitment to follow the data did not please everyone. Despite a lack of evidence, servicers and their allies demanded either
that Fannie Mae and Freddie Mac provide them with cheap funding or that
such cheap funding be offered by the Federal Reserve. Given both the trou-

bled state of Fannie and Freddie and the relatively healthier state of mortgage servicers, the former was not an option. The FHFA's first responsibility was to protect the safety and soundness of Fannie Mae and Freddie Mac. In particular, since I had staked my reputation on changing the FHFA's occasional disregard for the law, I was not about to start ignoring our statutory obligations, especially for entities that we had no control over or responsibility for.

Important decisions should rarely be based on a single piece of data. While I was very comfortable with our economists' estimates of future forbearance numbers and our accounting data for servicers, it was critical that we supplement these data by hearing directly from industry participants. Before March 2020 had closed, John Roscoe had organized one-on-one calls with the CEOs of all the major mortgage servicers. I wanted to hear from them what they were seeing. I also recognized that the accounting data we had on servicer liquidity were likely somewhat outdated. I wanted to know if such data for each servicer still reflected its actual financial condition. We also wanted to know how much extra servicing capacity each company had. We might need it to transfer servicing from a weaker company to a stronger one.

Over the course of March and into early April 2020, we spoke directly to the CEOs of some 20 mortgage servicers representing most of the industry. While the majority spoke in favor of a government lending facility, not one claimed to need it for themselves, nor did any of the CEOs echo the more apocalyptic pronouncements of industry lobbyists. Most CEOs, in fact, made clear efforts during our calls to distance themselves from such dire warnings.

Perhaps they were just being shy, but the history of Bear Stearns and Lehman in 2008 shows that failing firms rarely hold back from asking for help in private. They might not want to admit weakness in public, but if the survival of your firm was on the line, you would say so to federal regulators.

Gauging the actual financial health of mortgage servicers was not the sole reason for these calls. I wanted to also gauge their ability to absorb the servicing of any companies that might collapse. Not surprisingly, there was a wide range of interest and ability. A few servicers expressed being close to "maxed out," but that was only a few. Many expressed a strong interest and ability to absorb the servicing of any failed companies. In addition to the aggregate industry capacity estimates we had calculated ourselves, these calls to the CEOs allowed us to come up with a rough range of how much servicing could be transferred without running into any systemic issues. At no time in 2020 did the industry ever appear at risk of breaching that range.

_____

After a few weeks, I reached the conclusion that talking to some Washington industry lobbyists was mostly a waste of time. They seldom, if ever, had any facts or analysis. Roscoe and the FHFA's number two, Adolfo Marzol, were kind enough to take many of the trade association calls. I wanted to get the facts. For that, I relied on regular calls with leaders within the mortgage industry.

My decisions would have been a lot less informed and deliberative had mortgage industry leaders like Sanjiv Das at Caliber, Jay Bray at Mr. Cooper, Mat Ishbia at United Wholesale, David Spector at PennyMac, Sandro DiNello at Flagstar, and Bill Emerson at Quicken[11] not been willing to share their expertise and observations with me on a regular basis. More than once, a CEO told me that a certain policy choice would cost their company revenue, but they saw it as the right thing to do and supported the final decision.

I have long found that when engaging with industry trade associations, it pays to go directly to the members. Throughout the pandemic, Kristy Fercho at Wells Fargo and Susan Stewart at SWBC Mortgage, the senior member leadership at the MBA, were a constant source of valuable on-the-ground information and insight. The same holds true for Vince Malta and Charlie Oppler during their presidencies at the National Association of Realtors (NAR). Bob Goldberg, CEO of the NAR, also provided regular feedback and insight.

Trade associations usually have a unique governance structure. Industry members rotate through leadership positions, generally holding terms for a single year. The 2021 president of the NAR, for instance, would be different from the one in 2020. This structure makes it crucial to build relationships quickly while also maintaining regular contact with staff leadership. It also means that sometimes association priorities can shift from year to year. That said, everyone realized that for 2020 and 2021, COVID-19 response was the priority.

The mortgage and real estate industries are overwhelmingly filled with great, hard-working, compassionate people. Most stepped up in a crisis and did their best to help borrowers. They worked long nights, putting in countless hours. What criticism I do have of those industries is the result of a small number of actors and a fragile system that no one person chose or designed.

I had the privilege of starting my career in Washington at two of the most influential trade associations in real estate—the National Association of Home Builders (NAHB) and the NAR. My years spent in the economics and research divisions of those associations laid the groundwork for everything I've done since. I owe much of the success that I have had in my career to my friends and former colleagues at the NAHB and NAR, and the leadership of both provided critical input throughout COVID-19. The NAR's 2020 president, Vince Malta, kindly provided his insights into the functioning of the real estate market during one of the most unusual home-buying environments in American history. The NAHB's president and fellow scuba-diving fanatic, Jerry Howard, was a constant source of wisdom. Between social distancing requirements and material shortages, the homebuilding industry faced one unique challenge after another. Jerry's willingness to share his concerns and observations kept me informed and allowed the FHFA to craft several policies to keep the mortgage market for new homes functioning.

———

The FHFA does not directly regulate mortgage servicers. Unless they are depositories—that is, banks and credit unions—no one really regulates financial strength. That is not to suggest that the safety and soundness regulators of banks have a great track record. The Consumer Financial Protection Bureau examines servicers for consumer compliance, but unlike, say, state insurance regulators, that really does not include a servicer's ability to continue meeting its financial obligations.

Despite the lack of a direct relationship with Fannie and Freddie, servicers are one of the most important players for those organizations. If servicers do not do their job en masse, this ultimately threatens the ability of Fannie and Freddie to do their jobs. Servicers also want to stay on their good side. While there is still a lot of business outside the

conforming loan space, having Fannie or Freddie stop doing business
with you can be the end of your company.

While the FHFA could not regulate servicers directly, we could set
some standards regarding the counterparties of Fannie and Freddie. Doing
business with Fannie and Freddie is not an entitlement. Because of the large
number of counterparties, going on reputation alone would not do. We
needed some minimal solvency and liquidity standards. Since I was worried
about the risk these nonbank servicers presented to Fannie and Freddie, the
FHFA in January 2020 proposed raising eligibility standards for nonbank
originators and servicers who wanted to do business with those companies.[12]

Much of February 2020 was spent hearing from nonbank servicers.
They believed our proposed criteria were too tough. I was told repeatedly
that the industry had rock-solid balance sheets. Imagine my surprise to
be told only a month later, once COVID-19 struck, that these balance
sheets would now need a government rescue.

————

A commonly heard refrain from Wall Street was that because forbearance was a decision made by the FHFA, along with Fannie and Freddie,
then Fannie and Freddie, not the Wall Street-owned mortgage servicers,
should pay for it. As one of the more prominent Washington lawyers for
mortgage servicers, Laurence Platt, argued, "Given the economic pressure
on servicers of 'federally backed mortgage loans' subject to the CARES
Act's forbearance provision, some might argue that Congress and the
federal agencies indirectly have deputized private mortgage servicers as
if they were public resources to mute the impact of COVID-19 on residential mortgage borrowers. Unlike government workers or government
contractors, however, they are not getting paid for their services."[13]

Platt was far from alone in this view. Michael Bright declared that
"it would be like telling restaurants they had to prepare food for the
unemployed but not paying the restaurants to do so."[14]

Such dire warnings were not limited to Wall Street lobbyists.
Even such an eminent scholar as Barry Eichengreen at the University
of California, Berkeley, cautioned, "I do think there are going to be
financial problems coming because mortgage servicers are going to

have trouble, big time."[15] Although Eichengreen has long been in the Keynesian, interventionist camp, he is a serious scholar and one of the leading authorities on exchange rates and macroeconomics. If only this were an exchange rate crisis.

Wall Street's campaign for a bailout was not limited to this side of the Atlantic. One of the nastier and more bizarre comments came from *Financial Times* columnist John Dizard. Here are a few highlights from his April 10, 2020, column, "US Is on Course for a Downward Spiral of Mortgage Failures":

> There was supposed to be a deal in place, admittedly not one that was well thought through, to keep housing finance ticking over. Unfortunately there is one man—an officious regulator named Mark Calabria, the head of the Federal Housing Finance Agency—who has decided that the simple fix to the financial problem caused by the coronavirus pause should not be simple.
>
> Despite the industry's pleas, Calabria will not arrange for Fannie and Freddie or the Fed to make secured bridge loans to the servicers, which keep track of the documents, mail the accounts to the borrowers and the checks to the bondholders, who own the mortgages.
>
> According to Calabria, the payments shortfall for the servicers caused by congressionally mandated loan forbearance is all "spin." The mortgage bankers who generate most US mortgages are extremely angry with him. For the moment, Calabria has the support of Treasury secretary Steven Mnuchin. Apparently, Calabria has decided that there has to be a "stress test" for the servicers this May, and perhaps for a few months after that.
>
> Calabria makes an unlikely villain, but he has become one in the world of housing finance. At this rate, he will do well to collect a fat severance payment at the end of May. For his safety, Congress may have to throw in anonymity through the witness protection programme, and maybe a job under his new name, perhaps teaching slide deck composition at a for-profit online college.[16]

Yes, in the view of the *Financial Times*, not bailing out Wall Street makes one the villain. For the record, Dizard never reached out to me or anyone else at the FHFA. We would have been happy to walk him through the data and analysis, as we did for several journalists. The real lesson here is that in a crisis, many voices will yell for a government rescue and assert that not providing bailouts is the "reckless" path. I can guarantee that you will hear that in the next crisis as well, perhaps even from Dizard. And for the record, there was never a "deal in place."

————

The massive hole in this argument is that the contracts that Fannie and Freddie have with mortgage servicers explicitly require the servicers to cover forbearance in stressed environments. Yes, you read that correctly. Wall Street was trying to wiggle its way out of obligations to which it had knowingly agreed.

What is even more appalling is that servicers had a choice that would have allowed them to avoid this outcome. That choice, however, was less lucrative. So, as usual, many in the mortgage industry went for the short-term quick profit and later complained about the results. Contrary to the claims of some industry advocates, servicers were already paid for covering forbearance shortfalls. To understand how requires an explanation of servicing options facing the lenders.

The primary job of a mortgage servicer is to forward payments from the borrower to the investor, or in the industry lingo, to "remit." The servicer, upon delivery of a loan to Fannie or Freddie, has some choice of remittance methods. That is, the servicer has full control over just how much risk it is willing to take in terms of future payment flows.

The crucial difference between methods is whether the servicer is obligated to advance the borrowers' contractually scheduled mortgage payment regardless of whether the payment was made by the borrower.

An "actual" remittance requires the servicer to remit only amounts collected from the borrower. Therefore, it does not require the servicer to advance a payment from its own funds. A "scheduled" remittance requires the servicer to advance the amount even if the borrower did not pay the servicer.

Remittance types may be scheduled or actual, depending on the treatment of interest and principal. The first half of the description addresses interest, and the second addresses principal. For example, a scheduled/actual remittance requires the servicer to pay scheduled interest but to remit principal only to the extent actually collected from the borrower.

Freddie Mac's primary remittance type for loans for single-family homes is scheduled/actual. Fannie Mae has two remittance types. For their mortgage-backed securities (MBS) program, remittance is scheduled/scheduled, obligating the servicer to remit both interest and principal even if no payment is collected from the borrower. For Fannie Mae's "cash window" program, the remittance type is actual/actual; therefore, servicers remit only the amount of principal and interest collected from the borrower.

On the basis of these schedules, servicers have no obligation to advance any mortgage payments under Fannie Mae's large cash window program. Fannie Mae assumed all the obligation to advance missed payments to MBS holders for mortgages purchased via the cash window. As the cash window business was made up predominantly of smaller lenders, the situation also meant that the smaller lenders, who might lack the balance sheet strength of larger lenders, would not be obligated to advance missed mortgage payments.

Freddie Mac servicing requires servicer advances only for uncollected interest but limits them to four missed payments by the borrower. Of note, for mortgages with low interest rates or some seasoning, a substantial portion of the borrower's scheduled mortgage payment is principal (which the servicer is not obligated to advance). The servicers' advancing obligation was most material under Fannie Mae's scheduled/scheduled MBS program.

That obligation was capped at four months to align Fannie Mae with Freddie Mac's existing process. This action alleviated significant market uncertainty, solidified mortgage servicing rights valuations, and enabled servicers to secure additional mortgage servicing rights financing if necessary.

———

Many servicers in fact chose the low-risk option. As one servicer wrote me directly in April 2020, "We had options to earn additional revenue by selecting Schedule/Schedule for our GSE [government-sponsored enterprise] servicing. [But didn't.] Thank you for waiting for the data and not just handing over solutions to, what in normal times are highly profitable, clever but vulnerable business models. Wait for the data and you will be right."

There is a tendency in financial crises to paint all institutions as experiencing the same troubles, hence the need for a rescue to avoid the collapse of an entire industry. Such assertions are hardly ever true. For instance, one of the forces behind the crash of Bear Stearns in 2008 was the growing mismatch between the durations of its assets and liabilities. To ride the yield curve, Bear Stearns increased this disconnect. That allowed a greater spread between assets and liabilities, increasing its profits. However, when the yield curve flattened and momentarily inverted, Bear Stearns was paying more on its liabilities than it received on its assets. Few financial institutions will survive long under such conditions. While the company continued these high-stakes gambles, other investment banks, such as Goldman Sachs, were reducing this mismatch and were able to survive a market environment that sank Bear Stearns.

We saw something similar in the spring of 2020. One servicer business model proved robust, while another proved fragile. There was no risk of an industry-wide collapse. There was only a risk that a small number of servicers would fail because of their chosen business models.

———

To fully understand why the risk of a systemic liquidity shock appeared extremely remote, if not zero, one must look at the overall obligations of Fannie and Freddie servicers.

At the time of the passage of the CARES Act, the total monthly principal and interest payments for Fannie and Freddie were approximately $32 billion. Of that, about 40 percent, approximately $13 billion, of the advance obligation rested directly with them. This is the result of lenders choosing a remittance structure that leaves the risk with Fannie and Freddie.

About $11 billion, approximately a third, rested with depositories, such as banks and credit unions. During the first few months of COVID-19, banks and credit unions were witnessing record inflows of deposits. That is, they were swimming in cash. And, of course, banks could access Federal Reserve lending facilities, and credit unions could access liquidity facilities operated by the National Credit Union Administration. Thus, the servicing ability of banks and credit unions was never in question.

Roughly $8 billion, approximately a quarter, of the potential monthly advance obligation rested with nonbanks. At a 6.5 percent forbearance rate, which is what the FHFA was projecting in March 2020 and what ended up occurring, this translated to approximately $520 million of nonbank incremental advance needs per month. As a result of the FHFA's four-month limit on servicers' obligations to advance principal and interest payments on loans in forbearance, nonbanks' total four-month obligation equaled approximately $2.1 billion.

The FHFA's median forecast of 6.5 percent forbearance for Fannie and Freddie loans turned out to be dead-on. According to Black Knight, one of the foremost service and data providers in the mortgage industry, Fannie and Freddie forbearances peaked at 6.9 percent, including borrowers in a forbearance plan but still paying.[17]

Now, we could have just gotten lucky. I recognized that any forecast is susceptible to error. Examining historical unemployment patterns and previous recessions, we estimated a series of possible outcomes. Within a very wide band of confidence, our figures suggested that Fannie and Freddie forbearances could reach as high as 15 percent. That outcome, however, was extremely unlikely. Even if it did occur, nonbanks' total four-month obligation would equal around $5 billion, still well within the industry's capacity.

Actual servicing needs were even less: consistently throughout COVID-19, about a fifth of borrowers in forbearance programs continued to make their payments, seeing the program as an option they hoped not to need.

To the degree that a servicer is also an originator, the lender can also use the "float" from mortgage prepayments as the borrower refinances to cover their servicing obligations. With the decline in mortgage rates, we expected 2020 to be a great year for refinance activity, even if our projections ended up being below the refinance boom that occurred. On the basis of our conservative refinance estimates for 2020, the float alone from expected mortgage prepayments would more than cover nonbanks' total Fannie and Freddie servicing obligations. That is, a full consideration of all the relevant projected cash flows indicated that net nonbank servicing liquidity needs for Fannie and Freddie mortgages would be approximately zero.

Industry lobbyists claimed that nonbank servicer obligations could reach "as much as $100 billion."[18] The Urban Institute went so far as to claim that costs would be $162 billion.[19] So how does one get from $2.1 billion to $100 billion? The short answer is one cannot. If 100 percent of Fannie and Freddie loans went into forbearance, with the four-month cap the nonbank obligations would be around $33 billion. Even adding in the rest of the mortgage market—Federal Housing Administration (FHA), private label—would not get you to $100 billion. That was not even a reasonable outside estimate.

Why were industry and some think tank estimates so wildly inaccurate? Let's set aside the possibility that they were intentionally so. Some commentators simply took the overall monthly principal and interest payments, around $42 billion in spring 2020, multiplied that by 25 or 30 percent, and got a monthly cost of $10 to $13 billion. Then they assumed that borrowers would take all or most of a full year of forbearance. Add in property tax and insurance payments from escrow, and sure, you can get to a range from $100 to $162 billion.

There are several flaws in this analysis. Foremost, it ignored that Fannie and Freddie were already responsible for large portions of these payments. Perhaps think tank analysts can be forgiven for not knowing how mortgage servicing remittances work, although the authors of the Urban Institute estimate are industry veterans. It is also possible that industry advocates did not understand the breakdown of Fannie and Freddie remittance schedules. For these reasons, we did share our analysis with industry and think tank commentators. Nevertheless, we did not witness any pro-rescue commentators changing their story after we explained the remittance schedules.

Industry forecasts were also widely off about what percentage of borrowers would take forbearance and for how long. The overall peak for all mortgage types was about 10 percent, and most mortgages in forbearance exited within six months. And as previously mentioned, we capped Fannie and Freddie servicer obligations at four months. Freddie's four-month cap was already in place before the CARES Act— that is, when the industry was first putting out estimates. We quickly announced that we would soon align Fannie and Freddie policies, with details finally being released to the public on April 21, 2020.

Even after I had presented this analysis to the Senate Banking Committee in June 2020, there were still loud voices arguing for a bailout of mortgage servicers, even into July 2020, long after it became clear that the FHFA's estimates were the most accurate presented.[20]

Any estimate of liquidity need must be weighed against the availability of liquidity. Here, the FHFA was at an informational advantage over any other market observer, including Fannie and Freddie. The FHFA regularly receives balance sheet and income statement data for all 346 (as of January 1, 2020) nonbank servicers that did business with Fannie and Freddie.

What did our data tell us? Liquidity for the industry was not only sufficient but also increasing. Total nonbank liquidity increased by 9 percent to $36 billion in the first quarter of 2020. Of that, unencumbered cash and equivalents made up $13 billion, an increase of 19 percent from December 31, 2019.

The mortgage servicing industry was sitting on $36 billion to cover what the FHFA believed would be about $2 billion in needs. Even if the industry did not want to sell off liquid assets, there was still more than sufficient cash available.

Although the FHFA was privy to more data on nonbank servicers than any other organization, we were not hiding this information, at least not the aggregates. The preceding data were shared within the FSOC. On March 30, 2020, a conference call of the FSOC's Task Force on Nonbank Mortgage Liquidity was made to discuss conditions in the mortgage servicing markets.[21] FSOC attendees, in addition to me, included Treasury Secretary Mnuchin, Federal Reserve chair Jerome Powell, Comptroller of the Currency Joseph Otting, FDIC chair Jelena McWilliams, and Consumer Financial Protection Bureau director Kathy Kraninger. I presented these data, along with more confidential data on the health of specific servicers and a discussion of the condition of Fannie and Freddie.

The Department of Housing and Urban Development (HUD) is not a member of the FSOC, but both HUD and the FHA attended this task force meeting to update the FSOC on liquidity needs facing nonbank servicers supporting the FHA and Ginnie Mae. FHA commissioner Brian Montgomery and Ginnie Mae principal executive vice president Seth Appleton led that presentation.

I had also walked numerous members of Congress through this analysis. We regularly discussed these aggregates with industry representatives. I also presented this information to the public during testimony before the Senate Committee on Banking, Housing, and Urban Affairs. Of course, we vetted these data extensively with Fannie and Freddie, which had collected them. Not once can I recall anyone telling us where our analysis was off. We would have welcomed such corrections if they had been needed.

Since there clearly was no systemic liquidity risk to the nonbank mortgage servicing sector, why all the industry lobbying and effort, especially during a pandemic? There were a handful of smaller servicers that, according to our monitoring data, might have run into some liquidity problems. This was never more than a small portion of the industry. For the first several months of COVID, I also received daily updates on "at-risk" servicers. We would let the data do the talking. While the industry certainly did not need a rescue, an extremely small segment might express considerable stress.

———

Given the lack of systemic importance, I believe the actual driver of the industry's demand for a liquidity facility is a simple one: profits. Recall that the FHFA had estimated that lenders' float from the refinance boom would be more than sufficient to cover their needs. However, this would mean that the float would be forwarded to investors a lot sooner than usual. Normally, lenders invest the float in short-term instruments, adding significantly to their profits. Since a sizable portion of industry profits derived from the float, the industry felt entitled to those profits. In some cases, lenders would also have to draw on their lines of credit from commercial banks. Obviously, those lines of credit are not without cost. The bottom line is that there was no systemic risk to the nonbank mortgage servicers, just a dent in their profits, for which they believed the public should make up.

I believe another factor is the rivalry between banks and nonbanks. While I am no more a fan of bailouts for banks than for nonbanks, it is fair to say I am a minority voice in Washington on that front. Part of nonbanks' feeling that they had arrived, so to speak, was a sense that if banks get rescues, then so should nonbanks. You have not really made it until Washington is willing to throw money at your mistakes.

Part of the trade's growing animosity toward me derived from my unwillingness to be their advocate. At least one insider was kind enough to express as much, saying they had hoped I would be a "voice for the industry." Somehow, my response that I was an independent, arms-length regulator and not a cheerleader for any industry was not the answer they were looking for.

I can see where the nonbanks were coming from. The Office of the Comptroller of the Currency often advocates on behalf of the big banks, the National Credit Union Administration has a long history of reflecting the interests of credit unions, and the Federal Reserve is a reliable voice for Wall Street's primary dealers. You can usually get the Wall Street take by picking up the phone and calling the Treasury Department. Even the Consumer Financial Protection Bureau is a consistent voice for the trial bar. I don't like it, but it is certainly common for industries to co-opt agencies to be their advocates. This is not even necessarily the result of undue influence or bad intent, but simply from the fact that regulators engage with their regulated entities more than any other party. In this case, familiarity generates common assumptions.

Such had been the case for much of the FHFA's history. The FHFA did not regulate the nonbanks, but both Fannie and Freddie viewed the nonbanks as their clients and core constituency. As depositories would always have the option of holding whatever mortgages they originated, they were viewed by Fannie and Freddie as unreliable political partners.

Both companies viewed the nonbanks as critical advocates for a large government-sponsored enterprises footprint. As Fannie and Freddie further influenced the FHFA, the views of the nonbank mortgage industry became more and more the conventional wisdom within the FHFA, at least until I came along.

———

Our inability to get accurate, reliable data from the mortgage industry became a major frustration. While I should not have expressed that feeling to the press, I did, in two interviews the first week of April 2020.[22] I had hoped that doing so would encourage the mortgage industry to be more reliable, but instead, industry lobbyists played the victim. How dare I call out their intentional campaign of misinformation?

I had tried to maintain my relationship with industry and advocacy representatives as one based on openness. I believed we had brought to the FHFA a level of transparency unmatched at any other financial regulator. Foremost, I regularly explained that our guide was the statute that Congress had created, not my desires or those of the mortgage industry. Thus, the degree to which many industry advocates placed getting government subsidies ahead of containing a pandemic was disheartening.

I must emphasize that not all lenders—not even most—behave this way. The real estate and mortgage businesses are full of well-meaning, hard-working individuals. But the fact remains that the mortgage industry does a very poor job of weeding out unethical actors. All too often, its representatives have advocated not for the best of the industry but for the worst.

———

Since Wall Street was having trouble securing a rescue on the basis of its own needs, it had to roll out the old "it's really about Main Street" line.[23] Essentially, the argument was that if servicers had to honor their obligations to forward missed payments, then they would either lack the funds to originate new mortgages or they would increase their credit standards to avoid making loans to borrowers who might later take forbearance.

This begs the question of whether we really want to encourage lenders to make loans that are unlikely to perform. One of the big changes to come out of the Dodd-Frank Act was the requirement that lenders document the borrower's ability to pay the mortgage. Since the basis for entering forbearance is an inability to pay, it should be obvious that making lots of loans that might not be repaid was in direct conflict with the consumer protections put in place after the 2008 crisis, not to mention irresponsible. We can debate the wisdom of the Dodd-Frank Act, but by requiring lenders to account for borrowers' ability to pay, which changes over the course of a business cycle, the act is clearly structured to make mortgage lending more pro-cyclical. That effect had nothing to do with servicer liquidity.

Since depositories such as commercial banks were experiencing a massive influx of deposits, and hence greater liquidity, if servicer liquidity among nonbanks was adversely impacting the mortgage market, then we should have witnessed at least two trends: declining market shares for nonbanks and tighter credit standards for nonbanks than for banks. We witnessed neither. The nonbank share of Fannie and Freddie mortgage originations increased over the course of 2020. As measured by borrower credit scores, nonbanks were operating throughout 2020 with weaker credit standards than banks. This trend held for Fannie and Freddie loans as well as for the traditionally weaker credit at the FHA.[24]

As noted above, much of the industry could avoid the responsibility for advancing missed payments. Fannie sellers could have simply made new loans via the cash window, for instance, or just chosen a remittance schedule based on what was received from the borrower. This would have been less profitable, but lenders were free to make that tradeoff.

———

With Fannie and Freddie not aiding servicers, the attention turned to both Congress and the Federal Reserve. Despite intense industry lobbying, Congress resisted the call for a mortgage servicer rescue. Although several representatives and senators did call for a bailout, I do not believe that they ever convinced Senate leadership, particularly the leads on the Senate Banking Committee, chairman Mike Crapo and ranking member Sherrod Brown, of the need for a servicer rescue. While not ironclad, a general rule on Capitol Hill is that it is hard, if not impossible, to get something done if both the chair and the ranking member (the senior member of the minority party) of the committee of jurisdiction oppose it. I also believe that Mnuchin opposed inclusion of mortgage servicer support in any COVID-19 legislation.

Secretary Mnuchin was the most pivotal player in this drama, perhaps fitting for an occasional movie producer. Steven was the administration's point person with Congress on COVID-19 legislation. He regularly interacted with House and Senate leaders and was widely seen by senators and representatives across the political spectrum as speaking for the White House. In short, his views carried considerable weight on Capitol Hill. His history in the mortgage industry was also significant. While he was strongly criticized by Democrats during his confirmation hearing for foreclosure practices during his time at OneWest, most of Congress considered that experience as at least suggesting that he was an expert on the mortgage market. All that said, mortgage servicers' efforts to lobby the Hill were not paying off. Such a lack of progress clearly added to their frustration.

Secretary Mnuchin also played a critical role in that his approval was needed for any Federal Reserve relief for mortgage servicers. After the passage of the Dodd-Frank Act in 2010, Congress required the Federal Reserve to gain the approval of the Treasury secretary before engaging in any aid to nonbanks under its so-called 13-3 powers. This provision was passed in reaction to the bailout of AIG and the assisted purchase of Bear Stearns by JPMorgan Chase and was mirrored in a similar, long-standing process at the FDIC.

Although Jay Powell was the face of the Federal Reserve's response to COVID-19, many others played important roles. Investigating and researching the liquidity needs of mortgage servicers fell primarily to Federal Reserve Board governor Lael Brainard, with some occasional assistance from the vice chair for supervision, Randall Quarles. Both regularly inquired about what we were observing and shared what they were hearing from the banks regulated by the Federal Reserve. Despite our political differences—Brainard being a well-known Democrat who received some notoriety for donating just enough to Hillary Clinton in 2016 for it to become public, a rarity for Federal Reserve Board governors, who prefer to maintain the public illusion of being nonpolitical—I found working with Brainard to be straightforward, professional, and productive. She and Quarles regularly reached out for data and analysis on the mortgage market. One of my core objectives as director was to elevate the FHFA to be the public and interagency place to go for mortgage data and analysis. The frequency with which both the Federal Reserve and the Treasury turned to our agency became a real testament to how far we had come in such a short time.

Mnuchin consistently opposed a rescue of mortgage servicers. The Federal Reserve displayed no such resistance. Perhaps it is just part of the culture, but the usual "bail out first, ask questions later" approach was on full display. The Federal Reserve made it extremely clear to us and to the Treasury Department that a liquidity facility for mortgage servicers was ready to go. All they needed was Treasury's permission to "turn the key." Although I believed and publicly stated that it was the Federal Reserve's and Treasury's call whether to establish a 13-3 facility for mortgage servicers, I must admit to being somewhat disappointed in the Federal Reserve's readiness, despite the data so clearly indicating that it was unnecessary.

I played a modest role in vetting Federal Reserve Board governors, including the chair, while working for Vice President Mike Pence. The vice president had long been opposed to Wall Street bailouts, having for years talked in his speeches as a House member about being the "first member of Congress to publicly oppose" the Troubled Assets Relief Program bank assistance in 2008. The vice president's office had regularly pushed back on potential nominees whom we believed would be pro-bailout. There were several possible Federal Reserve and other financial nominees whom we blocked for that very reason. Thus, it was with considerable disappointment that I watched an institution I had helped to shape so quickly fall into rescue mode. It is further evidence that the Federal Reserve ends up changing the governors more than the governors change the Federal Reserve.

The Federal Reserve is not the only institution in Washington that is susceptible to financial industry pressure. HUD often, perhaps too often, tends to reflect the views and interests of the mortgage industry. Nowhere is this more pronounced than within the FHA and within Ginnie Mae. Over the years, I have reflected many times that the FHA appears to operate as a subsidiary of the mortgage industry, regardless

of who is in the White House. It did not take long for the industry to
get to HUD. In our internal interagency meetings, HUD became a
vocal advocate for a bailout of the mortgage trade. Unfortunately for the
industry, and fortunately for the greater public good, HUD did not have
a say in the process. The decision was ultimately Secretary Mnuchin's.

Secretary Mnuchin may have been the ultimate obstacle to relief for
mortgage servicers, but he was prepared to let the public criticism fall
to me, which was perfectly fine. Well, kind of. Mnuchin was not trying
to dodge responsibility for the issue. He simply did not feel it was necessary to publicly express his opposition. All of that is very understandable,
especially in a pandemic when you have countless issues coming at you.
There are enough painful choices without asking for more.

So why make me a target for Wall Street? Of course, that was not the
objective, even if many of my friends, including those at the White House,
derived considerable amusement from the headlines reading "Wall Street
Puts Blame on Calabria for Blocking Mortgage Aid,"[25] or perhaps my
favorite, from *Politico*, "Trump's Libertarian Housing Regulator Refuses
to Bail Out Mortgage Firms with Public Money."[26] At *Politico* there is
probably no bigger insult than "libertarian," other than being "Trump's"
appointee. Despite the never-ending hours spent trying to educate publications like *Politico* that the FHFA was then an independent regulator,
and therefore not anyone's regulator, our media continue to go for the
clickbait. I have long been adamant about protecting the FHFA's independence, even from a White House of which I was previously a part.
However, it was still nice to hear nothing but supportive messages from
the White House in opposing another Wall Street bailout.

The reason to be public was to encourage any troubled servicers
to go out and raise funds in the private markets. It may be counter to
conventional wisdom, but I believe the biggest lesson of the failure of
Lehman Brothers is that if you lead a company to expect a bailout, it
will not take the actions needed to avoid one. As we know, there were
several offers to acquire Lehman, which would have avoided the need for
a rescue. After the assistance to Bear Stearns's shareholders and creditors,
Lehman was given plenty of reason to expect similar treatment.

Lobbyists, analysts, and other commentators continued to tell the
mortgage industry that a rescue would happen eventually. They were

not just the paid advocates giving their spiel. Even Isaac Boltansky, who is one of the most reliable and consistent commentators on Washington financial policy, continued to tell his clients that a bailout was forthcoming. Isaac was clearly getting his information from lobbyists who had a vested interest in that outcome. Since the industry had put its collective head in the sand and no one else was stepping forward, it fell to me to wake it up with a message it most certainly did not want to hear. The cavalry wasn't coming to the rescue.

Some of this message took place via the press. For instance, I had discussed with several journalists our plans and procedures for transferring the activities of any failed servicer to a healthy servicer. And, we had just completed such an exercise in September 2019, when Ditech entered bankruptcy and its servicing was acquired by New Residential Investment. In fact, Fannie and Freddie could transfer servicing without having to resort to bailouts. A considerable part of March and April 2020 was spent on the phone with the CEOs of servicing companies, including depositories. Fannie and Freddie were engaged in a similar effort to line up capacity in case of servicer failures. I saw this repeatedly in 2008: the claim that some firm must be rescued by the taxpayer because it performed a critical function or because a ready buyer was not there. We did not intend to either wait or be forced to choose between uncertainty and bailout. We worked with Fannie and Freddie to create resolution planning for failed servicers, including recapture of the mortgage servicing rights and conversion of failed servicers into subservicers.

Bizarrely, some of the loudest voices for a bailout had only a few years earlier presented servicing transfers as the appropriate route in the event of a servicer failure. Karan Kaul and Laurie Goodman of the Urban Institute wrote in 2016, "Traditionally, nonbanks have not been subject to the same level of supervisory financial regulation and capital requirements as depositories. Nonbanks don't hold consumer deposits and don't have a retail presence, thus limiting the potential for customer disruption in the event of insolvency. Further, disruption of servicing upon failure of a nonbank servicer is typically avoided by transferring servicing rights to a financially sound servicer, thus ensuring continued collection of mortgage payments from borrowers and uninterrupted remittance of principal and interest (P&I) to MBS investors."[27]

Perhaps Kaul and Goodman believed the above applied when a single servicer or a small number of servicers were facing failure, not large segments of the mortgage trade. That, of course, is why we continued to monitor the health of the industry and would have engaged in systemic solutions if the problem itself became systemic. But again, there was never any evidence supporting the warnings of system-wide failure.

Fortunately, we were not flying blind when it came to which servicers might find themselves in trouble. As part of our supervision of Fannie and Freddie, we focused attention and resources on counterparty risk. Perhaps there is no bigger co-contractor risk to Fannie and Freddie than mortgage servicers. For that reason, the FHFA regularly receives balance sheet and income statement information on all the nonbank servicers that do business with Fannie and Freddie. Yes, such data can sometimes be stale, so we requested more frequent updates from Fannie, Freddie, and the servicers. Every weekday morning during the first six months of the pandemic, I received a troubled servicer watchlist detailing which servicers were close to the line and could find themselves in financial trouble.

Private equity and hedge funds were major investors in a few of the troubled servicers. Now, I am a big believer in the net positive role played by them both. Thus, I am certainly not hostile to that industry. However, I do object to the idea that investors can spend years pulling money out of a company and then, when that company needs funds, request that the government provide them. Fortunately, when investors came to realize that we would transfer the servicing rights of these companies—their main assets—and that they would have almost no value left, those investors decided to inject funding sufficient to protect their investments. A win all around, without the use of a single penny of taxpayer assistance.

Chapter 7
Social Distancing in the Housing Market

The great COVID-19 housing boom appears to have been driven not only by the desire to move away from certain urban areas, such as New York City, but also by the additional free time experienced by many now-remote workers.[1] One in four households reported wanting to move in response to the pandemic restrictions imposed by their local governments,[2] the biggest impetus of which was school closings.[3]

Some buyers also appeared to be moving from COVID-19 hot spots to areas of the country with fewer cases.[4] Not surprisingly, this trend drove more buyers to rural areas, relative to pre-pandemic trends.[5]

For some, time formerly spent commuting was used to surf real estate websites, such as Realtor.com, Zillow, or Redfin. Virtual three-dimensional walk-throughs on Redfin increased 563 percent in 2020, for just one example.[6]

Perhaps the most surprising development was the explosion in home purchases made sight unseen. Personally, I could never imagine buying a home without having visited it first. Apparently, I am in the minority. Redfin reported that by December 2020, 63 percent of offers to purchase were being made sight unseen.[7] This was a housing boom driven by the laptop class.[8]

Contributing to the willingness to buy sight unseen was the large amount of down payment assistance provided in the form of federal

COVID-19 relief payments. One in four homebuyers during the pandemic reported using federal stimulus money for their down payment.[9] Another 23 percent cited an increased ability to save due to the pandemic, as they were no longer incurring commuting expenses or spending on that European vacation.[10]

One of the more interesting shifts was the use of self-guided tours, limited mostly to vacant properties.[11] Having spent a few years early in my career at the National Association of Realtors (NAR), I have never underestimated the creativity of real estate agents when it comes to closing a sale.

The pandemic was a stark reminder that much of the real estate and mortgage transaction was still face-to-face. A great deal of that would have to change.

———

The purchase of a home, particularly when it is financed with a mortgage, is a complex legal process. The most critical link is the transfer of deed. This is the most fundamental legal aspect. If the deed is not properly transferred, you do not own the property in the eyes of the law.

A deed transfer is not as simple as having the homeseller hand you the deed. That would be too easy—and too risky from a legal standpoint. Deeds must be signed by both parties before a notary. The signing is usually done at the office of a settlement agent or notary. Traditionally, this has been a process characterized by half a dozen people crammed into a small conference room. If you think that sounds like an ideal environment for COVID-19 to spread, you are correct. Obviously, that process would have to change.

Before the pandemic, 34 states allowed the deed transfer to take place online.[12] Those were predominately rural states, such as Alaska or North Dakota, where there would be few notaries spread over large geographies. For them, moving to only online, or remote, notarization would be relatively easy. Unfortunately, the 16 without this flexibility were some of the nation's largest housing markets, such as California and New York.

California would let the notary come to you, however. Hence the occasional real estate closing taking place in a front yard, in a driveway, or on a porch, with appropriate social distancing.

The federal effort to create a national standard for remote online notarization did gain some momentum, led by Sens. Kevin Cramer, a Republican from North Dakota, and Mark Warner, a Democrat from Virginia. Both senators were on the banking committee and were point persons for much of the real estate and mortgage industry.

Senator Warner, in part due to his efforts at reforming Fannie and Freddie, was seen by many in Washington as the most astute senator in the Democratic caucus on mortgage issues. While I have had occasional disagreements with him, I always found him friendly and thoughtful. He was among those on Capitol Hill with whom I spoke most often during my tenure at the Federal Housing Finance Agency (FHFA), especially during the pandemic. Most of the Democratic senators, such as Sherrod Brown and Elizabeth Warren, with whom I regularly interacted, focused their questions on renters and, to a lesser degree, on homeowners. Warner would inquire about those issues as well, but also about the state of the mortgage industry and the future of Fannie Mae and Freddie Mac. He has been far more optimistic than I, for instance, in terms of recouping the taxpayers' investment in Fannie and Freddie.

Unfortunately, the senators' efforts on notarization stalled, partly because their bill was referred to the Senate Judiciary Committee. As neither Senator Cramer nor Senator Warner was a member of the Committee, their ability to push the bill was limited. It also probably did not help that the most senior Democrat, the ranking member on the Committee at the time, was Senator Dianne Feinstein, representing California, the state most opposed to remote notarization.

As with many issues, and appropriately so, states moved when the federal government could not. Whereas California would not adopt remote notarization, states such as Illinois, New Hampshire, and New Jersey did. Fannie and Freddie would also have to adjust their policies to be more accommodating to remote notarizations.

States would also largely determine which businesses were deemed "essential" and therefore somewhat free of lockdowns. Following guidance from the Department of Homeland Security suggesting that real estate and mortgage services were essential, most states followed suit.[13] To add to the confusion, some cities issued essential-business directives that differed from those at the state level. Early in the pandemic, it was not unheard of for real estate services to flip from essential to nonessential and back, all depending on the local political dynamics.[14]

A far greater problem was the shutdown of local courthouses. After a deed transfer is signed and notarized, it generally must be recorded with the local courthouse or county recorder. Local governments were among the first to close or transition to remote work. One reason for the many foreclosure and eviction moratoriums, for instance, was that the courts that process those legal actions had gone into lockdown.

This might be one of the rare instances in which the length of the real estate and mortgage processes became an asset. Despite a lot of creative thinking, both at the FHFA and in the real estate industry, there simply was no fix for closed courthouses. Since the closing process can take weeks, and sometimes a month or two, the recording of deed transfers and new mortgages would await the reopening of courthouses. Fortunately, by May 2020, most of the approximately 3,000 county courthouses would be back to some level of service.

The shutdown in county courthouses immediately reminded me of my time at the White House during a federal government shutdown. During the 35-day shutdown from December 2018 to January 2019, many government services either slowed or halted. Numerous airports were disrupted, for instance, because of the shutdown's effect on the Transportation Security Administration. At one point, I was hearing from the major auto companies that the new models would not be ready for release unless the Environmental Protection Agency reopened soon. My most immediate takeaway was that far less of the private sector should be dependent on government permission to simply function.

———

The biggest concern would be with the parts of the mortgage process that require someone to enter your home. Before the pandemic, a home inspector or appraiser could easily spend an hour or more inside your house, usually with you following close behind. Sometimes the two of you were in cramped quarters, such as getting a closer look at that crack in the bathroom tiles or squeezing into that small closet that holds your water heater. None of that sounds attractive if you are trying to avoid an airborne virus.

Both Fannie and Freddie had already been implementing alternatives to traditional appraisals. It was not a move I was particularly comfortable with. A home's appraised value directly affects how much can be borrowed against that home. The pressure appraisers felt from lenders and real estate agents to "hit the number" was a direct but modest contributor to the 2008 financial crisis. Alternative valuation methods appeared to be more about gaining a competitive advantage for Fannie and Freddie and less about getting accurate home appraisals. The costly missteps at Zillow, losing almost a billion dollars in the hottest housing market in a generation, illustrate the dangers of relying too heavily on automated valuations.[15] And these efforts were being made with little input from external stakeholders.

Because of these concerns, I directed the FHFA's staff to begin evaluating changes to the appraisal process. This would start with a public request for input, followed by public listening sessions.[16]

In the interim, we would have to find a way to allow some mortgage activity to continue without requiring an appraiser to enter the house. As I did not want Fannie and Freddie to take additional risk, the solution was to allow external, or "drive-by," appraisals but to lower the allowable loan-to-value on the mortgage, with the assumption that more flexible appraisals would result in upward bias in estimated values. We would monitor loan performance. If early payment defaults increased, we could adjust. As part of both our request for input and ongoing monitoring, staff would conduct a full analysis of the performance of flexible appraisals.

The waiver of a full appraisal worked most easily for a simple rate reset refinance, because in most cases there would be no reduction in homeowner equity. We would be less flexible on cash refinance or purchase loans since they would present additional credit risk beyond that of a simple rate reset. We would also limit the appraisal waivers to loans already guaranteed by Fannie or Freddie, so as to limit any new credit risk.

The most difficult part would be new construction because the buyers do not have an existing mortgage and there may be few comparable properties. Most jurisdictions declared residential construction to be an essential activity and allowed it to continue during the initial lock-downs. Although many new homes are purchased with all cash, a sizable number still depend on conventional financing. We would increase our documentation requirements to help us ensure that the homes had actual-ly been constructed, while providing enough flexibility to keep the mar-ket moving. Since Fannie and Freddie provide financing not for home construction but only for home purchase, the greatest risk in the process was still with the construction lender, usually a local community bank.

Although it is too early to know for sure, I do remain concerned that the appraisal flexibilities we implemented during the pandemic con-tributed to the record home price increases. I still believe the tradeoffs were worth it, but there were significant risks in reducing the use of full appraisals. That is why we limited appraisal waivers to loans already guaranteed by Fannie or Freddie—and only to loans with significant homeowner equity, usually 30 percent or more. The main risk, however, is that such practices will become standard as the pandemic recedes, especially if applied to loans with little to no equity.

———

The home value is a critical input in the processing of underwriting a mortgage. Another crucial component is the borrower's income. After all, you do want to make sure the borrower has the capacity to pay back the loan.

The usual process for verifying a borrower's income and employment involves contacting their employer. As you might imagine, that became a lot harder when so many employers had shut down or switched to remote work. Moreover, we were faced with the possibility that the bor-rower had lost his or her job during the shutdown after the mortgage had already closed or had been purchased by Fannie or Freddie. Even more difficult were cases where the borrower was a small business owner, such as a restaurant owner. Was the business still open? Would it reopen soon?

In many instances, the mortgage would simply not be made. There really was no way around that, especially for many self-employed workers and small business owners. In other instances, we would accept alternate documentation or verification by the lender.[17] However, we would also reduce how old asset and income documentation could be, since everything was changing so fast. Fortunately, the job market and overall economy quickly started to recover in June 2020. Otherwise, we would have been forced to find another approach, especially for the self-employed.

Often the purchase of a home is contingent on the results of a home inspection or appraisal. I highly recommend not buying an older home—really, anything more than 10 years old—without having a home inspection. Whether the result of the increased flexibilities offered by Fannie and Freddie or of competitive market pressures, buyers during the pandemic increasingly waived inspection and appraisal contingencies, essentially agreeing to buy as-is. According to the NAR, almost a third of buyers during the pandemic were doing so.[18]

The most important waiver might have been the decision by many buyers to go without a mortgage. Normally, between 15 and 20 percent of buyers pay all cash for their home. That number surged to 25 percent by early 2021.[19] Although an even larger share of all-cash sales occurred in the early years of the Great Recession, those were predominantly distressed sales. The cash purchases during COVID-19 were not. Skipping the mortgage does significantly reduce the number of social interactions involved in the process, but it means giving up the chance to enjoy record-low mortgage rates.

The desire to maintain social distancing likely also explains the stronger recovery in new home sales than in existing home sales. Between the beginning of 2020 and late summer, the percentage of prospective homebuyers wanting to buy a new home instead of an existing one nearly doubled.[20] From April to July 2020, new single-family home sales increased over 60 percent, after being relatively flat during 2019.[21] Newly constructed homes are vacant, so there is no need to work around the schedules of occupants. Just as important, new homes were more likely to be available in parts of the country with lower COVID-19 numbers and more open schools. Building a new home far from anyone else might have been the ultimate in social distancing, especially if you added the optional underground bunker.[22]

To some degree, the housing market kept humming along during the pandemic by cutting corners and waiving long-standing protections for both consumers and lenders. In some areas, such as the servicing rules of the Consumer Financial Protection Bureau (CFPB), flexibility was needed to offer borrowers better options to avoid foreclosure.[23] In other areas, such as contingency and appraisal waivers, it remains to be seen whether the proper balance was struck.

In most situations, additional protections were added to offset some of the expected increase in risk. While I was surprised to learn such was not already the case, early in the pandemic the FHFA formed a partnership with the CFPB—the Borrower Protection Program—to ensure that we at the FHFA were getting timely information regarding consumer complaints about Fannie- and Freddie-guaranteed loans.[24] This sharing of information allowed the FHFA, working with Fannie and Freddie, to correct practices at several servicers before they became widespread.

The real estate and mortgage industries were generally supportive of our efforts to keep the housing market going.[25] Not surprisingly, there was also the occasional complaint that we were not being flexible enough. While most industry participants appeared to acknowledge the need to balance flexibility and risk, I suspect that most would also have placed less emphasis on managing the risks at Fannie and Freddie. But then again, I was the safety and soundness regulator. They were not.

Another issue was striking a balance between public health and maintenance of as much normalcy as possible for the housing market. Did we really want to encourage a roaring housing market when so much of that market typically depended on face-to-face interactions? Unfortunately, some families might have been forced to sell because of the financial pressure of the crisis—for instance, to keep their small businesses afloat. Others may have been forced to move to keep their children from missing too much in-person school. The best thing we could do to support potentially distressed buyers and sellers was to keep the housing and mortgage market liquid.

Chapter 8

Refi Rebound

As someone trained in economics, I am a big fan of meteorologists, since they make economists look like good forecasters. Humor aside, economists do not have the best track record of predicting turns in the economy. Drawing a line with a ruler would be just as accurate most of the time. Forecasting the housing and mortgage markets in 2020 would be especially difficult.

Despite my concerns about forecasting, when I walked through the doors at the Federal Housing Finance Agency (FHFA) in April 2019, I was shocked that the agency lacked a housing or mortgage market forecast of its own. It had simply used whatever projection Fannie and Freddie provided. It was as if the Federal Reserve based decisions on forecasts provided by Citibank or Wells Fargo. Establishing that capacity would be a top priority, as the predominant risks facing the entities regulated by the FHFA were declines in the housing and mortgage markets.

——————

When COVID-19 hit, the FHFA was still building its prognostic function. We were stuck, to some degree, with relying on the forecasts of Fannie and Freddie. I knew the chief economists at both Fannie and Freddie (Doug Duncan and Sam Khater, respectively) and had worked with Sam early in my career. Their immediate instincts matched mine.

Homesellers would pull back, taking their properties off the market. After all, who wants to hold an open house during a pandemic? Many sales would be made by pressured sellers, who had little choice but to sell, perhaps at distressed prices. Normally, a decline in supply would suggest price increases, which is what eventually occurred, but in March 2020, most of us expected demand for homes to fall as well. That expectation, to a large extent, assumed that mandated remote work would end by late summer 2020. Even when workers were fleeing New York City for the Catskills, for instance, most housing forecasts, including mine, did not see that resulting in a massive jump in home sales.

Well within the consensus was the Mortgage Bankers Association (MBA) prediction, in April 2020, that existing-home sales for 2020 would be slightly below those for 2019, falling about 2 percent, from 5.3 million to 5.2 million. Instead, existing-home sales surged to 5.6 million in 2020.

In April 2020, both Fannie and Freddie were expecting home prices to fall for 2020. The MBA was a little more optimistic, forecasting a 4.3 percent increase, down from the 5 percent witnessed in 2019. As it turned out, prices instead surged by about 9 percent in 2020.

At first, the assumption of declining demand did play out. Between February and May 2020, existing-home sales dropped by almost 30 percent on an annualized basis.[1] The second half of 2020 would witness a boom in home sales, as many families recognized that the economy was reopening but that many of them would not be required to return to work in person. Geographic differences in pandemic response drove a boom in migration from mostly the Northeast and West Coast to the Southeast and Western areas, which were already reopening (especially the public schools, which remained closed in much of the Northeast).

———

Even more off the mark were forecasts of the mortgage market, which to be fair has always been harder to predict than housing activity. In April 2020, the MBA was forecasting a total of $2.4 billion in mortgage originations for 2020. Half of that would be purchase mortgages, and the other half refinancings. Instead, 2020 would see one of the largest years ever for mortgage originations, with a total of $3.7 billion, over 60 percent of which were refinancings. To the MBA's credit, its estimate for purchase originations, at $1.2 billion, was not far off from the eventual number of $1.4 billion. The surprise would truly be in the refinance market.

Most refinance activity comes down to interest rates. Even with a pandemic, in April 2020, the MBA was forecasting only a modest decline in mortgage rates, from 3.7 percent for 2019 to 3.5 percent in 2020. This would spur some refinancing activity but not a record boom. What is perhaps a little surprising is that the MBA, again not out of the consensus range, was predicting only a modest decline in mortgage rates even after the Federal Reserve's massive purchases of mortgage-backed securities (MBS) had started in March 2020.

Some of the lowest mortgage rates on record were seen in 2020. The 30-year fixed rate would start 2020 at around 3.7 percent and would end the year at around 2.7 percent. These rock-bottom rates were even more amazing after subtraction of inflation, running just over 1 percent at the end of 2020. Inflation would spike in 2021 and 2022, leaving many borrowers paying negative real mortgage rates. Essentially, lenders would be paying people to borrow money. What could go wrong?

———

The record-low mortgage rates would be a boon to the 8.8 million borrowers who refinanced their loans in 2020. Researchers at Freddie Mac estimate that borrowers who refinanced in 2020 saved, on average, $2,800 in annual mortgage payments.[2] Averages, of course, can mask considerable variation. Borrowers in Washington, DC, for instance, saved an average of $4,095, whereas borrowers in Atlanta saved an average of $2,509. For many families, the benefits of refinancing were comparable to the relief payments received under the Coronavirus Aid, Relief, and Economic Security (CARES) Act.

In addition to lowering their mortgage payments, about a third of homeowners refinancing in 2020 also took equity out of their homes in the form of a "cash-out" refinance. A total of about $160 billion would be withdrawn in cash-outs in 2020, roughly half that witnessed in the record year 2006.

The cash-out sum might have been much greater had we not pushed back. Unfortunately, it was not all that uncommon for borrowers to extract large amounts of cash in 2006 and 2007 and then go on to default in 2008 or later. With a simple rate reset refinance, Fannie and Freddie owned the credit risk, at least for loans they already held. And we made every effort to tilt their refinance activity toward those loans. You could even make the argument that a simple rate reduction that reduced monthly payments would reduce the credit risk of the loan.

On new loans, or for cash-outs, that would mean new credit risk for the companies. Sadly, this was new credit risk that the companies simply did not have the capital to support—the result of Washington not having fixed the companies when times were good.

So we set different terms for rate resets versus cash-outs. It was less a difference in pricing and more a change in what flexibilities we would allow. Considering the social distancing concerns of the pandemic, for instance, flexibilities on appraisals would be easier on a rate reset but harder to get on a cash-out. That is just one example. We also made it difficult, but not impossible, for the companies to refinance each other's loans. The result was that the vast majority of Fannie refinancing was on Fannie loans, and the case was the same for Freddie.

Not surprisingly, there were some complaints from the mortgage industry. The new terms certainly made it harder for some lenders to play the companies off against each other, a longtime practice that usually resulted in a race to the bottom. The argument from the lenders was that all the risk was already owned by the taxpayer, meaning, "What's the difference?" Setting aside the fact that the taxpayer did not legally stand behind that risk, the more important fact is that the FHFA was managing two conservatorships, not one. Under our statutory framework, you could not just dump risk from one company to the other.

Some lenders also grumbled that we were not doing enough to stimulate the overall economy. Their concern, of course, was their revenue, not the overall economy. With the massive leverage at Fannie and Freddie, we managed to support a record refinance wave without taking much additional credit risk. It appeared that a modest tightening in loan parameters, such as loan-to-value, had no noticeable negative effect on the mortgage market.

———

We know approximately how much borrowers saved and how much cash they took out of their homes. In addition to the $160 billion in cash-outs, borrowers reduced their annual payments by about $25 billion. What they did with that money is harder to pin down. Most important for economic policy is how much of it they spent.

Although economists usually assume that households will spend a greater percentage of their income during an economic downturn, there is reason to believe that the pandemic was different. Most of the savings from refinance activity went to households that did not suffer job losses. In fact, it was difficult, if not impossible, to refinance if you had lost your job. Many of those families also cut back on spending, such as on vacations or commuting costs. For these reasons, researchers at the Wharton School of the University of Pennsylvania believe that at the margin, consumers during the pandemic were spending only an additional 27 cents out of every new dollar received.[3] Reviewing the literature on this issue, I find that to be a credible assumption. If that applies to savings from mortgage refinancing, then consumer spending increased by about $50 billion in 2020 because of refinance activity.

Over the first six months of 2020, consumer spending declined by over $500 billion. By the end of 2020, almost all of that decline would be reversed. At most, 10 percent of that recovery in consumer spending can be attributed to the stimulative effect of mortgage refinance activity.

Not all households spent income equally, just as not all homeowners display the same propensity to refinance. The generally accepted assumption within the economics profession is that lower-income households are more likely than higher-income households to spend out of income received. If refinance activity was concentrated among higher-income borrowers, then the 27 cents per dollar estimate may be considerably higher than what would be expected for savings from refinance.

Researchers at Wharton have provided a breakdown of marginal propensity to consume during COVID-19 by income quintile. The highest two quintiles display a marginal propensity to consume of about half that of the overall population.[4] This suggests that instead of 27 cents spent per dollar of refinance savings or equity extraction, a more likely estimate is 13 cents, resulting in an increase in consumer spending of only $24 billion, rather than $50 billion. That amounts to less than 5 percent of the decline in consumer spending witnessed in the first half of 2020.

Of course, one person's spending is another person's income. The same applies to interest payments. While the extraction of equity via cash-out refinancing did not necessarily reduce anyone's income, the reduction in mortgage payments did reduce the income of investors, such as retirees. This effect is likely small but does imply that one should view the 2020 bump in spending of $24 billion that resulted from refinancing as an upper estimate.

Total consumer spending had mostly recovered by the end of 2020, in both real and nominal terms. We witnessed a robust increase in consumer spending in 2021, however: 13.7 percent in nominal terms and still a strong almost 8 percent once adjusted for inflation. Given the spike in inflation starting in 2021, it is likely that any increased consumer spending resulting from mortgage refinancing in 2021 contributed to inflation.

———

Even in normal times, the likelihood of borrowers refinancing their mortgages is positively related to their income. As higher-income households, on average, have larger mortgages, their total savings from refinancing is greater. Since lenders are often compensated in part based on loan size, they have a strong incentive to devote their attention to larger loans.

This typical difference was magnified during COVID-19. One group of researchers estimated that difference to have increased by a factor of 10 during the pandemic.[5] Their study found that a combination of time spent at home (remote work), unemployment, and forbearance explains most of this change.

I felt that much of the 2008 response had been structured to benefit most the households that needed it the least, while leaving behind those who were worse off. I was concerned that the 2020 response was turning into a repeat. While I could not do anything about remote workers reaping the most rewards, we could offer some relief to those who took forbearance.

Under normal circumstances, Fannie and Freddie do not allow a borrower in forbearance to refinance. In fact, the companies usually require borrowers to make a year of on-time payments before being eligible for a guaranteed refinance.

One pleasant surprise throughout the pandemic was the sizable proportion, usually around a fifth, of borrowers who continued to pay their mortgage while in forbearance. We would allow those borrowers to refinance immediately if they were current on their mortgage payments.[6] Additionally, borrowers exiting forbearance would be required to make only 3 payments, instead of 12, before being eligible for a refinance. I had hoped this would help narrow the income gap in refinancing that we were seeing, while also providing an incentive to remain current and exit forbearance.

More flexibility for borrowers in forbearance, surprisingly, would also reduce some of the costs of forbearance. Since the primary avenue for forbearance exit was our payment deferral option, which acted as an interest-free balloon, a refinancing would functionally end the period of free interest on the missed payments, which Fannie and Freddie were still making to MBS investors.

———

Not unexpectedly, the record refinance boom of 2020 was a record year for mortgage lenders. The mortgage industry may seem competitive from the outside, but like many, it faces supply constraints and bottlenecks. Many lenders, for instance, outsource their backroom operations overseas. When India went into lockdown, so did part of the operations of numerous mortgage lenders.

Rather than be held back by supply constraints, lenders priced to the market. The MBA reported that the average per-loan profit of $1,470 in

2019 surged to $4,202 in 2020.[7] Capacity constraints allowed lenders to capture about half of the overall decline in interest rates. Usually the difference, or spread, between what lenders charge a borrower and the rate charged to the lender by Fannie and Freddie is about 100 basis points, or one percentage point. In the early months of the pandemic, this spread widened to around 250 basis points. Had mortgage rates declined one-for-one with the decline in Treasury rates, borrowers would have witnessed a savings of twice what they received.

The record profitability for mortgage lenders in 2020, as well as the record spread paid by borrowers, is partly the result of regulatory changes implemented in response to 2008. The Dodd-Frank Act and other regulatory changes reduced the role of depositories, such as commercial banks and credit unions, in the mortgage business. In the first quarter of 2020, Federal Deposit Insurance Corporation (FDIC)-insured institutions held just over $2.2 trillion in single-family mortgages on their balance sheets.[8] A year later, in the first quarter of 2021, after a record refinance wave, that figure *declined* to $2.18 trillion. Despite being flooded with deposits, which would increase by an astonishing $4 trillion over the pandemic, commercial banks were not using those deposits to fund mortgages.

Wells Fargo, historically one of the nation's most aggressive mortgage lenders, was sidelined with a regulatory asset cap. The fear of Dodd-Frank oversight chased insurance companies such as MetLife out of the mortgage origination business. The record-low mortgage rates of 2020 hid from mortgage consumers the fact that they were instead paying unusually high spreads. This was all because of the 2008 response, which was supposed to benefit consumers.

The record profits also lessened the calls for a mortgage servicer rescue. As mortgage servicing and origination are occasionally separated, not everyone in the industry benefited to the same degree. Servicers who also originated loans had no trouble covering their servicing obligations, since every refinance provided them with several weeks of "float" that could be used to fund those obligations. Specialty servicers were not so fortunate. Nevertheless, the overall industry's record profits made calls for a rescue far less credible.

The refinance boom was generated not solely by the Federal Reserve's reduction in short-term interest rates, but also by its large-scale purchases of MBS. Although these purchases provided short-term benefits to both households and financial market participants, they did leave the Federal Reserve with a large balance sheet of long-dated assets, whose values are very sensitive to interest rate changes. From 2020 to 2021, the expected duration of MBS held by the Federal Reserve almost doubled, from 3.1 to 5.7 years.[9] Without selling, the Federal Reserve would be stuck with a lot of MBS for some time.

The Federal Reserve could sell MBS, of course. The sale of assets from its balance sheet has long been an important tool for monetary policy. The difficulty, however, is that almost all of the MBS would have to be sold at a loss. With current (2022) mortgage rates over 5 percent, a considerable discount would have to be offered to entice investors to purchase MBS, with an average rate of about 2.5 percent. At the end of 2021, 99 percent of the Federal Reserve's MBS holdings were paying interest rates below the current outstanding mortgage rate. This is new territory for the Federal Reserve.

Since the Federal Reserve is not like a commercial bank, losses can be absorbed indefinitely. At least that is the financial aspect. The political one is different. Taking tens of billions in losses from selling MBS at less than par could expose the Federal Reserve to adverse attention that it would prefer to avoid. While such concerns are unlikely to change the direction of monetary policy, they could affect the timing and magnitude of policy changes, resulting in more economic volatility.

While I am skeptical of the net economic benefit of the COVID-19 refinance boom, one important result was that it allowed Fannie and Freddie to reprice their books of business. The companies charge a guarantee fee on each mortgage they acquire. That fee is received on an ongoing basis if the mortgage is outstanding.

Before 2008, the companies were charging guarantee fees that were insufficient to cover the credit risk on the mortgages. A large portion of outstanding mortgages was guaranteed before the companies had rationalized their pricing. A significant obstacle in restructuring the companies and making them attractive to future investors was the mis-pricing of their legacy business. The years 2020 and 2021 presented an unexpected opportunity to reduce that obstacle. So, while borrowers were receiving historically low rates, Fannie and Freddie were also able to reprice most of their outstanding guarantees. That will provide great-er future income and hopefully offset much of any future losses. The COVID-19 refinance boom, remarkably, may be the most important contributor to the future stability of Fannie and Freddie. It certainly helped the mortgage industry.

Chapter 9

Who's Got the Check?

One perhaps can be forgiven for thinking that Fannie Mae and Freddie Mac were created to lose money. Judging from the usual Washington dialogue, one might think these were two giant charities, rather than shareholder-owned private companies. Like many companies, Fannie and Freddie were adversely affected by COVID-19. Not to minimize the difficulties that so many businesses faced, the efforts of Fannie and Freddie to cover pandemic costs became another Washington political football, where hypocrisy would again become the dominant feature of government-sponsored enterprise (GSE) debates.

The actions taken at the Federal Housing Finance Agency (FHFA) under my direction in response to COVID-19 were never meant or structured as charity. They were designed to minimize losses to Fannie and Freddie while also supporting the functioning of the mortgage market. I believe our response was what any reasonable business would have done. This conclusion should be obvious from the fact that the vast majority of mortgage lenders and servicers not covered by the Coronavirus Aid, Relief, and Economic Security (CARES) Act adopted very similar borrower mitigation strategies.

While it is still too soon to have a full accounting of COVID-19's financial impact on Fannie and Freddie, our initial estimates at the FHFA indicated that costs would range from $6 billion to $15 billion, depending mostly on how many borrowers would exit COVID-19 forbearance without difficulty. Some costs were close to certain, such as the $500 per forbearance exit that we would pay mortgage servicers. Others, such as the "free interest" provided by our payment deferral option, would depend on how quickly borrowers exiting forbearance would go on to refinance their loans. With time, the range of estimates narrowed, as expected, most recently falling in the area of $7 billion to $8 billion. Early estimates by the Congressional Budget Office were very similar to ours.

Considering the range of potential losses and the fact that such losses would be recognized over a two- to three-year period, I concluded that we needed to design a COVID-19 cost recovery of approximately $5 billion annually. At that rate, we could spread the total cost over a few years rather than impose it all at once. Additionally, we hoped that the economy would be in a better spot by then. I also felt it was important that these costs be recouped during my tenure. All too often in Washington, officials hand out benefits and leave the costs for their successors. That was not my way. The range of costs was wide. We could reevaluate every six months or so as we gained more clarity on final losses.

Businesses throughout the economy adjusted their prices to cover COVID-19 costs to the extent possible. Some of us even felt compelled to increase our generosity in the face of the pandemic. I suspect, for instance, that I was far from alone in tipping more than I used to when ordering carry-out or dining at local restaurants. I valued them and wanted them to survive. Having started my first paid work in restaurants, I was also keenly aware of the difficulties in running a restaurant in the best of times. We would have to adjust pricing at Fannie and Freddie as well.

In addition to the usual requirements of business, we had the legal mandate to cover the losses of Fannie and Freddie via increased income. You might not guess it from today's congressional debates, but when Congress wrote the statutory charters of Fannie and Freddie, it required all costs and expenses to be covered by income. If you hear someone invoke "subsidies" to Fannie and Freddie, don't forget that Congress has never voted to extend any such assistance. Congress has never appropriated funds to cover the losses of Fannie and Freddie. Congress made it extremely clear that Fannie and Freddie were to cover their own costs. In keeping with my campaign to have the FHFA and the GSEs operate fully within the law, I intended to follow that congressional directive as well.

Despite public perception, the largest net cost of the 2008 Troubled Assets Relief Program (TARP) bank bailout was the assistance provided to delinquent borrowers. While I continue to believe that the bank bailouts themselves were a mistake, I would be the first to admit that the TARP assistance to banks was paid back. One can and should debate the appropriate rate of return, but the principal was repaid. This was not the case with the homeowners' assistance. In addition to our legal mandates, I felt that the ethical approach would be to have costs incurred within the mortgage market recouped within that market.

I believed that it would also be feasible to structure a program of assistance in which those most in need were prioritized. The 2008 response often focused on giving help to those who did not need it, while doing little for those who needed it the most. Many, like me, were able to refinance at a lower interest rate in 2009 thanks to the federal response. But I did not need that help, nor did many others. For most, it was simply a windfall, and one that was often saved. The hope was a sort of Keynesian trickle-down in which subsidies to the well-off would increase spending, thereby eventually increasing the employment of lower-income workers. In 2020, as in 2009, those not suffering a job loss or income loss tended to save this subsidy, with little if any positive effect on the macroeconomy.

If anything, the increase in disposable income from reduced mortgage payments added to the inflationary pressures experienced later in the pandemic. The dramatic surge in house prices, driven partly by the low interest rate environment, also added to inflation via the increase in consumer spending that resulted from higher home values.

Fortunately, I had 11 months on the job before COVID-19 struck. That time ended up being crucial. Under a previous agreement between the Treasury Department and the FHFA (on behalf of the GSEs), retained earnings were capped at $3 billion for each GSE. Once confirmed, I immediately worked to remove that cap and start building capital. By the time COVID-19 hit, we had managed to reduce the leverage at

Fannie and Freddie from around 1,000 to 1 to about 160 to 1—still dangerous, but enough to give us time. Had we not started to retain earnings in 2019, Fannie and Freddie would have failed in 2020.

———

I am not known for being too generous toward Fannie and Freddie in my commentary. That said, they do deserve credit for trying to be responsible in absorbing losses in the face of a pandemic. Both Fannie and Freddie came to me in early March 2020, asking to raise the guarantee fees, or pricing adjustments, on the loans they purchase. They were committed to surviving whatever COVID-19 might bring without asking for a bailout. Regaining earnings faster would be key.

I spent several weeks in early March 2020 discussing pricing increases with the executives and the boards of both companies. There was widespread agreement that a modest pricing increase would help the companies recover from any COVID-19-related costs and that such a policy could be implemented in a manner that would not have a noticeable effect on the mortgage market. I asked both companies to submit straightforward proposals as soon as possible.

Apparently, that request was lost in translation, as the Fannie and Freddie proposals were not only wildly different, but also overly complex. The back-and-forth consumed about three weeks. By that time, the public and political perceptions of the pandemic had shifted. I felt that to increase pricing in late March 2020 would have posed significant reputational risk to both the GSEs and the FHFA. The question was, given the financial state of the companies, how long could we wait?

Included in the CARES Act was significant accounting relief for financial institutions, including Fannie and Freddie. I was not a fan of these flexibilities—not for the banks and not for Fannie and Freddie. This relief allowed financial companies to delay the recognition of COVID-19-related losses. Generally, I do not think Congress should get involved in setting accounting rules. That is not to say that the Financial Accounting Standards Board does not occasionally get it wrong, but I have never seen Congress get involved in specific accounting issues and have the result be greater transparency for investors and financial markets.

Since such relief was allowed for the banks and for Fannie and Freddie under the CARES Act, we allowed it as well. However, we would do our best to make sure the public accounting releases for the GSEs reflected economic reality as closely as possible.

The big issue for Fannie and Freddie would be the treatment of interest due on loans in forbearance that had not actually been received. Or, as the accountants would put it, accrued interest income. Because of the CARES Act, Fannie and Freddie were able to count as income large amounts of interest that had not yet been, and might never be, received. For much of COVID-19, about half of the GSE reported earnings were in the form of either tax losses or interest accruals. None of that is loss absorbing. Moreover, it gave the public the perception that Fannie and Freddie were in better financial health than they were. Former Freddie Mac executive Dave Stevens pointed to the companies' earnings as a reason to oppose recovering COVID-19-related costs, stating: "Fannie Mae and Freddie Mac released their Q3 earnings last week, reflecting a combined $6.7 billion in net income, up significantly from the previous quarter. This strong performance was not unexpected, but makes the upcoming 50 basis point adverse market refinance fee more puzzling."[1]

The net income figures touted by Stevens represented mainly income not yet received, as a large portion of it was from loans in forbearance. For this reason, among others, I instituted an internal practice in which we had regular financial reporting that reflected not only the companies' public accounting statement, but also their true economic status. Unfortunately, the GSEs are far from being alone in these practices. The accounting statements of any financial institution should be taken with a grain of salt. Despite my misgiving, however, the new reporting did give the FHFA more flexibility in addressing its financial condition.

Having served as staff on the Senate Banking Committee during the 2008 crisis, I had witnessed how firms like Lehman Brothers were far too slow to recognize losses and attempt to increase capital before it was too late. I did not want to see Fannie and Freddie make similar mistakes this time around. It is far easier to build or raise equity for a financial company when earnings are strong than when they are declining. As

President Kennedy stated in his 1962 State of the Union Address, "The best time to repair the roof is when the sun is shining."

———

Throughout 2020, both Fannie and Freddie regularly requested pricing increases to cover expected COVID-19 expenses. One of the downsides of a decade-long conservatorship was that the companies stopped giving much thought to reputational risk. They acted, perhaps correctly, as if any negative public reaction would hit the FHFA and not them. But to be ready to exit conservatorship, these companies needed to be able to think about risks to their reputation. The inability or unwillingness to do this would come back to bite us all when the pricing adjustments were eventually announced.

As the summer of 2020 passed, we gained considerable clarity as to COVID-19's financial impact on the GSEs. Forbearance had peaked in May. The labor market had long since hit bottom, showing considerable strength in June and July. We were seeing significant numbers of borrowers exit forbearance. By the beginning of August, we finally had the feeling that the worst was behind us, at least in terms of the mortgage market. We thought we should be able to move toward addressing the financial stress at Fannie and Freddie.

By the end of the summer of 2020, we also had a clearer picture of the direction the mortgage market was taking. Early in the pandemic, both Fannie and Freddie were forecasting house price declines and a weak housing market. As I mentioned earlier, I knew the chief economists at both Fannie Mae and Freddie Mac (Doug Duncan and Sam Khater, respectively), and I had worked with Sam for a few years earlier in my career. I sometimes read the data differently, but I did feel that the companies were trying to get an accurate handle on the housing market.

As it turned out, the mortgage market would see one of its best years ever in 2020. I believed that the best avenue for minimizing the impact of a pricing increase would be to spread that cost over as many mortgages as feasible. We knew we would have to raise a fixed amount: our target of $5 billion annually. If we missed the bulk of the refinance boom, then the per-mortgage price increase would be higher. For this reason and others, August 2020 looked to be the right time for a pricing adjustment.

———

To minimize the impact on homeownership opportunities, we would apply the COVID-19 recovery fee, which the GSEs called an adverse-market fee, only to refinancing. We would also exempt lower-income borrowers. The beauty of applying the fee only to refinancing also meant that loans subject to the fee would still offer borrowers a considerable savings on their monthly payments in the event of a refinance. And of course, no one is obligated to refinance. All parties would be better off. It is rare that one sees a policy that is close to a "free lunch." The fee could also be completely avoided by not selling the loan to Fannie or Freddie.

I considered this an extremely progressive approach. According to the FHFA's internal data, the fee would apply largely to the mortgages of wealthier households. The charge would allow us to continue to fund assistance to predominantly middle- and lower-income households. Also, it is worth remembering that to refinance, one had to be employed. Hence, we were creating a system in which those who had been fortunate enough to keep their jobs would see a slightly smaller savings from refinancing so that those who did lose their jobs could remain in their homes during the pandemic.

The reduced savings from the fee would also fall mainly on white borrowers, while the benefits of the assistance it paid for would go mainly to borrowers of color. In a time of racial turmoil, it would be the right thing to do. At that time, presidential candidate Joe Biden had included in his campaign platform a new fee for Fannie and Freddie borrowers that would be used to help provide housing for lower-income borrowers. That was exactly what we were doing with the COVID-19 recovery fee, although the proposed Biden mortgage fee was several times larger than our COVID-19 fee. A true progressive might complain that our fee was too small, rather than what we heard, which was that it was too big.

———

Despite the progressive structure of the fee and its similarity to one proposed by Biden, the rollout was widely attacked. It was an election year, after all. Rep. Maxine Waters, a Democrat from California, objected: "Imposing thousands of dollars in additional costs on borrowers at a time when the Administration is supposed to be working on methods to help families stay in their homes is just another example of tone-deaf policies put in place by Trump Administration officials who could care less about helping the American people weather this pandemic. I am urging the FHFA to reverse course immediately and allow homeowners a fighting chance."[2]

Setting aside that the FHFA was then an independent regulator, and therefore not part of the Trump administration, Waters' argument was that our funding assistance to keep families in their homes during a pandemic was actually hurting those families. Sound a little Orwellian? Yes, that's politics.

Of course, it is not as if Waters, or rather her staff, was engaged in original thinking or deep analysis. They were largely cutting and pasting from the press releases of Wall Street lobbyists. For instance, and do not be surprised if you recognize similarities, the Mortgage Bankers Association argued that "tonight's announcement by the GSEs flies in the face of the Administration's recent executive actions urging federal agencies to take all measures within their authorities to support struggling homeowners."[3]

Contrary to these Wall Street talking points, the fee did not apply to "struggling homeowners," because you had to be employed and have a mortgage balance greater than $125,000 for your loan to be covered by the fee and, more absurdly, the fee-funded assistance went to actual struggling homeowners.[4] Furthermore, of course mortgages covered by the fee would still result in borrowers seeing savings when they refinanced their loans.

The real issue was twofold. First, the fee would make mortgages intended for sale to Fannie and Freddie more expensive than other mortgages. There are many Wall Street players whose entire business model is passing along mortgage risk to Fannie and Freddie. Anything that makes Fannie and Freddie more expensive than other options reduces the market share of lenders dependent exclusively upon Fannie and Freddie. For instance, mortgages made by commercial banks and held on their balance sheets would be exempt from the fee, giving commercial banks a

Federal Housing Finance Agency Director Mark Calabria, Federal Reserve Chair Jay Powell, and Treasury Secretary Steven Mnuchin meet as part of the Financial Stability Oversight Council in September 2020. (Photo from personal archive)

Participants practice social distancing during a hearing before the Senate Committee on Banking, Housing, and Urban Affairs on June 9, 2020. (Photo by Win McNamee/Getty Images)

Secretary of Housing and Urban Development Ben Carson and Federal Housing Finance Agency Director Mark Calabria participate in the hearing before the House Committee on Financial Services on October 22, 2019. (Photo by Tom Williams/CQ-Roll Call Inc. via Getty Images)

Federal Housing Finance Agency Director Mark Calabria and Vice President Mike Pence attend Calabria's swearing in ceremony in the vice president's ceremonial office, April 2019. (Photo by Andrea Hanks, @ahanksphoto)

Federal Housing Finance Agency senior leadership on day of the *Collins v. Yellen* decision. Director Mark Calabria sitting. From left to right: Sheila Greenwood, Clinton Jones, John Roscoe, Chris Bosland, Raffi Williams, Lydia Mashburn, and Ann Conant Rulon. (Photo from personal archive)

Federal Housing Finance Agency Director Mark Calabria and Vice President Mike Pence attend Calabria's swearing in ceremony in the vice president's ceremonial office, April 2019. (Photo by Andrea Hanks, @ahanksphoto)

Treasury Secretary Steven Mnuchin, Housing and Urban Development Secretary Ben Carson, and Federal Housing Finance Agency Director Mark Calabria testify before the U.S. Senate Committee on Banking, Housing, and Urban Affairs in September 2019. (Photo by Zach Gibson/Getty Images)

Sheila Bair, chair of the Board of Directors for Fannie Mae and former chair of the Federal Deposit Insurance Corporation. (Photo by Michael Nagle/Bloomberg via Getty Images)

U.S. Senator Sherrod Brown (D-OH) served as both chair and ranking member on the Committee on Banking, Housing, and Urban Affairs and is a vocal advocate for affordable rental housing. (Recording from the U.S. Senate Committee on Banking, Housing, and Urban Affairs)

U.S. Senator Mike Crapo (R–ID) served as both chair and ranking member on the Committee on Banking, Housing, and Urban Affairs and led housing finance reform efforts in Congress. (Recording from the U.S. Senate Committee on Banking, Housing, and Urban Affairs)

U.S. Rep. Maxine Waters (D-CA) served as both chair and ranking member on the Committee on Financial Services. (Recording from the U.S. House Committee on Financial Services)

U.S. Rep. Patrick McHenry (R-NC) served as both chair and ranking member on the Committee on Financial Services. (Recording from the U.S. House Committee on Financial Services)

Andrew Olmem, deputy director of the White House's National Economic Council. (Photo by Kyle Grillot/Bloomberg via Getty Images)

Lynn Fisher, deputy director of the Federal Housing Finance Agency's (FHFA's) Division of Economics and Statistics, appears on one of FHFA's frequent public video releases, highlighting pandemic-driven changes in the FHFA House Price Index. (Recording from the quarterly release of the FHFA House Price Index report)

competitive advantage. Of course, any such advantage was an unintended consequence. The hard reality is that almost anything you do to make sure Fannie and Freddie bear the full cost of their activities will have a competitive effect on the primary mortgage market. Most of the complaint was about market share and had nothing to do with actual homeowners.

Second, lenders were charging record spreads, hence earning record profits, on mortgages. Yes, the Federal Reserve drove down interest rates in 2020, but only about half of that decline in longer-term rates was passed along to mortgage borrowers. The rest went into the pockets of Wall Street mortgage lenders. The reason these companies were able to do so was the high degree of concentration among lenders. There were very real capacity constraints in the mortgage market, allowing lenders to capture value that would have gone to the consumer. Since the lenders were already charging what the market would bear, the bulk of the COVID-19 recovery fee would come mostly out of their pockets, at least in the short run.

This was confirmed in my many conversations with lenders during the rollout of the fee. A few were able to offer exact dollar figures on how much the fee would eat into their profits. Despite the hit to the bottom line of mortgage lenders, I was pleasantly surprised at how reasonable and cordial these CEOs were over the phone. A few told me directly that even though it would cost them, they understood the need for the fee, and some even agreed that it was appropriate public policy. The request from most of the mortgage CEOs was simply for more time to implement the fee, so that they could adjust the pricing of their mortgage pipeline. I made clear that a delay could mean we would miss the bulk of the refinance wave and would then have to increase the size of the fee. With that in mind, lenders seemed to accept the tradeoff.

It was another instance of what was becoming a repeated pattern: sensible, thoughtful conversations with CEOs focused on solving a problem, contrasted with hyperbolic, occasionally dishonest rhetoric from their trade associations.

———

The mortgage industry and congressional Democrats were not the only ones complaining. Despite Waters' claim that this was an action of the Trump administration, the White House, or at least parts of it, was opposed as well. My good friend Larry Kudlow, director of the White House National Economic Council, asked me to drop the fee. I explained that we were legally obligated to recover these costs and therefore I could not drop it. Larry also told me that White House Chief of Staff Mark Meadows was very unhappy about it. I thanked Larry for his views and said that we were certainly open to finding other ways to cover these costs, but cover them we must. Meadows and the White House communications team later leaked to the *Wall Street Journal* their disapproval of the fee. While I was disappointed with their attempts to pressure an independent regulator, I continued to carry out my statutory obligations. Having served as the vice president's chief economist, I had my own sources of information within the White House, and what I was hearing was that neither the president nor the vice president had an issue with the fee. I believe that President Trump and Vice President Pence supported me for this job because they knew I could resist the pressures of Wall Street lobbyists. They were correct.

Not surprisingly, the Wall Street backlash to the COVID-19 recovery fee resulted in several calls from members of Congress. After explaining the dynamics, I found that most members, while not pleased, understood the issue. I had explained that the CARES Act, which imposed costs on Fannie and Freddie, did not provide any funding to cover those costs. Some members expressed surprise at the notion that passing a law that imposed costs would result in increased costs. I never asked Congress to cover these costs. I felt we could and should do so within the mortgage market.

Several members, however, requested the opportunity to ask Congress to fund these expenses. After repeated pleas, I announced a delay, but a delay with a hard date. I was giving Congress about two months to fix the problem. Pushing anything beyond that would have been a failure to meet our statutory obligations.

With all the Wall Street money at stake, there was no way Congress was going to let this pass without a circus. A virtual hearing was scheduled for the House Financial Services Committee at noon on Wednesday, September 16, 2020. You can tell by the hearing title, "Prioritizing

Fannie's and Freddie's Capital over America's Homeowners and Renters? A Review of the Federal Housing Finance Agency's Response to the COVID-19 Pandemic," that it was all meant to be a setup.

I suspect that members of the Committee, along with the K Street lobbyists, were hoping that the pressure of a four-hour hearing with me as the single witness would cause me to fold. They were in for quite the surprise. Several members went at me right away for the COVID-19 recovery fee. I repeatedly countered that I was following the law for which many of them had voted, and that they had provided zero funding to offset the costs of that law. I constantly let them know that the fee would go away if they funded it. I think many of them were surprised that I had the audacity to point out that it was I who was giving assistance to borrowers and renters, while they simply bickered.

A problem many agency heads run into is that they willingly take ownership of problems created by Congress. I was more than willing to own any problems I had created, but I was not going to own those of Congress. More importantly, I was not going to let Congress off the hook.

Having worked on the Hill for seven years, one of the things I quickly noticed was that members of Congress like to take credit and avoid blame. That is human nature. What is interesting, however, is that if you put them in the position of having to own an issue, many will recoil, almost hide. That was my general approach in hearings. "Yes, Congressman So-and-So, you are correct, a certain policy is broken, and it would be great if Congress fixed that." It can be shocking how often suggesting that Congress just do its job changes the nature of the conversation.

Several members of the Committee, including the senior Republican, Patrick McHenry of North Carolina, came to my defense, reminding Democrats that all of this was indeed the result of legislation for which they had voted. Although I did not like having to delay the implementation of the COVID-19 recovery fee, doing so gave several members a degree of comfort and willingness to work toward a solution. There were also a few members, like Trey Hollingsworth, a Republican from Indiana, who commended my making the tough choices and encouraged me to keep at it. Sadly, such members are usually a minority.

Late in this four-hour hearing, one of the more absurd attacks came from Rep. Katie Porter, a Democrat from California. I should not have been too surprised. Porter represented a district with a median income almost twice that of the national average. The population of her district was also less than 2 percent black. One of the great tragedies of COVID-19 has been the disproportionate impact, during the height of the pandemic, on blacks, with much higher fatality rates.[5] The fact is that her well-off constituents would see less savings when they refinanced, with the assistance to families in need going mostly to people outside her district. Despite all the talk about being progressive, Porter was against her wealthy voters subsidizing the struggling families we were working to keep housed during a pandemic. Perhaps the most absurd part of her questioning was demanding why I had not informed her that the CARES Act, which clearly imposed costs on the mortgage market, would result in higher costs for that market. Time ran out before I could remind her that the Congressional Budget Office existed for that very purpose. I try not to take too much pleasure from the misfortune of others, but I must admit taking some enjoyment when Waters had Porter kicked off the House Financial Services Committee. Karma.

The hearing ended with the ball clearly in Congress's court. I came out stronger than I went in. The lesson for future agency heads is to not let Congress hang their mistakes on you. Make them own them. Not surprisingly, Congress did nothing to fund the GSEs' COVID-19 costs. But then, why would they? I had taken the heat. I came up with the funding. I am sure they managed to do several rounds of fundraising off the issue. Everyone is a winner.

———

The rollout of the COVID-19 recovery fee was also a painful lesson about whom I could trust. Since Fannie and Freddie had both been advocating for this fee since March 2020, and the usual method of communicating such changes is via a lender letter, I let the companies take the lead in announcing it. Boy, was that a mistake. They completely misrepresented the purpose of the fee, stating that it was prompted by increased risk in the refinance market, not COVID-19. We also heard informally that despite their requesting the fee on paper, they were orally telling mortgage lenders that they were forced to do it. None of this was true.

Sadly, it was another instance of when working with Fannie and Freddie felt like the old fable about the scorpion and the frog: some people will hurt others even when it does not benefit them. Such behavior just seemed to be in their nature. This was also one of several events that led me to express to both of their boards that their corporate cultures were broken. Those were painful meetings. In the case of Freddie Mac, I believe it eventually resulted in the resignation of the CEO. While those were not fun conversations, they were crucial and did result in both boards starting new corporate culture initiatives. I believe both are much stronger companies now after having begun those strategies. Only time will tell whether they have really turned over a new leaf.

Assistance that helped keep just under 3 million families in their homes during a pandemic was provided by Fannie and Freddie, at the direction of the FHFA. I remain extremely proud of that effort. In comparison, the Home Affordable Modification Program (HAMP), created in response to the 2008 crisis, provided permanent assistance to 1.5 million borrowers, and even about a third of those eventually defaulted. Perhaps most shocking was HAMP's slow rollout. A year into HAMP, just over half a million borrowers had received permanent assistance, whereas the FHFA helped almost six times that number in the first year of COVID-19.[6]

If the sluggish rollout of HAMP were not bad enough, the program proved expensive, costing taxpayers well over $20 billion.[7] That does not even reflect the $25 billion in borrower assistance that was promised under the settlement with major lenders, or the almost $10 billion appropriated by Congress to local governments under the Hardest Hit Fund.

We created a funding mechanism that ensured that we could provide assistance at no cost to the taxpayer. It was also done without any visible disruption to the mortgage market. The COVID-19 recovery fee also brought to government a level of transparency that is rarely seen. All government choices have costs. Making those costs explicit is not an excuse for inaction. We acted—and we acted quickly. And we paid for it, not the taxpayer. This should be the model for future responses, not the endless subsidies and bailouts that have all too often become the norm.

Chapter 10
Preexisting Conditions

COVID-19 did not affect everyone equally. One's risk was in part a function of any comorbidities or preexisting conditions. Certainly, as someone whose body mass index is higher than I would like, that was hard for me to ignore. Industries and individual companies had their own comorbidities. While airlines, restaurants, and retail establishments come to mind, both Fannie and Freddie had several preexisting health issues when the pandemic started.

Their lack of capital was the most pressing problem, but it was far from the only one. Despite the conservatorship of Fannie and Freddie for over a decade, on most days it felt like almost nothing had been done in that time to actually fix the problems. Sadly, in many ways the situation had been made worse.

———

I have read quite a few stories of institutional disaster or failure. Think AIG, Lehman Brothers, Continental Illinois, Enron, GE, or the *Challenger* space shuttle explosion. It's not always thrilling reading, but I recommend it. The most important thing I have taken away from this study, as well as my experience in government, is that organizational culture really matters.

In almost every instance of organizational failure that I have examined, someone somewhere within the organization had the right information or insights. That information was either ignored or never got to the right decisionmakers. This was true for both Fannie and Freddie leading up to the 2008 financial crisis.

My friend and colleague Adolfo Marzol is just one example of a person with such insight. Adolfo, who served as my number two at the Federal Housing Finance Agency (FHFA), had spent much of his career at Fannie Mae. He eventually served as the chief risk officer there, responsible for identifying and measuring dangers. Adolfo was among the first to spot growing problems in the early 2000s mortgage market. Unfortunately, voicing such concerns was not welcomed within Fannie Mae. If you cannot steer the ship away from the reefs, then at some point it is time to jump ship. Adolfo wisely did so in 2005.

Adolfo also brought tremendous market and government experience apart from Fannie Mae. Immediately prior to joining the FHFA, he served as Housing and Urban Development (HUD) Secretary Ben Carson's primary adviser on mortgage finance issues. That was an important element in cementing the FHFA's relationship with HUD. Adolfo had also founded a mortgage insurance company, Essent. His vast contacts in the mortgage industry would be a critical asset during my entire tenure.

Another example, this time from Freddie, is that of Susan Wharton Gates, who documents the problems there in her book *Days of Slaughter: Inside the Fall of Freddie Mac and Why It Could Happen Again.*[1] There are many others.[2]

Although both companies had gained some small degree of modesty in the early days of their conservatorship, that was all gone by 2019. In fact, Freddie had adopted a strategy of constantly fighting the FHFA and never admitting error. Their general counsel at the time had been hired with the explicit command that the FHFA is always wrong, and Freddie is always right.

This wasn't just a matter of the companies' relationship with the FHFA, although it is never wise for a large financial institution to maintain a confrontational attitude with its regulator. It was a matter of the survival of the companies. It would be a mistake to release them from conservatorship if they were simply going to return to it at some point. The fact was that their corporate cultures raised legitimate concerns about their safety and soundness. Those had to be addressed before an exit from conservatorship.

I am a big believer in having a diverse organization. Not as a form of quotas or redistribution, but because no individual ever sees the full picture on their own. Different experiences and backgrounds help challenge group-think and reduce blind spots. None of that matters, though, if an organization is not built to process that information. Although Fannie and Freddie regularly touted their employee diversity, the truth was that it was mostly surface level. Employees at the companies often felt they couldn't raise concerns or objections, something we later confirmed via employee surveys.

After several months of problems accumulating at the companies, I raised the issue of corporate culture to the boards. To its credit, the Fannie Mae board got it immediately. Many of its members had seen the damage a broken corporate culture had inflicted on other companies. While it started out tense, that Fannie Mae board meeting was a breakthrough. Members of the board who rarely spoke during meetings suddenly found their voices. While they did not fully agree, they also didn't disagree, and they committed to taking ownership of the issue.

Freddie was another story. The general view was disbelief. Who, us? A few board members asserted that the problem was the FHFA. No shock there. A handful of board members regularly acted as if their jobs were to protect Freddie management, rather than to represent the conservator. Replacing some board members would be critical if we were going to get the companies ready to exit conservatorship and meet the standards expected of any large financial institution.

Freddie's then CEO David Brickman appeared to take it personally. I liked David. We both had doctorates in economics, although I would admit he was the better technical economist. But then, neither of us was being paid to play that role. During our conversations, he remarked that he saw no culture problems at the company. Perhaps that is to be expected, as he had been with Freddie for decades. With the election results, which suggested that an exit from conservatorship would be unlikely, and their potential impact on the company, I believe the problems around Freddie's culture ultimately led to David's decision to leave the company. From his perspective, if there was not going to be an exit from conservatorship, because of opposition from the Biden administration, then he would never be able to be a real CEO. Perhaps even worse, he would still have to deal with constant management of the company by the FHFA.

Considering the short notice of David's departure, board chair Sara Mathew stepped into the breach, taking over many of the CEO's responsibilities. That ended up being a blessing. Problems that were not apparent to the board suddenly came into full view. The situation was not sustainable, however, for either Sara or the company. Fortunately, former Prudential Insurance CFO Mark Grier, who also served on the Freddie board, agreed to fill the role of CEO on an interim basis while we searched for a permanent replacement. Both Mathew and Grier had been either executives or members of the boards of other large highly regulated financial institutions. They understood where Freddie needed to be. Many of the recent improvements at Freddie are due to their efforts.

I have occasionally been critical of the culture of some of our largest banks. The repeated rescues of Citibank, for instance, have been both a contributor to and the result of cultural problems at that company. I have regularly quipped that my objective was for Fannie and Freddie to be only as highly leveraged, poorly regulated, and mismanaged as Citibank. The fact that this would be a big improvement at both Fannie and Freddie should tell you all you need to know. They simply did not have the culture, particularly one of regulatory compliance, that is needed at systemically important financial institutions of their size.

That is changing, thanks to the boards. Whether the revamping sticks is an open question. Before I left the FHFA, both companies conducted extensive surveys and focus groups among their staff. The results were enlightening. The two board chairs, Sara Mathew at Freddie, and Sheila Bair at Fannie, took personal ownership of the corporate culture. That may be one of the few differences that lasts.

———

An aspect of corporate culture that consumed far too much of my time was the issue of executive compensation. Even before I walked in the door at the FHFA, there were complaints from Congress and other stakeholders about the compensation of executives at Fannie and Freddie. The issue was repeatedly raised during my introductory visits with members of the House Financial Services Committee.

In one of my first meetings with senior Freddie executives in April 2019, they begged me not to scrutinize the company's compensation practices too closely. At one point, a Freddie executive said, "Mr. Director, I do not feel you really appreciate just how hard it is for someone to get by in the Washington area on only $500,000 a year." I guessed I didn't, as my response was to suggest that the executive and I must travel in different social circles. I am hard-pressed to think of anyone I know who wouldn't be overjoyed to earn such a salary.

The argument was that the companies needed to compete with Wall Street for talent. I wasn't buying it. I immediately told both companies' executives and boards that compensation practices would have to change. I repeated my view that if you paid people like they were on Wall Street, they'd act like they were on Wall Street, and that such behavior was the last thing the government-sponsored enterprises (GSEs) needed. In fact, it contributed to their failures. Freddie still tried to run its balance sheet operation like a hedge fund, even with the conservatorship's limits on balance sheet size.

Freddie also based some percentage of executive compensation on its market share relative to that of Fannie. Now, I could somewhat understand this position in normal times, but these were two failed companies essentially in bankruptcy, and here we were incentivizing them to compete aggressively with each other? While it was a relatively small percentage, the bigger problem was that it represented a core cultural failing at Freddie: the obsession with keeping up with Fannie. I am a major advocate of competition, but not when the taxpayer is taking the downside. This race to the bottom had to stop.

The companies' mutual obsession resulted in one bad behavior after another. During the conservatorship, we had eliminated the companies' long-time practice of giving lenders volume discounts to buy market share. It was not uncommon before 2008 for the companies to charge the largest mortgage lenders half of what they charged community banks and credit unions to provide the same guarantees. Such behavior drove consolidation in the mortgage business, benefiting massive lenders like Countrywide while forcing smaller lenders out of the business.

You must give the companies some points for creativity. Since they could not formally give volume pricing discounts, they found other avenues to favor some lenders over others. They offered special terms of business available to only select lenders. They also entered bundling agreements in which various services were combined, such as mortgage acquisition and an upfront credit transfer on the same loans. These agreements allowed them to hide volume discounts. It was a never-ending whack-a-mole. We would never truly fix it until we fixed the culture.

———

There were also no limits on the companies' revolving door with lenders. An account manager could handle all the business for a particular lender and then leave the very next day to work for that lender. I don't blame the account managers for responding to incentives; it was the companies that had put their staff in a position where their loyalty would be to lenders and not the companies, and certainly not the taxpayer or conservator.

This activity was also counter to their statutory charters. Congress did not intend for Fannie and Freddie to drive the mortgage market. Congress meant for the companies to be a backstop. For that reason, both companies' charters require them to conduct their business, especially in terms of pricing, in a way to "discourage excessive use of their facilities." Congress intended them to be the mortgage buyer of last resort, not first. It was as clear as day in the law, even if it had been ignored for decades.

The culture of prioritizing the satisfaction of Wall Street lenders also resulted in regular leaks from the companies to the mortgage industry. The FHFA was often subject to industry lobbying on topics that were still under development and not public. On more than one occasion, industry lobbyists even admitted they had received such information from Fannie and Freddie.

This was obviously a problem in terms of the companies' relationships with the FHFA. They reeked of disrespect and arrogance. It would also be a problem with conducting a public stock offering as part of an exit from conservatorship. The companies had been subject to our primary federal securities laws only since 2008. They had even been exempted from the Sarbanes-Oxley Act of 2002, only a few years before their own accounting scandals. Fannie ended up being the second largest corporate restatement in U.S. history, behind only WorldCom. If the equities markets were going to trust these companies, there needed to be considerable improvement in their internal controls.

In addition to the problematic executive compensation, there were also claims of gender disparities in payment at both companies. While my first instinct was to lower the salaries of some of the men at the companies to match those of female peers, this did not come without its own problems. In the end, I directed each company to come up with its own solutions to the problem. Unfortunately, one company submitted a proposal, cleared by both its legal team and the FHFA's, that was later criticized by the FHFA's inspector general. Accordingly, it was eventually rescinded. No good deed goes unpunished. During my last few months, we released a public request for input on compensation practices at the GSEs, including the Federal Home Loan Banks. The system, including the FHFA's internal process, was broken. We needed a long-term fix, not continued ad hoc adjustments.

————

A badly needed change was to get Fannie and Freddie to take some moral responsibility for practices in the mortgage market. The companies did not see it as their role to police bad behavior. In fact, they felt that they had no obligation whatsoever to borrowers. Their goal was to keep Wall Street lenders happy.

Fannie and Freddie, along with the Federal Housing Administration (FHA) at the Department of Housing and Urban Development, dominate the U.S. mortgage market. It is impossible for bad behavior to become widespread in the mortgage market unless they turn a blind eye to it. Since few others had any incentive to police the mortgage market, Fannie and Freddie had to step up.

Both companies, for instance, like to brag about their environment-social-governance efforts. Despite their regular claims to support "green" lending, when I asked them what types of lending they intended to stop supporting, such as funding for projects that led to the destruction of vulnerable wetlands, I was met with silence. They showed the same attitude toward the sustainability of their mortgage lending.

Efforts to alter this unwillingness to take responsibility were made, however. Working with the Fannie Mae board, particularly its chair, Sheila Bair, we established a new low-income streamlined refinancing product. To make sure that borrowers were not simply churned through the process to generate fees for the lender, we required a net benefit test for the borrower. There had to be a minimum reduction in monthly payments before Fannie would buy the loan. For once, we were going to push responsible behavior in the mortgage market. Unfortunately, this important consumer protection was later rescinded by the Biden administration.

————

Back in 2008, Congress had also directed the FHFA to establish a process for approving new products at the companies. Fannie and Freddie, like commercial banks, have limited corporate charters. Most public companies, like Amazon or Walmart, have general corporate charters that allow them to enter most lines of business. Financial services have long been different. The lines dividing what banks can and cannot do are the subject of countless legal and political battles. The same holds for the GSEs.

GSE executives would often suggest increasing profitability at the companies by entering adjacent lines of business and undercutting incumbents by leveraging their funding advantages. I, however, didn't see anything innovative about leveraging an implied government guarantee to run someone else out of business. I was all for transformation within their charters, but not creative reads of those charters.

The companies also failed to see the benefits of a transparent approval process for new products. Fannie and Freddie had engendered considerable ill will over the years as to how they stepped on the business of others. In fact, there had been an entire lobbying effort, FM Watch, created to monitor charter violations. Ultimately, I felt, and tried to convince the companies, that a more open process would reduce hostility toward the companies. It is surprising what people will accept if they've had an opportunity to make their case.

Transparency would be good for the companies. Unfortunately, I think they still don't see it that way.

Clarity over the product approval process would be helpful, however, if a large public equity offering was part of the conservatorship exit. Equity underwriters, as well as investors, would be better able to price an offering if the charter was clearer. The basic business model of the companies was fairly straightforward. But that basic business was relatively mature. The GSEs dominate the market segments in which they are allowed to operate. While I did not see it as my responsibility to position the companies as "growth" stocks, I did feel that greater regulatory certainty would facilitate equity pricing.

Fundamentally, I made it plain to the companies that they would be the ones selling equity. I was not going to be joining any road shows or ringing the bell to open the exchange. The FHFA was an independent, arms-length regulator, not a cheerleader. I was going to do my best to make sure it stayed that way.

———

I like to think that every cloud has a silver lining. One positive that became apparent from the pandemic was that given a unifying public goal, Fannie and Freddie could rise to the occasion. The problem was not so much the companies, their boards, or their employees (not that there weren't any problems there); it was a lack of leadership, especially from the FHFA.

Congress had created a direction and purpose for the companies. It is all there in the law. The problem is that such guidance had long been ignored, even violated, by the FHFA and Fannie and Freddie. I was simply amazed by the companies' response to COVID-19. There was finally something larger than the constant demands of Wall Street lenders to motivate the companies.

The companies always paid a lot of lip service to their mission, but before COVID-19 it was hard to see any evidence. They acted as if the public purse was there to be looted. Freddie had even included in its financial statements a claim of explicit taxpayer backing, which of course did not exist. Both companies had structured their activities with the expectation of another bailout. That had to go. I spelled out that any request for a Treasury draw had to include the resignations of the CEOs and board chairs and, as importantly, that any such request would likely be denied, with or without their resignations.

The focus on protecting borrowers and renters from the pandemic brought out the best in Fannie and Freddie. It was also proof of what the companies were truly capable of. The question was how we could take that experience and ensure that the companies continued this focus after the pandemic. For all our sakes, I hope this trend persists.

———

An occasional refrain from Wall Street was that the companies had already been fixed. It is probably obvious that I disagree with that claim. But to be fair, why would anyone make such a claim? Putting aside ignorance of what was going on within the companies, much of which even I was shocked to discover, what could be the basis for asserting that the GSEs had been fixed? If you put yourself in the shoes of a Wall Street asset manager, you care most about getting back the money you have invested in Fannie and Freddie debt. The contention about the companies being fixed is fundamentally an allegation that the taxpayer is now fully on the hook for Wall Street's speculations in GSE debt. Wall Street simply wants to get paid; it is not any more complicated than that.

The complications come in because, in fact, the taxpayer is not legally responsible for Fannie and Freddie's debt. That debt is still sold today with a clear disclaimer of any taxpayer backing. The emergency authority for the Treasury Department to purchase GSE securities has expired, despite whatever novel legal arguments the Treasury and its Wall Street friends present. The first word in the statutory section approving that authority is "temporary."[3] And the law distinctly states an expiration date. The implied guarantee may have hardened, but the taxpayer has no legal obligation.

None of this is novel. There is a long history of Wall Street misleading investors into believing a government guarantee is there when it is not. Considerable litigation occurred in the 1970s, for example, after investors were sold commercial paper in Penn Central with the assurance that a government loan guarantee would be forthcoming. After all, the then Interstate Commerce Commission had to approve debt issuance from Penn Central, so evidently there was an implied government backing. Then there are former Treasury secretary Bob Rubin and former New Jersey senator and governor Jon Corzine making fortunes from betting on a bailout of the Farm Credit System, sister GSE to Fannie and Freddie. Corzine was willing to bet almost everything on implied guarantees during the Eurozone crisis. One of my first meetings as a staffer on the Senate Banking Committee involved lobbying on why the United States needed to back a rescue of Argentine debt holders. And of course, there's Puerto Rico. It is the same script: Penn Central, Farm Credit, Argentina, Greece, Puerto Rico . . . Fannie, Freddie.

———

What all these entities needed was to have their balance sheets restructured. Despite some creative, but legal, accounting that allowed the companies to present financial statements in which the two sides of the balance sheet were in balance, the reality was that the liability side presented a huge overhang in the form of Treasury's preferred equity. Any investor putting new money into the companies would essentially be paying off Treasury without injecting any real economic capital.

The advantage of a receivership, whether in 2008 or now, is that such a designation would have offered a quick avenue for cleaning up the companies' balance sheets and releasing them back into the markets. To grossly oversimplify, cram down the liabilities to match the assets and then presto, you are good to go.

If it were so simple, why wasn't this done earlier? First, Treasury secretaries Henry Paulson and Timothy Geithner both wanted to protect GSE creditors, even if they were legally at risk and willingly assumed the possibility of a GSE failure. That position, while offensive, had some logic while creditors were at risk. But eventually the companies started to make money, so why not address the issue then? I believe there are at least two reasons. First, many Wall Street asset managers wanted Congress to provide an explicit guarantee on their GSE debt holdings, even the unsecured corporate debt. I had several say as much to me. Those investors believe that having the GSEs in conservatorship hardens the implied guarantee, increasing the likelihood that taxpayers would be forced to make them whole. Second, I also believe that once the government had built up a substantial stake in the companies, Treasury did not want to bear the political criticism from reducing that stake to match its actual economic value.

Despite the political risk to Treasury, Secretary Steven Mnuchin expressed full support for the restructuring of Treasury's preferred share holdings when I arrived at the FHFA. We set out to hire financial advisers, along with allowing the companies to hire their own advisers, to work out a variety of options. On February 3, 2020, the FHFA announced the retention of Houlihan Lokey, one of the world's foremost firms in the area of corporate restructuring. This work continued throughout the pandemic.

Fortunately, both Fannie and Freddie had already done some analytical work on exit options. Although that work was almost always self-serving and usually shifted considerable costs to the taxpayer, it was still extremely helpful in raising considerations. Building on that work, we were able to formulate a small number of executable options by the summer of 2020. We ruled out any choices that depended on congressional action, as they were a distant possibility under any circumstances.

Any option needed to bring the two sides of the companies' balance sheets into economic balance. Investors had to have an incentive to put money into these companies. Secretary Mnuchin generally felt that any option had to maintain Treasury's priority in the capital structure. Treasury could be heavily diluted, and almost certainly would have to be, but it did not want to see that accomplished by losing its standing.

Debt and equity are often discussed as two discrete states. That makes financial analysis and theory a lot easier to handle. Yet a better representation is to view debt and equity as ends of a continuum. Imagine individuals standing in a line. In terms of a corporate capital structure, your place in line determines when and whether you get paid. In the front of the line are secured creditors, and at the back are common shareholders. In the middle are unsecured debt holders and preferred shareholders. Each of these groups can be further subdivided. You can have a separate line within the unsecured debt holders. For Fannie and Freddie, there was also a separate line within the preferred shareholders, with the Treasury standing in the front of that line before other, junior preferred shareholders.

While Treasury was not willing to be behind other shareholders, Mnuchin was open to placing all the equity holders, including Treasury, in a similar spot. That is, he was willing to see Treasury's senior preferred shares given the same seniority as the existing junior preferred. I believed that, short of a receivership, the cleanest solution would be to convert all the preferred shares, even those held by Treasury, into common equity. This would have the benefit of having the equity markets determine value instead of trying to work with a par value for the preferred shares that was far above their economic value. It would also allow the Treasury to share in any equity appreciation, as well as more easily exit its position. I was deeply concerned about any outcome that left the U.S. government as a major equity owner of the companies in the long run. Common equity held by the government could be more easily sold into private hands than could preferred shares.

Although I thought a conversion of Treasury's position was the smoothest approach, at times it was difficult to explain. On one phone call with Sen. Mark Warner, a Democrat from Virginia, it took me some time to clarify that it simply was not economically possible for Treasury to recoup the par value of its preferred shares, as there was not a corresponding value on the asset side of the balance sheet.

A conversion would also allow a more accurate reflection of Treasury's claims without the political fallout of outright forgiveness. There had been some calls over the course of the conservatorship for Treasury to just forgive all or part of its claim. That was a nonstarter, politically, for Treasury. Moreover, Treasury claimed that it could not legally do so. A conversion of all preferred equity was one of the only ways to fix the companies' balance sheets in a manner acceptable to Treasury.

We were ready to conduct a restructuring by late summer 2020. Despite the pandemic, our financial advisers continued to make significant progress. I regularly met with Mnuchin to discuss restructuring options, as well as to exchange updates on the pandemic response. Most of these meetings were held in the secretary's small conference room.

As far as I could tell, the pandemic did not stop Mnuchin from coming into the office every day. I recall after one meeting passing American Airlines CEO Doug Parker coming in as I was leaving. Mnuchin clearly had a lot on his plate. However, that did not limit our ability to continue trying to fix Fannie and Freddie.

Despite all his responsibilities, Mnuchin was able to maintain his unique sense of humor. As he took his seat across from me during one of our regular meetings, he glanced down at the memo prepared by his staff. These memos usually contained a biography and picture. Glancing down at my picture, he remarked, "You're really not a bad-looking guy." To which I responded, "So I guess I will be in your next movie." Without missing a beat, Mnuchin retorted, "Yes, sure, we'll need a villain." Perhaps that was just Treasury once again speaking for the Wall Street asset managers.

A continued point of contention was Treasury's line of credit to Fannie and Freddie. As I was determined to see the FHFA follow the law, I could not agree to any extension of a backstop that had already legally expired. Treasury might be comfortable with creative legal maneuvers, but I was not.

Mnuchin didn't seem to mind letting the lines of credit eventually go if the companies were able to build sufficient capital. Neither of us wanted to unnecessarily disrupt the mortgage market. I believed we could find an avenue to bring the conservatorships to an end, restructure the balance sheets, and end the illegal line of credit, while preserving stability in the mortgage market. In fact, I believed we could do so in a manner that would improve the stability of the mortgage market.

Since we had well-developed restructuring plans by late summer 2020, why did none of them happen? First, I believe both the Treasury and the White House wanted to push the issue until after the election. Since any change had the potential to create short-run volatility in the mortgage market, I believe the administration did not want to run that risk.

After the election, I was ready to get back to business. I did not see myself as a lame duck. And not for a minute did I believe our legal responsibilities ended with the election. It was simply inconceivable to me that I would do anything other than my job for every day and minute I was there.

At first, it appeared that Treasury shared the desire to continue fulfilling our legal obligations. Regular meetings were held between Mnuchin and me from the election to Inauguration Day. Constant communications took place between our staffs. As I was led to believe that we were mainly in agreement on direction before the election, I did not see the need for much additional policy negotiation. Whether the continued back-and-forth with Treasury was in good faith on their part, I will never know. What I do know is that there was general agreement between the FHFA and Treasury on a restructuring plan. That would not immediately end the conservatorship, but it would place the companies in a position to raise outside equity, which I could complete later in 2021, depending on market conditions.

I have been a close observer of the Treasury Department for decades. Secretary Mnuchin and I have had our differences of opinion. He even lobbied the vice president in opposition to my consideration for the FHFA directorship, as he had his own preferred candidate. Despite that, we had a very productive working relationship. We saw eye to eye on the most critical mortgage finance issues, particularly the growing risk at the FHA. I believe that Mnuchin's service as Treasury secretary is greatly underappreciated; I consider him the best we have had since at least John Snow. He runs circles around Geithner or Paulson in terms of intellect and integrity. I had been told on a few occasions that Mnuchin had made partner at Goldman Sachs because of his father's stature there. I have had at least some interaction with a few Goldman partners, including former National Economic Council director Gary Cohn, Corzine, and Paulson. I found Stephen Mnuchin to be the sharpest of the handful I have interacted with.

All that said, once the election was behind us, Mnuchin's attention clearly turned to his post-Treasury plans. Any restructuring, to be successful, would have offended somebody. We did not get it done because Mnuchin did not want to upset anyone on his way out the door, including incoming Treasury secretary Janet Yellen.

We briefed the new Treasury team. As I was simply carrying out the law as intended, I was hopeful that Secretary Yellen and her team would see the necessity of fixing the GSEs quickly. Considering how long this housing expansion had run, I did not feel that we had many years left before a turn. Fannie and Freddie were not prepared to weather such a turn. I repeatedly raised my concerns about the mortgage and housing markets, both to Treasury directly and to the Financial Stability Oversight Council. I also emphasized that no part of our financial system was more vulnerable to climate change than the mortgage market. If we were to see significant coastal erosion, the losses to Fannie and Freddie could be extraordinary. Unfortunately, the response was generally a dull, polite smile and a nod. It appeared that new Treasury leadership would ignore the growing risks in our mortgage finance system.

Chapter 11
Capital in the Capitol

There are generally two ways that businesses fund their activities: owners' equity and debt. How much owners' equity financial companies should hold has been at the center of reform debates since at least the 2008 financial crisis. Because a lack of shareholder equity was the proximate cause of the failures of Fannie and Freddie, reforming the regulation of government-sponsored enterprise (GSE) capital is a central regulatory function of the Federal Housing Finance Agency (FHFA). It would also constitute one of the most difficult policy issues during my tenure at the FHFA.

When Congress established the FHFA in 2008, it required the FHFA to create a risk-based capital rule for Fannie and Freddie. Just as it sounds, a risk-based rule is calculated from historic loss estimates of the various assets held by a specific financial company. Accordingly, it differs across companies, since no two are the same. Even Fannie Mae and Freddie Mac, with their similar charters, have different business models and risk profiles.

Despite Congress's direction to create a risk-based capital standard in 2008, the FHFA waited until 2018 to propose such a rule. That proposal, by director Mel Watt, was still outstanding (i.e., unfinished) when I began my tenure in April 2019.

Why do financial regulators impose capital standards, anyway? After all, we do not see capital standards imposed on most companies by the government. There is no capital regulation of Amazon or Walmart.

Capital standards exist mostly because policymakers consider the failure, or bankruptcy, of some financial companies to be potentially disruptive to our financial markets and even possibly to our overall economy. The intent, therefore, is to reduce the chance of failure.

In a normally functioning market, the greater probability of failure would also increase the cost of a firm's borrowing. At some point, that cost would be high enough that issuing equity would be cheaper than issuing debt. To some degree, firms prefer debt to equity, since our corporate tax code subsidizes debt more than equity. This is because interest payments on debt are expenses that can be deducted from taxable income, whereas economically similar dividend payments to shareholders are not deductible.

Financial institutions also enjoy explicit or implicit guarantees behind their debt. The most common is Federal Deposit Insurance Corporation (FDIC)-provided insurance for depositors, which dampens the degree to which deposit costs reflect a bank's probability of failure. For some large financial companies, such as Citibank or Fannie Mae, there is also some likelihood that the federal government will rescue creditors even in the absence of an explicit guarantee to do so. For Fannie and Freddie, there is even a disclaimer that they will not be rescued should they be unable to finance their debt. Of course, such disclaimers can lack credibility.

Because of the tax advantages and possible guarantees, financial companies generally maintain much greater leverage—that is, debt to equity—than comparable nonfinancial companies. They also maintain much greater leverage than would be expected from the costs of bankruptcy that would be borne by parties outside the company.

Fannie and Freddie also have a special purpose that sets them apart from most other financial companies: they were created to serve as a counterweight to the rest of the mortgage market. Their job is to be there when others cannot.

The activities of most banks, for instance, increase during an expansion in the economy and contract during a recession. Fannie and Freddie are supposed to do the opposite: maintain some modest activity in a boom and be ready to step in when things get rough. They are the mortgage market equivalent of firefighters.

Or to take one back to one's college days, Fannie and Freddie are there to come by and help clean up after the keg party. Obviously, however, if they are at the party getting drunker than anyone else, they are not going to be much help cleaning up the next day.

Therefore, Congress required the FHFA to set risk-based capital standards not only to cover losses but also to maintain "sufficient capital" to support the activities of Fannie and Freddie. Congress wanted the GSEs to continue operating even during a deep recession. To do so, they needed to maintain a positive going-concern value. In plain English, they had to have enough capital to cover the losses from loans made in the good times as well as enough capital to keep making new loans in the bad times and still maintain the confidence of their creditors and other counterparties.

The last part is especially important. Creditors are most skeptical of a GSE's solvency during market turmoil. For example, the increase in the GSEs' borrowing costs and the associated difficulties that the GSEs faced in refinancing their debt were among the most immediate grounds for the FHFA to place the companies into conservatorship in 2008.

As I had not analyzed the FHFA's 2018 proposal before my tenure began, once I was in office, staff briefings were organized to bring me up to speed. The rule had been proposed. Comments had been received, many of which the staff had analyzed. But I had seen none of it so far.

I began the process with an open mind. Maybe the rule was well structured and thoughtful and carried out clear congressional intent. Unfortunately, it did not take me long to figure out that that was not the case.

The most glaring problem was that the rule, as proposed, failed to achieve the congressional intent to maintain a positive going-concern value. If we had another 2008—which, after all, was the reason the FHFA was created—the GSEs would fail again. Obviously, we needed a rule that allowed Fannie and Freddie to fulfill their intended purpose.

We also needed to create a capital rule to facilitate an exit from conservatorship. We could try to build capital solely via retained earnings. Our estimates were that such a policy could take a decade or more. Perhaps a decade is not that long. I thought that we would be unlikely to go another decade without a housing downturn, however. We had to beat that clock if we wanted the companies to not only exit conservatorship but also not come right back in during the next housing downturn.

A capital rule in place would be needed to help raise external capital. That was the only avenue by which we could render the companies safe and sound in a reasonable time frame. Letting the market know how much capital was required would allow estimates for a return on capital to be calculated, information investors would want, especially if these turned out to be the largest public offerings ever.

There was some suggestion, particularly from the companies, that we go with a weak rule to increase return on equity. First and foremost, that would not meet congressional intent. Second, it would guarantee the companies an eventual return to conservatorship, defeating the whole purpose of the effort. Last, as I regularly pointed out to the companies, investors care about the risk-adjusted rate of return. To hold onto the 2018 proposal would have resulted in a high probability that investors would eventually lose everything when the companies failed again.

We needed to get this rule right. And we needed to do it in a timely manner, as it had already been over a decade since Congress had directed the agency to do so. I felt that taking more than 10 years for an agency to fulfill a congressional mandate was unacceptable, if not a complete dereliction of duty. Fortunately, we had just brought over from the Treasury Department one of Washington's smartest young banking lawyers, Jonathan McKernan. I put Jonathan under the direction of the FHFA's number two principal deputy director, Adolfo Marzol, and tasked them with getting the rule into compliance with congressional intent. Since Adolfo had spent years as the chief risk officer at Fannie Mae, he knew these companies better than almost anyone. And given his decision to leave Fannie Mae in 2005 because he thought the company was taking too much risk and would not moderate, he also had the benefit of having been proven correct.

Jonathan and Adolfo spent months with the capital team, working out every detail. While I received regular briefings from the capital team, I had no time or inclination to micromanage the process. The flaws in the existing rule were obvious. The team was given considerable discretion to come up with options.

Eventually, we came to an impasse. To finalize a rule in a manner consistent with congressional intent would require substantial revisions. But would those revisions fall within the scope of the proposed rule? To finalize a rule, changes made to the proposal must be within the scope of the proposal on which comments were submitted. That is, the final rule should be a logical outgrowth of the process. It should not be outside the range of expected outcomes. Obviously, there is some subjectivity to expected outcomes. Our legal team thought that we could finalize a stronger rule without reproposing. However, even if we were on solid legal ground, the process lacked the degree of transparency I wanted for the agency.

The 2018 proposal was released for public comment under the assumption that it would be used primarily to help Fannie and Freddie price their mortgage purchases. It was not proposed with the expectation that the GSEs would exit conservatorship and must raise and maintain sufficient capital. Commentators participated in the process believing that the GSEs were not going to exit conservatorship. I felt that it was fairest to the public to allow for additional comment, considering the changed assumptions underlying the proposal.

What ultimately settled the issue for me was the slow realization that the initial proposal in 2018 had not been conducted legally. Agencies such as the FHFA are required to conduct rulemaking in compliance with the Administrative Procedure Act (APA). The APA is intended to ensure that the process is fair and open. No one is allowed special access. All have an equal opportunity, including length of time, to comment and provide input.

In briefing me on the 2018 proposal, the FHFA staff would regularly refer to analysis from Fannie and Freddie. At first, and for some time, I assumed that the reference was to the comment letters Fannie and Freddie had submitted. Eventually, it hit me. Fannie and Freddie had been extensively involved in the process before the proposed rule had ever been made public.

One thing I have noticed in the federal government is that career federal employees are generally happy and willing to discuss agency history. I find such histories interesting. They give one some sense of the agency culture and allow one to understand how certain decisions were made.

So I started to have a few somewhat casual conversations with members of the capital team. The more I heard, the more concerned I became. Not only had Fannie and Freddie had access to information that others had not, but they had also provided regular analysis during the process of developing the rule.

One such conversation was particularly jarring. It went as follows:

> M. C.: The leverage ratio options proposed in 2018 seem a little complex, yet also really weak. How did that come about?
> FHFA senior employee: Oh, I really agree. Anything under a 4 percent leverage ratio just is not credible.
> M. C.: Ok, then why didn't the proposal end up there? Why so much weaker?
> FHFA senior employee: Well, it did. At least at first. Four percent is what the team submitted to the director's office.
> M. C.: So, the director's office came up with the weak, convoluted approach?
> FHFA senior employee: Oh no, our proposal was passed along, by the director's office, to Fannie and Freddie. It was Freddie that drafted the approach that ended up in the proposed rule.

At that point, I was just stunned into silence. I am rarely speechless. I knew the companies had been given a lot of leeway, but I never imagined that they would be allowed to draft the very regulations they would be subject to. And as importantly, why was I hearing about this only now, months into the process?

Allowing private parties external to an agency, especially ones that will be directly subject to a regulation, to even see, much less write, parts of a proposed regulation is a massive violation of the APA. It just is not done. At most agencies, the very suggestion would be anathema. If nothing else, I now knew we could not legally finalize the proposed rule without putting it back out for comment. We essentially had to start the process over.

Given the legal cloud hanging over the 2018 proposal, I decided we needed to put all the elements into a brand-new rule and send it out for comment. That process began in the fall of 2019. I hoped that we would be able to have the proposal ready for public comment in the beginning of 2020.

I eventually discovered not only that Fannie and Freddie had been given access to the 2018 proposal as a veto, but also that the FHFA staff lacked some of the skills and resources necessary to complete the rule. Over the five years before my appointment, there had been almost no growth in the FHFA's staff, with a cumulative increase of about 2 percent. Perhaps that had made sense when there was little actual supervision of Fannie and Freddie, but that needed to change. We moved quickly to bring in the resources we needed.

It helped that Jonathan was familiar with the capital structure that the bank regulators used. The FHFA began a dialogue with the staffs at the bank regulators, particularly the Federal Reserve. We also began the process of hiring additional staff with the needed expertise.

To make the rule more understandable to potential investors and other financial market participants, we translated much of it into language similar to that used by the bank regulators. Basel-speak, as I called it. The bank regulators based their framework of capital regulation on international agreements crafted at the Basel Committee on Banking Supervision of the Bank for International Settlements, in Switzerland. If we did manage public stock offerings for the companies, many of the equity analysts covering the companies would also cover banks. Translating the capital rule into a bank framework should improve analyst coverage of the companies.

While we borrowed the language and some of the framework, we needed to improve on that framework. The mistakes and distortions created under Basel I and II were direct contributors to the 2008 financial crisis. After all, this was the same plan that had concluded (after considerable analysis, I am sure) that Greek sovereign debt was risk-free.

The Basel plan for residential mortgages had also contributed to the 2008 crisis. It artificially incentivized securitization and ultimately increased the amount of leverage in the mortgage market. Its accounting for mortgage credit risk was also rather blunt and primitive. We would use the framework, but we would enhance it.

The Basel system, as well as the stress tests that bank regulators used, tends to be pro-cyclical. The results look great when the economy is doing well but can quickly turn when the economy weakens.

This creates an incentive for financial companies to take more risk at the top and pull back at the bottom, obviously making the economy more volatile than it would be otherwise. In part, this is driven by basing capital and stress test results on current asset values. This is a particular problem for the GSEs, because so much of their stability is derived from the state of the housing market. Yet the role of the GSEs was to be a countercyclical balance to the market. We needed a capital regime to reflect that.

Our use of Basel-speak resulted in some commentators attacking the rule as too "bank-like." The argument was that banks were riskier than the GSEs, so smaller amounts of capital should be required of them. The main flaw in this argument is that our rule used only bank capital language; the actual levels of capital required were still below those of banks. And, of course, the GSEs were less diversified than commercial banks.

We also needed to address the issue of what counts as capital. The purpose of capital is to absorb losses to avoid insolvency. Yet much of what financial regulation allows as capital cannot absorb losses. Some of this problem results from generally accepted accounting principles, some from congressional choices, and some from regulatory choices. For a considerable part of 2008, for instance, Fannie and Freddie avoided insolvency by the use of deferred tax assets as capital. Obviously, some possible offset against taxes is not the same thing as equity. And, unfortunately, tax assets are not the only nonequity accounts that can be used as capital. We needed to focus our proposal as much as possible on having actual shareholder equity. Although I have been critical of the Basel approach to capital regulation, the efforts to better define what counts as capital under Basel III were a significant improvement.

There is also the flaw that the bank capital standards are themselves too weak. While the third round of the Basel process was an improvement over the first two, the standards did rather little to improve the strength of our banking system. And despite all the hype around the Dodd-Frank Act, it actually did little to improve the capital position of U.S. banks. While I was at the White House in 2017, some in the Treasury Department wanted to include in Treasury's financial regulation reports the argument that bank capital was too high. I am proud to have led the fight to have Treasury drop those suggestions. There were even drafts of the reports that described the current bank capital regime as "gold-plated"—a term I heard regularly used by Wall Street lobbyists.

———

This question of bank capital led to my first one-on-one conversation with Treasury Secretary Steven Mnuchin. The Treasury Department is located just east of the White House. The secretary asked me to come over one afternoon. He was a cabinet secretary, so I did not mind meeting on his turf. I also enjoyed the route.

From my office at the time, room 289 of the Eisenhower Executive Office Building (EEOB), I proceeded down the Navy steps and across West Executive Drive into the West Wing. A walk to Treasury afforded me the opportunity to travel via the West Wing to the basement of the White House residence, to the East Wing, and then to Treasury. Maybe it was the exercise, but that walk always energized me. It also afforded me the opportunity to drop in on the White House Congressional Affairs team, located in the East Wing.

The meeting was held in the Treasury secretary's small conference room. Like the EEOB, many of the rooms that constitute the Treasury secretary's suite had been furnished in a late-1800s American Renaissance Revival style. In addition, since it was the Treasury Department, there were old currency notes framed on the walls. I did not know at the time that it would be the first of many meetings in this room.

Unless you are the president or vice president, the Treasury secretary never arrives before you for a meeting. Only after everyone else is seated does the secretary appear. So it was for our initial in-person conversation.

After Secretary Mnuchin took his seat, he immediately turned to me and asked, "You were at the Cato Institute?" "Yes," I responded. To this day, I am still unsure whether he meant that as a good thing or a bad thing. The look on his face clearly expressed some opinion as to my previous employer. Regardless, I convinced him of the merits of dropping any call for bank capital reductions. My first direct engagement with Mnuchin was a success.

———

The capital rule would be another area where Sheila Bair's recruitment to the Fannie Mae board of directors would prove crucial. Having served as both chair of the FDIC and assistant secretary for financial institutions at the Treasury Department, Bair is one of the world's foremost experts on capital regulation. She lived the battles over bank capital regulation, helping us learn from them as we worked to improve the regulation of Fannie Mae and Freddie Mac.

Bair would also serve as a critical counterweight within Fannie Mae. Senior management and much of the board had been obsessed with hitting certain return-on-equity (ROE) targets, and hence strongly argued for the weakest capital rule possible. The whole debate was a distraction. Bair kept the company focused.

Perhaps most important of all, Bair understood that holding capital does not come at the cost of Fannie's mission. Just the opposite—capital is the foundation upon which Fannie and Freddie are able to fulfill their statutory responsibilities. The Wall Street lobbyists will claim that larger capital holdings impede Fannie and Freddie's ability to operate, but the truth is the exact opposite.

Bair would also serve as a bridge to progressives, both on and off Capitol Hill. Senators Sherrod Brown and Elizabeth Warren, for instance, knew and trusted Bair. I believe Bair's comment letter in support of my proposed capital rule greatly lowered the opposition from progressives. This was another important policy area where Sheila's experience, wisdom, and credibility would prove essential in our attempts to build a world-class regulatory regime for the GSEs.

The need to retool so much of the rule resulted in our missing the hoped-for January 2020 release. As it turned out, the finalization of the new proposal slipped into March 2020. Then, of course, COVID-19 became our number-one agenda item. Even though our capital team was not engaged in the COVID-19 response, I felt that releasing the reproposal for comment in March 2020 would be a mistake. It would not be until May 2020 that I felt we had reached a place with the pandemic where we could continue improving the companies' regulatory regime.

Once we released the rule for comment, the upside-down world of Washington GSE politics started to assert itself. For instance, the lead Democrat on the Senate Banking Committee, Sherrod Brown, sent a letter to all the financial regulators, including the FHFA, asking that during the pandemic we suspend rulemaking that was *not* related to either safety and soundness or COVID-19. I felt that was a reasonable request, so we complied. Imagine my surprise when he personally asked me why we were moving forward with a capital rule, considering his letter. There is perhaps no area of financial regulation more important to safety and soundness than capital. At that time, Senator Brown was also criticizing other regulators for offering capital relief because of the pandemic.

Senator Brown's flexible approach to when capital regulation is for safety and soundness and when it is not, wasn't all that unusual. A handful of members of both the House and the Senate, who had been vocal advocates for higher bank capital, complained to me about requiring higher capital at the GSEs. This makes one wonder if the debate is really about safety and soundness. In more candid moments, some have even conceded that the GSEs are so special that the American taxpayer should bear the risk of their failure. Of course, Congress had already explicitly decided the opposite. Broader debates were beyond my job responsibilities. Carrying out the law as written was my job.

On some level, we all got the joke. One amusing time was in September 2020 during the opening of a hearing before the House Financial Services Committee. Chair Maxine Waters raised the issue of the FHFA's proposed capital rule, questioning its possible effect on lending costs. In response, I read from a letter that Waters had recently sent to Federal Reserve chair Jay Powell, in which she praised higher capital standards for banks and how they would support more lending. After reading excerpts of the letter, I expressed how much I agreed with her comments and said that I would work to achieve those ends. In response, she smiled at me and laughed. We moved on to the next issue.

At least Waters had a sense of humor. I believe she did appreciate the occasional absurdity of it all. I cannot say the same for Sen. Chris

Van Hollen, a Democrat from Maryland. During a heated hearing in June 2020, conducted in a virtual and in-person hybrid setting, the senator claimed that he had a study from Moody's Analytics showing that the FHFA's capital rule had assumed too much risk in the market. Perhaps Senator Van Hollen can be forgiven. He was not in the Senate before the 2008 crisis. I, however, was on the Banking Committee's staff leading up to 2008. I very much recall Moody's telling me pre-2008 that there was little to no risk in the housing and mortgage market. Needless to say, I did not share Senator Van Hollen's comfort with once again outsourcing the safety and soundness of our mortgage market to Moody's.

Senator Van Hollen also pressed me on the point of cost-benefit analysis for the rule. This was perhaps one of the stranger flip-flops. It has historically been the case that Democrats on the Senate Banking Committee have been uniformly and strongly opposed to the use of cost-benefit analysis in financial regulation. They were certainly correct on the existing law. There is no legal requirement for financial regulators to conduct cost-benefit analysis on proposed rules. One could legitimately argue that doing so would violate the law, if the analysis were used to ignore congressional intent or delay congressionally mandated deadlines, as Congress had already made the decision to promulgate certain regulations. It is fully within congressional authority to direct regulators to take action when the costs exceed the benefits, assuming that the underlying law is constitutional. Senator Van Hollen was not alone in this change of heart. One of the most vocal critics of cost-benefit analysis, Senator Brown, once said that "cost-benefit analysis just helps the powerful people in this town resist any kind of regulation that makes people's lives better, whether it is health, whether it is safety, whether it is safety and soundness of the financial system."[1]

He later asked me when we planned to conduct cost-benefit analysis on our proposed capital rule. Reminding him of his own past views and the lack of any legal requirement to do so, I made clear that we had no intention of doing so.

The fact that the FHFA did not conduct cost-benefit analysis—after all, we were simply carrying out the orders of Congress—did not stop others from doing so. The issue came up several times in my confirmation hearing. For instance, from Sen. Mark Warner:

> I guess one of the concerns I have, if we go to a bank-like capital requirements [sic], that that is going to dramatically increase the cost of borrowing . . . currently, borrowers are basically requires [sic] to pay about 30 basis points on the mortgages guaranteed by the GSEs. My calculation, and I am trying to do this on a conservative basis, would be that if you raised GSEs' capital to bank-like capital, you would be talking about at least a tripling of the capital requirements. You can take this from about 30 basis points to 90 basis points. That is close to a full 1 percent increase.[2]

Unfortunately, Senator Warner never showed his math, so we do not know how he came up with such numbers. However, there is an extensive amount of peer-reviewed research done on the relationship between borrowing costs and capital standards. Some of this work has been done by the banking regulators, but much of it by independent academics. I had FHFA staff survey that literature. The result was that nowhere is there support for Senator Warner's calculations. The consensus of the academic literature is that a capital increase of the amount proposed under the FHFA's rule would have an impact of somewhere from 0 to at most 20 basis points. And of course, more damning to Senator Warner's estimates is that banks currently can make and hold mortgages on their balance sheet, obviously backed by bank-like capital standards, and do so at costs far below the senator's estimate. Indeed, the banking regulators significantly increased regulatory capital standards following the financial crisis, independently of the Dodd-Frank Act. Wall Street lobbyists predicted significant increases in borrowing costs, but they did not come to pass. It was just bizarre, however, to hear senators and representatives who rejected the argument that higher capital increases lending costs in the bank context suddenly become converts to the same logic in the context of Fannie and Freddie.

One of the more disappointing aspects of promulgating a GSE capital rule was the almost complete lack of stakeholders' interest in or knowledge about what the research said. I believe only one comment letter, from former FDIC vice chair Tom Hoenig, even referenced the academic literature. There were a handful of comments that offered their own cost-benefit analysis. But these, like Senator Warner's analysis, had no basis in the scientific literature and did not even reference or recognize such. All these analyses fell apart once one started looking into their assumptions.

Another letdown was the unwillingness of many vocal advocates for higher capital to even weigh in. There is a group of mostly progressive academics and former regulators who write, research, and comment on bank capital. Many are quite thoughtful. I spoke to several and expressed our desire to hear from as many commentators as possible. We welcomed their expertise. Sadly, the general response was, "Great rule, you're doing the right thing, keep it up, but it's too political for me to get involved." So much for profiles in courage. And this from a group that is generally quite outspoken.

In fairness, one can certainly criticize some Republican members of Congress, who were generally against higher bank capital but suddenly supported higher GSE capital. That is a fair observation in some cases. But it certainly is not a universal one. My views on bank or GSE capital are consistent with those of my former boss, Sen. Richard Shelby, a Republican from Alabama. Working with then Maryland Democrat Paul Sarbanes, Senator Shelby was instrumental in getting U.S. bank regulators to delay implementation of Basel II. This holdup meant that U.S. banks had much better capital positions going into 2008 than their European counterparts. The bipartisan efforts of Shelby and Sarbanes saved U.S. taxpayers billions and shortened the Great Recession in America relative to that in Europe.

———

This is not to say that all the Republicans on Capitol Hill supported the FHFA's capital rule. A handful of Republicans raised concerns about the proposal's impact on the use of credit risk transfers (CRTs) by Fannie and Freddie. Over the course of the conservatorship, the FHFA and the companies worked on a variety of mechanisms that they believed would reduce the risks that taxpayers faced. In general, I have been supportive of these efforts.

The most prominent has been the use of CRTs. Like too many feats of financial engineering, CRTs do not actually perform as they are labeled.

You might think that CRTs, as the name suggests, transfer credit risk outside the GSEs. They do not. CRTs are derivatives whose value is based on the performance of a reference asset, in this case a designated pool of mortgages. I guess I should not have been surprised at the structure, as some of the same people who helped JPMorgan Chase create the credit default swaps (CDSs) that were behind the failure of AIG designed the CRTs.

I am not against financial engineering. CDSs, for instance, had a valuable function. The problem is when they became a source of regulatory arbitrage, resulting in greater leverage of our financial system. And of course, by linking AIG more deeply with our financial system, CDSs increased the interconnectedness and ultimately systemic risk. CRTs were on the road to doing the same.

The FHFA's 2018 proposal, in a vein similar to the way bank regulators used capital regulations to reward the use of CDSs before 2008, drove the use of CRTs. They were being used not for purely economic reasons but for gaming of the regulatory system. Our proposal treated them less generously, but still far more so than did the bank regulators. Many CRT advocates argue that we should give dollar-for-dollar capital relief. Such an argument ignores the fact that equity capital is fungible— that is, it can cover losses from any asset, whereas CRTs cover only losses on the specific assets referenced.

The supervisory staff had already begun an evaluation of CRT before I arrived at the FHFA. I sensed that there was a big divide within the agency. The capital team was quite enamored with CRT and wrote glowing reports about its performance, studies that I would later discover were shoddy and misleading. I felt misled by that work, which was more like Wall Street sales spin than serious analysis. The supervisors and examiners who went into the companies every day were skeptical of CRT.

Once I had established an independent research and evaluation function within the FHFA, I asked that team to evaluate CRT performance. I made it clear that they should write and report whatever they found. There was to be no molding of the facts to fit any preconceived conclusion.

Unfortunately, that analysis was not completed until after the capital rule had been finalized. I was stunned by the results. As the housing market had been mostly strong during the use of CRTs, I certainly expected to see short-term costs exceed short-term benefits. But I was not expecting the efforts to have a net cost of around $15 billion. That is real money. The analysis included stress tests as well. Most shocking was that if we again experienced a 2008 scenario, the net costs would go up, not down.

The clearest way to think about CRT is as insurance. You pay premiums, and if something bad happens, the insurance covers the cost. Yet the way that CRT worked was that you paid massive premiums and then when something bad happened, your coverage would immediately expire and you would get almost nothing back.

The FHFA's estimates in April 2020, for instance, projected that because of COVID-19 losses, the companies would receive about $1 billion from CRT. Immediately, we were lobbied by CRT investors to forgive our claims. The FHFA had done so in response to previous hurricane losses. I was aghast. We had paid our insurance premiums, if you will, and now when we needed to collect, Wall Street begged, and even lobbied Capitol Hill, to get out of its obligations. At my confirmation hearing, Sen. Robert Menendez, a Democrat from New Jersey, asked if I had ever called any financial company a "deadbeat." If Senator Menendez is reading, CRT investors not wanting to honor their obligations are exactly what I would call deadbeats.

Wall Street need not have worried or bothered to lobby. The CRT deals had been structured in such a manner that when interest rates declined and mortgage refinance activity increased, much of the CRT protection disappeared as the reference pool mortgages were refinanced. What was supposed to be $1 billion in payments turned into around $10 million. The fact that the companies were essentially robbed on their CRT deals is one reason we had to impose a COVID-19 cost recoupment fee.

During recessions, when mortgage credit losses increase and CRTs would be expected to pay out, interest rates tend to decline, because of both Federal Reserve easing and a decline in the demand for credit. That often results in an uptick in mortgage refinancing. It slowly dawned on me that the CRTs were structured to almost never pay. I finally understood why Wall Street was lobbying so hard against our capital rule. It threatened a multibillion-dollar gravy train. With so much money at risk, of course, Wall Street threw millions into lobbying against our rule. They funded think tank "research" against the rule and spread money around to members of the House Financial Services Committee, including numerous Republicans. The contributions were a bipartisan affair. There are even staff members within the Biden White House whose previous work had received funding from CRT investors.

In the late spring of 2021, after it became apparent that the companies had essentially been looted, we started to investigate the details of how CRT transactions were underwritten. Our first shock was learning that the Wall Street underwriters earned fees that were multiples of the net values of CRTs to the companies. These Wall Street underwriters—you can guess the firms—were supposed to protect Fannie and Freddie, but instead they joined in robbing their clients. Of course, the CRT investors, primarily hedge funds and real estate investment trusts, were also clients of these Wall Street firms.

We also learned that at least one senior GSE executive working on CRTs held equity in one of the very Wall Street firms selected to underwrite the CRT deals.

We had just begun putting the pieces together when the *Collins* decision (discussed in Chapter 14) was made and my tenure came to an end. Given the connections between the Biden administration and the Wall Street players profiting from CRT, I suspect that any investigation has come to an end. In fact, one probable reason the Biden administration wanted me out so quickly was to bring an end to it.

———

Congress lays out several duties for the FHFA. At the top of that list is the "maintenance of adequate capital" for the entities regulated by the FHFA. Capital is not an afterthought. It is the foremost obligation of the FHFA. Debates around capital have often relied on a false narrative—namely, that there is a tradeoff between the mission of the GSEs and holding capital. That is simply false. It is by holding sufficient capital that the GSEs achieve their mission. Insufficient capital leads to failure. The FHFA has a duty to see that Fannie and Freddie maintain enough capital. The FHFA does not have any statutory duty to expand homeownership or lower mortgage rates. The statutory charters of Fannie and Freddie apply to them, not to the FHFA. The FHFA's mission is to see that Fannie and Freddie stay within their charters, not to abandon its prudential duties in furtherance of the GSEs' charters.

Capital should be the simplest issue in financial regulation. Have more of it and have it in the form of shareholder equity. End government policies that favor debt over equity. The 2017 tax reform made some progress in reducing corporate tax subsidies for leverage. But more needs to be done to reduce the incentives to hold debt. Our financial system—not just the GSEs but also our largest banks—remains dangerously leveraged. Banking weathered COVID-19 mostly because of massive assistance, including accounting relief. We may not be so lucky next time. Perhaps it should not be startling that the simplest issues in financial regulation remain the hardest to achieve.

Chapter 12

Leading a Federal Agency

I have a long public record of being extremely skeptical of government. Some of this comes from my study of economics, notwithstanding the profession's obsession with market failures. But most of this is the result of almost three decades of seeing the federal government up close. I was not always this way. Indeed, my first college internship was at U.S. Public Interest Research Group, where I had the pleasure of meeting Ralph Nader. My family also has a long history of government work. My parents met while serving in the Navy. My mother spent about 20 years working for the Fairfax County government in Virginia. My sister has been a longtime employee of the Virginia state government. I am very proud of the service my family has given to our fellow citizens.

However, by the time I was confirmed as the Federal Housing Finance Agency (FHFA) director, I was deeply suspicious of government. Rather than being a hindrance to leading a federal agency, this outlook was an asset to me. My close study and experience with government allowed me to take a principled and focused approach to running a federal agency. An awareness of the limitations of government allowed me to better navigate around trouble spots. Your ship is more likely to make it to shore if you know where the reefs are, rather than pretending they do not exist.

Now, one might think that having such a skeptic of government lead a federal agency is a recipe for failure. I believe the clear policy success of the FHFA's response to COVID-19 should put that argument to rest. Two additional measures of success are respect for leadership within an organization and respect for leadership outside an organization, especially among peer agencies.

The internal respect for management is the easier to identify. It is measured regularly by employee surveys, such as the Federal Employee Viewpoint Survey. Table 1 provides a comparison of several survey questions early in my tenure and over a year later. In just over a year, the percentage of staff having a high level of respect for leadership increased by 18 points. The belief that the agency administration maintained high levels of honesty and integrity increased 21 percentage points. Motivation of staff by senior leadership increased by 23 percentage points.

These are impressive and unusual magnitudes of improvement in the federal government. They are perhaps even more dramatic considering that I was nominated by President Donald Trump in an era when many federal employees viewed themselves as part of the resistance to his

Table 1
FHFA Federal Employee Viewpoint Survey Results

Statement	% Positive Responses		
	2019	2020	Change
In my organization, senior leaders generate high levels of motivation and commitment in the workforce.	43	66	23
My organization's senior leaders maintain high standards of honesty and integrity.	50	71	21
Managers communicate the goals of the organization.	64	78	14
Managers promote communication among different work units.	55	66	11
Overall, how good a job do you feel is being done by the manager directly above your immediate supervisor?	61	71	10
I have a high level of respect for my organization's senior leaders.	53	71	18
Senior leaders demonstrate support for work/life programs.	68	87	19

Source: Federal Employee Viewpoint Survey for Federal Housing Finance Agency.

administration. Further, the FHFA is an agency where, all else equal, a Republican would normally be met with some skepticism, if not hostility.

So how exactly did my team turn around a troubled federal agency? I did have some unique factors working in my favor. Foremost, I had helped to create the agency while I served as a staffer on the Senate Banking Committee. In fact, I had spent the better part of five years of my career working to create the FHFA. At a minimum, there was a general recognition among the staff that I both valued the work of the agency and intended to strengthen it.

As a rule, it is difficult, if not impossible, to lead an organization if you do not support its mission. In my case, I fully supported the FHFA's mission of ensuring that Fannie Mae and Freddie Mac are properly regulated. In contrast, many people on the staff expressed to me that my predecessor had regularly questioned the value and purpose of the FHFA and the work of its staff. My impression from staff discussions and from having observed my predecessor's previous congressional service is that he did not believe that Fannie Mae and Freddie Mac needed to be regulated. In fact, it appears that he generally considered the executives of Fannie Mae and Freddie Mac more credible than the FHFA staff. The result was that I entered an agency with low morale and little confidence in the management.

Rule number one for leading a federal agency: you must believe in the staff or at least in their potential. I firmly believed that the FHFA and its staff could be successful. Or, as I repeatedly phrased it, a "world-class regulator." You cannot lead an organization to a destination to which you think they are incapable of going.

It is also crucial to communicate to the staff regularly and clearly what exactly that destination is. You cannot really know if you are successful if you have not first defined success.

Underlining success is also critical. In our day-to-day work, it is easy to lose sight of the big picture. Caught up in delivering project Y by date X, one can forget how project Y fits into the broader view. The FHFA is the most important federal regulator of the U.S. mortgage market. Since the federal government guarantees, implicitly or explicitly, most of the residential mortgage market, any potential for market discipline on the part of investors is pretty much destroyed. Coupled with the fact that most of the real estate and mortgage businesses are compensated on the basis of transaction volumes, with little retention of risk by the private sector, there is essentially no one in our current system with an incentive to care about mortgage quality. That also means there is really no one with an incentive to care about borrower outcomes. Therefore, I repeatedly emphasized to staff that they could not count on others to police the mortgage market. They alone held the responsibility of protecting millions of families from a mortgage crisis. It might have sounded a little heavy, but I believe it helped give the staff focus and added a larger meaning to their work. The bottom line is that staff need to know why their work is important.

There is always the temptation in government to pursue a personal agenda. I was regularly described by press and lobbyists as advancing my own private agenda. While that may often be the case with agency heads, I do not believe that accurately described me. I certainly have my views about how I wish the mortgage market were structured and regulated, but during my work on the Hill, I came to understand how important it is, under our democratic form of government, that Congress establish agency priorities and that agencies follow those priorities. If agency heads decide that they should set the priorities, they are interfering with Congress's constitutional duties, ultimately undermining the will of the voters.

My agenda, to the extent that I had one, was to carry out the express will of Congress. If I felt that Congress should have decided A instead of B, that was irrelevant to the job. The job was to implement B.

For example, I do not happen to like the housing goals and trust fund obligations of Fannie and Freddie. A better system would be to limit their overall activities to low- and moderate-income borrowers. That would achieve the same objective as the current goals without some of the negative effects of weakening underwriting quality. But that decision was not mine to make. In fact, the largest-ever housing trust fund contribution was made during my tenure. Success in running a federal agency requires you to clearly recognize which decisions are yours to make and which belong to others, particularly Congress.

Accepting that division is much easier if, like me, you believe in the fundamental role of Congress. I submit that you cannot be a faithful

follower of the oath to uphold the Constitution if you do not recognize
and act according to the central role of Congress established in Article 1
of our Constitution.

Among some agency heads, there is an obsession with maintaining
"optionality." The most articulate presentation of this view is former
Treasury secretary Robert Rubin's book *In an Uncertain World: Tough
Choices from Wall Street to Washington*. The issue that many policymakers
face, however, is that Congress has often intentionally limited their
options. Recognizing this fact, I believe, is key to being a successful
agency leader. For instance, I spent very little time thinking about what
a different mortgage finance system would look like. Should we have a
Fannie Mae or a Federal Home Loan Bank system? That simply was not
the job Congress had assigned me.

Unfortunately, from its beginning, the FHFA had gotten caught
up in various agendas. Foremost, Congress had decided that a failed
government-sponsored enterprise (GSE) should be resolved by a receivership, rather than an endless conservatorship. Even former Treasury
secretary Henry Paulson has recognized that in ignoring the receivership provisions created by Congress, he was directly going against congressional intent. Paulson believed his gut reactions during a crisis were
superior to years of deliberation and compromise by Congress. Don't be
like him. Such behavior undermines trust in government and erodes the
democratic accountability of our government.

Congress had also given the FHFA several mandated tasks, such as
to construct a risk-based capital rule. Yet for years, the agency ignored
the assigned duties. The agency also pursued several expensive and
time-consuming tasks for which it lacked congressional authority, such
as the creation of a single security backed by GSE mortgages. I believe
the regular flouting of congressional directives undermined morale
within the FHFA and reduced external respect for the agency.

At my confirmation hearing, I told the Senate Banking Committee
that whatever the issue, my first question would be, "What does the
statute say?" And that was the manner in which I directed the FHFA.

In addition to being the appropriate thing to do, following the law has
several practical benefits. The statutes authorizing agency action are public.

Therefore, anyone can access them. The most efficient and effective leader should be able to paint such a clear picture of the agency's direction that staff members already know the answers to most questions before they are raised with the agency head. Direct and consistent following of the authorizing statutes aids greatly in that communication.

A critical aspect of leading any organization is deciding what not to think about. One's time is limited. One's ability to make well-informed decisions is also limited by the number and complexity of those decisions. Admit to yourself that you cannot do it all. If you leave the congressional determinations to Congress, you will better allocate your time and resources.

Leaving the job of Congress to Congress also greatly improves one's relationship with Congress. While many members are happy to delegate decisionmaking to agency heads, members are generally protective of decisions that they have reserved for themselves. If you believe Congress made the wrong judgment, you can always say so. But that is not a license to override Congress.

More than anything else, as I have noted, one must have a distinct, understandable destination where one is taking the agency. In my case, Congress had plainly expressed its intent that the FHFA become a "world-class regulator." Since we had many staff members who came to the FHFA from such agencies as the Federal Reserve, the Office of the Comptroller of the Currency, the Office of Thrift Supervision, and the Federal Deposit Insurance Corporation, there were known benchmarks for our objectives.

Once the top-line goal is stated, articulating what that means on a day-to-day basis is the next step. I approached that by laying out the principles and objectives of world-class financial regulation. The next objective was communicating that to the staff, as well as to external audiences.

———

A common mistake agency heads make is to limit their interaction with junior staff, meeting and communicating with only their direct reports—their deputies. I believe if you want your message to be followed throughout the agency, junior staff need to hear it directly from you as often as possible.

First, there is the issue of information reaching all the staff. I inherited a weekly executive meeting, consisting of my direct reports. I had expected that my directions from that meeting would then be shared by the direct reports to their staff. I discovered that was not always the case. Even when a message was conveyed, it was not always conveyed accurately. So, one of my first changes in process was to request that my direct reports bring along *their* deputies, or at least one of their senior staff, to our weekly executive meeting.

This request served at least two purposes. First, my deputies' deputies would hear what was discussed and agreed to directly from me, reducing the chance of miscommunication. Second, including more staff created a team mentality throughout the agency, not just among the most senior staff. I remembered from my time at the White House that few things were as thrilling for junior staffers to be included in, say, a Roosevelt Room meeting with the President, even if they were sitting along the wall, out of sight. I took that to heart. Many agency staff members are never in the same room as the agency head, and I worked to change that. I believed it greatly increased the flow of information within the agency, while also increasing morale and dedication among the staff.

Expanding attendance at the weekly executive meeting was only the beginning. Agency leadership, to be effective, must be seen regularly by the agency staff. One of my first actions was to simply walk all the floors of the organization. I suspect that a few employees were caught off guard having the new director poke his head in their office door to shake hands and say hello. I was told that this was the first time any director had been seen on certain floors of the agency.

In addition to regular all-staff meetings, we instituted staff lunches, for which a dozen or so people would sign up to have lunch with me. These events were open to everyone and gave them an opportunity to ask questions and hear from me personally about agency policies. It also gave staff members an opportunity to talk about themselves, as the format was explicitly informal.

I had planned to meet every employee at some point during my tenure. I did manage to meet a significant number during our staff lunches. Then COVID-19 hit, sending us all into telework. The solution, at first, was to take these lunches online, which met with some modest success. We also did separate lunches for new staff, since we did significant hiring during the pandemic. Finally, we set up virtual coffees with each office in the agency. By the time we were done, I had had a conversation with about 675 individuals out of an agency of about 700. One of the most enjoyable parts was encouraging staff to show off their pandemic puppy, COVID cat, or other newly acquired pet during our virtual lunches. Several staff members also shared their experiences of learning how to play instruments. I still get a little teary thinking about the FHFA employee who told me that he bought a piano and learned to play during the pandemic because when he was growing up in China, his family was not allowed to have a piano.

In addition to constant and repeated communication of agency objectives, there must be constant follow-up and monitoring of progress. A practice I borrowed from the Office of Management and Budget (OMB) was to have a specific person in the director's office assigned to work with a career staff deputy. I had heard repeatedly how previous directors' advisers would give conflicting advice to career staff, depending on the adviser. I made it clear on day one that each of my advisers had a separate portfolio, reducing the possibility of conflicting directions to career staff. To reinforce this, I never met with any of my career deputies without having the corresponding adviser in the room. If I met with the agency's general counsel, then my chief legal adviser was also in the meeting. This reduced the risk of misunderstandings and improved execution, as the adviser would be responsible for later following up with the career deputy to see that what was agreed on was carried out.

Your staff—both immediate advisers and the agency's career staff—will be effective only to the degree that you back them. One of the more shocking moments early in my tenure was the discovery that my predecessor regularly allowed the chief executive officers of Fannie and Freddie to directly call him to overrule decisions relayed to the companies by FHFA staff. If employees believe that they can be overruled regularly and arbitrarily, they lose morale and stop trying to do their jobs. Because it is the agency staff that carry out the actions of the agency, you also render yourself ineffective as a leader if you constantly undercut the members of your staff. They will not be seen as speaking for you or the agency. Such a result will greatly diminish your effectiveness, as you can no longer leverage others to express your objectives. I told the staff early and often that I had their back. I would never overrule or contradict them in front of the organizations we regulated. If we disagreed, that disagreement would occur internally at the FHFA.

Most of Washington does not want to see the FHFA become an effective safety and soundness regulator. I've long quipped that there's "no constituency for safety and soundness." The situation is bad enough for bank regulators but significantly worse for the FHFA. There is at least a small group of academics, think tankers, and pundits who advocate for strong and efficient bank regulation. Sadly, most of those voices fall silent when it comes to strong regulation of Fannie and Freddie. For instance, some commentators, including senators, who had a strong public record against cost-benefit analysis for bank regulation asked me why the FHFA was not doing more cost-benefit analysis.

To put it simply, I made sure the FHFA's staff understood that my primary job was to be their protector. I would work to create both external and internal environments in which they could do their jobs. I would go before Congress and take the hits during an oversight hearing. I would defend the agency's very purpose of safety and soundness before audiences that wanted us to mostly eliminate those constraints. I have found that few things encourage loyalty more than a willingness to take some punches on someone's behalf. I believe that, more than anything, my willingness to take public criticism on behalf of the agency's core mission is what led to my successes with the FHFA staff.

Most federal agencies stage events on a variety of topics. The FHFA's Office of Minority and Women Inclusion conducted a monthly lecture series. For instance, during Asian and Pacific-Islander Month, a panel of FHFA employees shared their personal and career experiences. The FHFA also held an annual Veteran's Day lunch to honor the FHFA's large number of staff with military service.

Rather than simply show up, give a few remarks, and leave, I went from table to table, asking each of our veterans about their experience. It is essential that an agency head attend these events. It is one of your best opportunities to connect with employees and demonstrate a sincere interest in them as individuals.

Too many leaders view spending time at organizational events as a drain on their calendar. Obviously, the time of attendance is time you do not spend on something else. But if you begin with the premise that it is ultimately the employees who carry out the agency's activities and that you are at best steering the direction, then you recognize that prioritizing their work and well-being, if done appropriately and effectively, is necessary to achieve the agency's goals. You might have your hands on the steering wheel, but if the tires are flat, you are not going anywhere.

———

At the risk of overgeneralization, there are three types of government employees: (1) those who can and will work hard to advance the agency's mission, (2) those who will actively work to undermine the agency's mission, and (3) those who do not do much of anything. Your immediate focus should be on types 1 and 2.

I have found that there are a lot of great federal employees who are first-class professional civil servants in the highest sense of the term. They understand fundamentally that they work for the American people, as the views of the public are articulated through their elected officials. They know that their job is to help implement that expression of public will. Often, they have been lacking guidance and recognition. I have talked about the leadership aspect. Recognition is critical as well. When I walked in the door at the FHFA, almost 90 percent of employees were rated "outstanding" or "excellent." That struck me as rather unlikely to be an accurate picture. If everyone is outstanding, then no one really is. Or at least no one is truly being recognized as such. So we rescaled the employee evaluation system to achieve a more realistic distribution. Frankly, I feared this would get a lot of pushback from those who received less positive ratings.

The result, however, was an improvement in morale and performance from those who were truly outstanding. Since often a small segment of the staff does a disproportionate amount of the work at any organization, anything you can do to improve the productivity of that group should be considered.

I wish we had made more progress on the type 2 employees. There were some individuals who were simply in the wrong job and would perform better in another. We made some important changes there. The truth, however, is that the resisters or saboteurs were rarely open about their actions. Even those who were not competent were not always easy to spot. As I was only 11 months into my tenure before COVID-19 forced the agency into telework, and we were in a pandemic, my ability to remove staff that were hurting the agency's mission was limited. If I had it all to do over, I would move more quickly to address staff members who were undermining the agency's performance and mission.

Unfortunately, all federal agencies suffer from some degree of capture.[1] The FHFA and its precursors have long been unduly influenced by the entities they regulate. The immediate harm, of course, is that agency actions can be driven toward benefiting the regulated entities rather than focusing on the public. Another harmful effect is a decline in employee morale. For employees who do want to work on behalf of the public—namely, seeing that the GSEs are appropriately regulated and supervised—their morale suffers when they witness their colleagues doing the opposite. Eventually, a highly captured agency will lose the staff members who prioritize the public good. I regret not making more progress on that front.

Another necessity for building employee loyalty, as well as for overall organizational success, is a sincere willingness to listen and to be open to criticism. Like any good Hayekian, I approach any situation with the assumption that there is more that I don't know than I do know. The most important aspect of leadership is humility. That does not mean you do not also project confidence and competence. In fact, my usual quip around the office was that I had such confidence in my opinions that I did not need anyone to repeat them back to me. What I did need was to hear what I might be missing.

Setting a clear aim, grounded firmly in congressional intent, is the first step. There can be several obstacles along the way. Some of these can be structural. For many federal agencies, the Office of the General Counsel (OGC) can be a graveyard. Documents flow in and there they stay, or at least remain for extended periods. I knew early on that we needed an OGC that was quick-moving and responsive, both to me and to other parts of the FHFA. To accomplish this, my legal adviser, Clinton Jones, began a review and reorganization of the OGC. Clinton later went on to serve as the general counsel of that office.

Another important change was the creation of an executive secretary. At the White House, I had witnessed up close the importance of this often-hidden job. Having someone whose sole function is to keep work moving greatly increases the speed at which an organization operates. We have all heard stories of documents sitting on someone's desk for weeks, even months. I was very fortunate to find Kate Tyrrell, who had previously been executive secretary to Treasury Secretary Steven Mnuchin. Kate served as the FHFA's executive secretary and deputy chief of staff. Rather, I should say how lucky I was that my chief of staff, John Roscoe, knew Kate from her time at Treasury and brought her to my attention. Having a strong chief of staff whom you deeply trust is essential to the success of any agency.

Despite being an agency with a single head, we made most decisions as part of a core group of three: Roscoe; the agency's principal deputy director, Adolfo Marzol; and me. No one worked harder than John. His eye for detail and constant communication with staff complemented my policy and economics experience, along with Adolfo's deep industry experience. John had held previous positions in both personnel and event management. I have long recognized myself as a big-picture person and knew I needed someone who was more a details person; John fit that bill perfectly.

———

A common concern among the public, and Republicans in particular, is that federal agencies have often taken actions beyond their congressionally authorized responsibilities. That was certainly the case with the FHFA. An effective avenue for both leading an agency and implementing small-government principles is to align agency actions with congressional intent, especially when there is clear statutory language. I would argue that one can make a significant difference simply by getting an agency to live by and within the actual language of its authorizing statutes.

Acting within the law is also an effective shield from attack. I was often asked, especially by members of Congress but also by external stakeholders, to take actions that lacked any legal basis. My established reputation for following the law reduced the intensity of those requests. When the petitioners could feel that it was not about them or their requests, it made the rejection of those pleas easier for them to accept. Of course, this works only if you are consistent about following the clear letter of the law. Deviate once and you lose that shield. Once external stakeholders know you are willing to ignore or bend the law, the requests to do so will multiply. In addition to undermining the integrity and legitimacy of agency action, it will be a huge drain on one's time, limiting one's resources and effectiveness in implementing actual congressional directives.

———

Focusing on congressional mandates also improves one of your most important relationships as an agency head: your relationship with Congress. It is essential to have working relationships with the chair and the ranking member of your oversight committee in both the House and the Senate. You should resist the temptation to work or communicate only with members of your own party. After my confirmation, my first Hill visit was to see Rep. Maxine Waters of California, chair of the House Financial Services Committee. As House floor votes were called during our first meeting, Chair Waters was delayed for about an hour. Despite her staff and mine suggesting that we reschedule, I believed it was critical for me to wait. As it turned out, Chair Waters appreciated the gesture and our relationship started on a good note. Whatever you may think about a member of Congress, you should recognize that they carry with them the legitimacy of having been elected, something you lack as an appointee. To disrespect that is to disrespect the very process of representative government.

I also tried to meet with as many of the nearly 70 members of the House Financial Services Committee as possible, starting with the chairs and ranking members of the subcommittees.

Accessibility does not begin and end with initial meetings. Whenever the FHFA planned to make a major announcement, I would offer to brief, in person or by phone, the chair and ranking members of my oversight committees. We would also have FHFA staff offer to brief committee staff on our announcements. I am proud to say that the numerous times I asked Chair Waters whether she and her staff were getting all the information they needed from the FHFA, she always said yes.

Regular communications with the Hill also reduce the ability of special interests to get legislation passed that is harmful to the agency's mission. There were several such attempts by special interests that would have undermined the safety and soundness of the GSEs or limited the FHFA's ability to accomplish its statutory goals. In fact, I cannot recall once getting "rolled" by legislation that would have undermined our efforts. I believe a significant reason for that is that I was constantly on the phone with members, explaining what I was doing. As much as possible, we also shared data with the Hill, demonstrating that our efforts were solidly based on facts and analysis as well as the law. While special interests might have had campaign contributions or constituents on their side, I was pleasantly surprised how often I succeeded by providing sound evidence for my views.

A common vehicle for congressional communications is the member letter. Generally, if you have a good relationship with a member of Congress, they will call you if they have a concern. Letters are generally the route used when they do not really know you or they want to have something to show publicly. Even with that in mind, I emphasized from the beginning of my tenure that congressional correspondence would be handled in a timely manner. And, just as importantly, if we could answer the question directly, we would. I have always hated the common practice of agencies taking months to reply to a letter and then saying nothing of substance in the reply. It is disrespectful. Do not stonewall or ignore congressional letters. We did our best to avoid that.

Just as having a seasoned communications team is critical, so is having an experienced Hill veteran manage your congressional outreach efforts. I was fortunate that Sarah Dumont Merchak, with whom I worked on the Senate Banking Committee my first year on the Hill, was willing to lead that effort. In addition to having both House and Senate staffing experience, Sarah had been on one of our oversight committees and had spent years as a well-respected lobbyist in front of our committees. She knew how the Hill worked and understood how members and their staffs thought. Such experience is priceless to a federal agency. Because of Sarah's motivation and expertise, she and our congressional affairs team provided more briefings and support to our oversight committees than all the other financial regulators combined.

Most of the congressional relations staff at an agency are career staff that you inherit. Some of them will have previously had political positions. In such cases, it is most likely that they served as Democratic staff. That was the case at the FHFA, where most of the career congressional relations staff had worked for Democratic members of Congress. Even with that history, I found that Sarah's and my professionalism and commitment to a strong, healthy relationship with Congress inspired our career staff. They felt needed, useful, and influential. Of course, that is because they were, and we treated them as such.

The FHFA does not receive its funding in the usual congressional appropriations process, so that reduced the number of senators and representatives of primary focus. If you head an agency within the congressional budget process, you must give the members of the relevant appropriations subcommittee the same attention and deference you would give to your own oversight committee. You are also likely to have to interact with OMB, an office of the executive branch. One of the toughest exercises will be balancing the demands of congressional appropriators, who probably want to increase funding for your agency, with those of OMB, who manage the overall budget. Just remember that as part of an administration, you must always and everywhere support the numbers presented in the president's budget.

———

Perhaps the most important step in becoming head of a federal agency is confirmation by the Senate. Of course, this assumes that you are nominated by the White House in the first place. Given my extensive written record, much of it controversial by Washington standards, it may be surprising that I was able to get confirmed. But then again, I did have a few things going for me.

My most helpful experience was having served for seven years on the staff of the Senate Banking Committee, the committee that would consider my nomination. Having done the committee staff work for several nominations and having experienced an even greater number of nomination hearings, I'd had plenty of opportunity to see what works and what doesn't.

If you start with the premise that most senators of the same party as the president are inclined to vote for you, then you quickly realize that your job during the confirmation process is to not give them a reason to vote against you. Foremost, that means keeping your head down. Nominees who try to gain confirmation by writing opinion pieces in their defense or arguing for their own nomination in the media generally hurt themselves. It is not a public relations campaign. So, once the White House lets you know you are under consideration, immediately stop tweeting or doing any sort of writing. Do not go on TV or radio or podcasts. Scrub any social media you have, or better still, shut down those accounts or set them to private.

Your immediate target audience is not the American public or pundits. It is the members of the committee. Before my confirmation hearing, I offered to meet with all members of the Banking Committee; I ultimately met with 18 of the 21 members. You should even meet with the members who are not likely to vote for you. In fact, it is especially important to meet with members who might oppose your nomination.

By meeting with members opposed, or potentially opposed, to your nomination, you achieve at least two things. First, those senators are almost always willing to tell you why they oppose your nomination or at least to offer a few clues. Such information will be priceless when it comes to preparing for your hearing. Second, most people, even senators, have a harder time attacking someone with whom they have met and had a nice conversation. That is just human nature. It is more difficult for someone to dehumanize you and treat you as the enemy once you have shaken their hand and exchanged pleasantries. Meeting opposing senators also signals a willingness to be accessible to them after you are confirmed, even if they vote against you. The intensity of opposition matters. Do everything possible to get those voting against you to just phone it in and avoid confrontation.

An important consideration for maximizing support and minimizing opposition is to not commit any process fouls. Meet any senator who asks for a meeting. Be willing to meet with senators' staff. Answer any questions from the committee in a timely manner. Provide all materials, such as writings or financials, that are requested by the committee. Be polite, nice, and deferential to the Senate. Bite your tongue and just take any abuse, in meetings or at your hearing.

An interesting issue to navigate is that many positions that are mainstream in an academic discipline are viewed as radical by members of the Senate. An example of this is the view widely accepted within academic finance and economics that government-provided deposit insurance creates a moral hazard. I was quizzed on this issue, as was my friend Judy Shelton during her nomination to the Federal Reserve. My own read of the literature on deposit insurance, as I believe is Judy's, is almost identical to that which has been expressed by Paul Krugman.[2] I was able to defuse the question by simply answering that all insurance, private or public, entails some degree of both moral hazard and adverse selection and that it is the job of a prudential regulator to account for such effects. The lesson here is to not deny what you said. Instead, generalize your answer in such a way that the observation appears less threatening or extreme. I took the same approach to capital regulation. When Democrats raised the question of my perspective on capital for Fannie and Freddie, my response was to say I believed that all large, systemically important financial institutions needed sufficient capital.

Since many Democratic senators had expressed similar views, it became hard for them to object in the context I presented.

It is vital to not appear to flip-flop or, worse, to be dishonest about positions you have held or written about. I have seen many a nomination stall or sink because the nominee came off as less than truthful. The senators are trying to judge whether they can trust you once confirmed. If you lie now, you will probably lie even more after confirmation. So, do not lie. Own what you have said in the past. Put it in context, explain it, but do not deny it. Use context to emphasize that you completely understand the difference between being an academic or pundit and being an agency head. Let Congress know that you intend to follow the agenda they have laid out in statute, not your own.

I was very lucky to have some influential advocates in my corner. At the time of my confirmation, I was working for Vice President Mike Pence, who also served as president of the Senate. Since he was regularly breaking tied votes, Pence spent a lot of time on Capitol Hill. He also usually attended the Senate Republican Caucus lunch on Tuesdays. It probably helped my nomination quite a bit that the vice president advocated on my behalf at one of those luncheons in front of the entire Caucus. He clearly signaled that my nomination was important to him. For that, among so many other things, I will be eternally grateful.

Another influential advocate for my nomination was my former boss Sen. Richard Shelby, then chair of the Appropriations Committee and hence one of the most powerful senators. It also helped that Senator Shelby was widely liked within the Senate. I was particularly touched when his staff told me they had made a laminated copy of my bio for Senator Shelby to carry in his pocket. He would apparently corner colleagues on the Senate floor and read from my bio. I was also deeply affected during my confirmation when Shelby mentioned that in his time as the longest-serving member ever of the Banking Committee, he had never seen a nominee more qualified for the position.

Few nominees can manage to get both the vice president and the chair of the Appropriations Committee personally vested in their confirmation. Fortunately, not everyone needs that. However, if a nominee can get at least one senator interested, even a little, it makes a huge difference.

That support can be based on modest connections. If you are from a small state with few nominees such as, say, Hawaii or Wyoming, then trying to get the senators from that state to advocate on your behalf helps. Since we now live in a world where many more nominations will require floor time, the Senate majority leader is constantly prioritizing nominations. Judges will certainly continue to be a high priority. But if you are not nominated for a judgeship and it isn't a high-profile agency, having a senator request that the majority leader prioritize your nomination can make a big difference in timing.

———

Before the 2008 financial crisis, the best research on the U.S. mortgage market was generally being conducted within the Federal Reserve System. The FHFA's predecessors, the Office of Federal Housing Enterprise Oversight (OFHEO) and the Federal Housing Finance Board (FHFB), were not viewed as being on the cutting edge of analysis or even as a deeply knowledgeable source on the mortgage market. In fact, Fannie and Freddie were generally viewed as having more expertise on the mortgage market than their regulator. Such a situation undermines the credibility of an agency among both the public and its peers. Officials at the Treasury or the Federal Reserve would go directly to Fannie or Freddie rather than work with OFHEO. I set out to change that dynamic.

The first step was to create a stand-alone research and statistics division. I was rather shocked that we did not already have one, but then, my predecessors had also looked at Fannie and Freddie as more credible than their own staff.

It helped that I was quite knowledgeable about mortgage issues. I had spent a considerable part of my career as a financial and housing economist. Granted, it had been years since I had run a regression or pulled together a data table, but I had done those things and I knew that there were tremendous amounts of data on the housing and mortgage markets available.

Because I brought that background and my personal connections to the FHFA, throughout COVID-19, the Treasury, the Federal Reserve, the Office of the Comptroller of the Currency, and even the White

House looked to the FHFA to explain what was going on in the mortgage market. I was flattered that Mnuchin would call me, instead of his own Treasury staff, for an overview of the mortgage market. Of course, I was a little out of practice as an economist, so I knew that I needed to get continuous updates from our economics team. If you oversee the regulation of a particular market, it is critical that you be in constant dialogue with market participants and keep monitoring relevant market data.

Another indicator of our success in improving the FHFA's standing among its peers was our treatment as a member of the Financial Stability Oversight Council (FSOC). A tangible example was a unanimous FSOC vote in support of the FHFA's efforts to strengthen the regulation of Fannie and Freddie. For the first time, the FSOC openly recognized the systemic risk to our financial system and economy from the companies. The FHFA was a critical part of that process, explaining to other agencies, particularly the Treasury and the Federal Reserve, how our regulatory regime would function. The very supportive public statements of all FSOC members, in particular Federal Reserve chair Jay Powell, were a real testament to the FHFA's status. On our drive back to the agency after one FSOC meeting, FHFA staffer Sandra Thompson, who had long represented us at the FSOC, expressed to me how great it felt to finally have the FHFA respected and treated as an equal at the FSOC.

While the FSOC is unique to federal financial regulators, almost all agencies, even independent ones, incessantly engage in interagency processes. Federal employees care how they and their agencies are viewed by their peers at other agencies. Being a respected and valued participant in interagency efforts also increases employee morale and respect for leadership.

———

You can be distrustful of government and still be successful at running a government agency. I believe skepticism is a benefit. But it can come with some baggage: agency employees, external stakeholders, and Congress might all be suspicious of you. That can be overcome, though. Ground your messaging and your actions in the language of the authorizing statute. If your mission is to simply have the agency act within the law, that is a big win for the cause of smaller government. I can assure you that there is a lot of government that could be eliminated by just having agencies follow the law. It is also an argument that stakeholders can understand and have a hard time criticizing. Even if there are a lot of stakeholders who want you to ignore or violate the law, most will be uncomfortable being explicit about it.

Skepticism toward agency leadership can best be surmounted by transparency, consistency, repeated messaging, and accessibility. Fortunately, the same characteristics will also improve employee morale and agency effectiveness. I am extremely proud of the FHFA's accomplishments and the performance of its staff during my tenure. We protected taxpayers, the financial system, and, just as importantly, families. And we did not have to sacrifice principles or integrity to do it.

Chapter 13
Challenging the Narrative

Leaders must lean against false or misleading narratives and establish a moral authority against them. . . . Policymakers should try to create and disseminate counternarratives that establish more rational and more public-spirited economic behavior.[1]

—Professor Robert Shiller, Nobel Prize winner in economics

Stories, narratives, serve as guideposts. They also serve as constraints and barriers. Every public policy question is embedded in a narrative. To successfully lead an agency through a crisis, knowing which narratives you should challenge and which you should accept can be the difference between success and failure.

The first step is to recognize just what the myths and beliefs surrounding your policy area are. There is a wide range of beliefs regarding Fannie Mae and Freddie Mac. Did they cause the 2008 financial crisis? Or were they just victims? Does their existence contribute to homeownership? Are they a stabilizing or destabilizing force in our financial markets? Can they be released from conservatorship without congressional approval?

The second step is to identify how these myths and beliefs are circulated. Are they the product of intentional lobbying campaigns? Do they reflect commonly held mistaken impressions among the public?

Beliefs can circulate like a virus, passing from host to host. What makes one set of beliefs contagious and another not?

In Washington, there are four primary sources of policy narratives. The first source is the agencies tasked with carrying out the policy in question. Every federal agency spends substantial time and energy creating a history and story of itself. For instance, the Department of Homeland Security specifically references September 11, 2001, in its history.[2] Responding to and preventing another 9/11 are core elements of its narrative. Similarly, responding to the Great Depression is a core element of the history of Fannie Mae and the Federal Home Loan Banks, just as the 2008 financial crisis is central to the creation of the Federal Housing Finance Agency (FHFA).

The second source of narratives is agency stakeholders, including Washington-based trade associations, advocacy groups, and broader business groups such as the mortgage and real estate industries. This source can take the form of lobbying campaigns but can also result from day-to-day transactions within the trade. Most of the mortgage industry, for instance, views Fannie and Freddie through the lens of their dealings. For some, Fannie and Freddie are just business partners.

The third source is the press, which can be both a distributor of narratives generated by others, such as lobbyists, and a creator of original narratives. There has been a small handful of journalists, such as Bethany McLean, whose writings have created new explanations or helped express an evolving portrait. McLean and Peter Elkind's book *The Smartest Guys in the Room: The Amazing Rise and Scandalous Fall of Enron,* nicely summed up the hubris behind Enron's failure.[3] Her work on Fannie and Freddie has similarly encapsulated the issues facing our mortgage finance system.[4]

The fourth source of narratives is the general public. While the public gets its information from the previous three sources and is often their target, the public can and does have beliefs apart from these sources. For instance, my experience is that much of the public sees the failure and rescue of Fannie and Freddie in a light similar to that of Citibank or AIG. Washington tends to see Fannie and Freddie as something separate; the public instead sees them as just another set of large, protected financial companies.

———

The place for an agency head to begin is the press. Engaging with the press is one of the most important and often frustrating tasks of an agency leader. How others in Washington see you is driven in part by your press coverage. Many a congressional hearing has occurred as a result of a news story. Whether you are viewed as an easy target or a hard one is influenced by the publicity you get. Choosing not to have a press strategy is itself a choice and not a very wise one.

Putting together an experienced external relations team is critical. I was lucky to recruit Sheila Greenwood to oversee my external affairs. I had seen Sheila do similar work for Don Powell when he served as the federal coordinator for the Hurricane Katrina and Hurricane Rita recovery efforts. Despite what was an ugly, partisan, racially charged debate about recovery and rebuilding, Powell left with his reputation intact and is generally viewed as accomplished in coordinating those efforts. Having Sheila manage the messaging was partially responsible for his success. I figured if she could handle that, she could manage the FHFA's external relations. It also helped that she served as chief of staff for U.S. Department of Housing and Urban Development (HUD) Secretary Ben Carson and was known widely among Washington finance and housing circles.

I was also fortunate in hiring Raffi Williams from HUD. Perhaps being the son of pundit Juan Williams, as well as being married to a reporter, led Raffi to constantly think about the press. Raffi did a superb job of making the agency's mortgage-speak more accessible and understandable. His energy and determination, combined with Sheila's experience and network, provided me with a top-notch communications team. John Roscoe was also deeply involved with our external affairs. You are unlikely to find everything you need in just one person. This is an area where a team of rivals is less likely to work than a group of complements. And you can take a chance on part of the crew being less experienced but full of spirit, but you cannot take that chance with the entire team. Successful crisis communication requires that at least one member of the group be battle-tested.

Although I had been in Washington for over 20 years before my appointment and had worked at some mainstream establishment organizations, my work at the Cato Institute and my willingness to regularly declare that "the emperor has no clothes" in relation to much of federal mortgage policy made it easy for some to paint me as a radical. While I was able to address such concerns at my confirmation hearing, I found it useful to build out a senior team that appeared, at least on paper, far more establishment than I was. In addition to Greenwood, I enlisted Clinton Jones, a long-time House staffer, as the head of our legal team. Clinton had over 20 years of experience on the House Financial Services Committee. He was widely viewed as an accessible, moderate, and extremely knowledgeable Republican. I appointed Adolfo Marzol, a long-time industry veteran, as my deputy. He had spent years at Fannie Mae before cofounding a successful mortgage insurance company. I brought in Chris Bosland, an experienced financial services lawyer, who had served multiple stints in government, including one of our precursor agencies, the Federal Housing Finance Board. Last, I brought in a long-time industry analyst, Lynn Fisher, to add to a research division. The senior team helped bring instant credibility to our efforts, even if their personal policy preferences were not all that different from mine. The lesson here is that it is important to choose some senior team members whom you can trust and who can serve as a bridge to the various stakeholders. I had even considered bringing in a well-known progressive working on financial regulatory issues to reach that community.

——

One thing you should just accept up front, especially if you are a Republican appointee, is that the press is never going to be fair, balanced, or even accurate in covering you. It is just not going to happen. This is truer still if you are somewhat at odds with many of Washington's special interest groups. That said, you cannot afford to ignore the press—not that you should anyway.

Most policy issues have a limited bandwidth with the press. There may be a handful of beat reporters who cover your agency. They may also cover other agencies and issues. For a regularly covered beat, like financial services or housing, some minimum number of words on the agency is going to be written weekly. For most policy issues there is also a maximum amount of coverage, unless a big scandal blows up.

My approach was to essentially fill up as much of that bandwidth as I could. That was made easier by the fact that the agency had so much unfinished business. I never felt as if I had to resort to manufacturing news. Part of this was timing. If you announce 10 things on a particular day, you are lucky if 3 are reported. Now, if you want to make an announcement without much press coverage, then, yes, release it along with other news. Since there was nothing I was trying to hide or downplay, I regularly put space between news announcements, making sure that each received maximum coverage. Regular announcements of policy also helped to create a sense of momentum, which was critical for an agency that had previously felt like it was going in circles.

There is no substitute for face time with reporters. While my communications group handled the day-to-day inquiries, I made a point of regularly meeting with the reporters covering the FHFA. I did my utmost to answer their questions in depth and with clarity. I believed our responsibilities as an agency were clear, so I could communicate openly what they were and how we would carry them out.

One of the most important reasons to interact often with the press is to correct any false narratives about the agency or about oneself. For instance, there is an entire mythology around Fannie Mae, Freddie Mac, and the FHFA that lacks any legal basis. The FHFA is first and foremost a financial safety and soundness regulator. You might not have guessed that from the press. Perhaps the worst offender was *Politico*, which regularly referred to me or the FHFA as a "housing regulator." The FHFA has no role in regulating housing. It does not set rules regarding lot sizes, zoning, or building materials.

Since mortgages are ultimately backed by houses, and the FHFA does regulate entities involved in the secondary mortgage market, maybe that is the explanation. But then, by that logic, the Federal Deposit Insurance

Corporation (FDIC) is an auto regulator, since the FDIC regulates institutions that make auto loans. It is obvious how absurd that conclusion would be.

The reason that the press often erroneously labels the FHFA a housing regulator is that the special interests that do not want to see Fannie and Freddie appropriately regulated for safety and soundness have created a narrative that the FHFA's job isn't that of a financial regulator. Nowhere in the FHFA's authorizing statute or in the statutory charters of Fannie Mae and Freddie Mac would one find language suggesting that the FHFA is a housing regulator, nor would one find any evidence to suggest that the FHFA or the government-sponsored enterprises (GSEs) have a responsibility to increase homeownership or lower mortgage rates. Such things simply are not found in the statutes, but they have become the common story around the GSEs.

I do not believe that the press intentionally sets out to create inaccuracies about the FHFA. The issue is that most reporters rely heavily on lobbyists as sources. Even experts presented by the press as objective may not be. They might sit on the boards of interested companies or have extensive consulting relationships. I have seen little evidence that reporters dig into the possible financial conflicts of experts. The fact is that if a majority of a reporter's sources say the moon is made of cheese, then that is what will be reported. It is a game of quantity, not quality.

Even if you've been dealt a losing hand, you still have to play, and you have to play better than anyone else at the table. Since the press will rarely read the statutes or the regulations, you must cite them ad nauseum. Just as endless repetition is key to changing an organization's culture, it is also essential to changing a public narrative.

What you do have going for you, as an agency head, is the bully pulpit. You may be outnumbered, but you can often choose the timing and place of engagement.

The foremost example from the FHFA is the narrative regarding an exit from conservatorship for Fannie Mae and Freddie Mac. During his tenure, my predecessor claimed that it was up to Congress to decide on such an exit. That claim is false. There is nothing in the statute to suggest a requirement for Congress to approve a release. A congressional approval process for a GSE receivership was even debated and rejected. The process Congress created was modeled on the FDIC's framework, which does not require congressional action for banks to be out of either conservatorships or receiverships.

One can understand not wanting to do the hard and controversial work of fixing the GSEs and releasing them from conservatorship, but that is no excuse to ignore clear congressional intent. What was most puzzling was the degree to which the media and various stakeholders treated such a blatant violation of the law as normal.

My first communications objective was to simply signal to the external stakeholders and the public that I intended the agency to follow the law. After repeating that intention frequently, it finally stuck.

The lesson is to have a coherent, consistent message—preferably grounded in the agency's authorizing statute—that you state time after time. You will know you have gotten there once the press, agency employees, and external stakeholders can finish your sentences for you.

———

Most of what Congress and the press are responding to is pushed by outside stakeholders. I would go so far as to say that Congress rarely goes after an agency head unless outside groups are urging it to do so. So if you want to have a good, healthy relationship with Congress and the press, you must have the same with outside stakeholders.

The primary reason to continually engage with outside stakeholders is to gather information on the impact of your agency's policies, as well as general information about the markets affected. While one must regularly monitor aggregate market data, such data are always stale, and aggregation misses important nuances. These interactions, whether in small meetings or speeches before large audiences, should entail as much listening as talking.

Of course, the great difficulty in engaging with outside stakeholders is that much of what they tell you is self-serving. They are lobbying you for a reason, after all. That is not to say that they are directly lying to you, although some will. The agency head and staff must be able to separate the facts, which do need to be heard, from the spin. It can be tempting to just cut off communications with some stakeholders once they have developed a pattern of dishonesty, and in fact there were a handful of people with whom I stopped meeting. But we did not cut them off completely. My staff continued to engage. Because an agency's involvement with any stakeholder is essentially a repeated interaction, occasionally punishing bad behavior can increase the likelihood of cooperation, as in the standard prisoner's dilemma game.

———

The schedule of an agency's head does not permit direct meetings with everyone who requests one. And, in general, outside stakeholder meetings should be structured and vetted. You do not want lobbyists to have your cell number or even your email address. There is only downside risk to that. In fact, once a few outside lobbyists had acquired my email address, we changed it. Every request should be filtered through a member of the external relations staff.

As a rule, especially with an outside stakeholder, minimize the use of email. On the few occasions that I received an email from a lobbyist, I did not respond and simply forwarded it to staff. Assume that anything in an email, whether internal or external, will become public. Assume that it will be misrepresented, if not edited. Even your internal email should be screened. I saved a great deal of my time and attention by giving only about a dozen agency staffers my new email address. Of course, you still need to be accessible, but that access must be filtered and managed.

It is critical that one not rely exclusively on Washington-based industry representatives for information. Foremost, they are not out in the markets in question. I have often been shocked by how little those lobbyists tend to know about the industries they represent. If you want real insights, you must speak to actual market participants. Washington lobbyists also have their own set of incentives, distinct from those they represent. I have seen lobbyists work against the interests of their clients or members on many occasions. Again, to get the real scoop, go directly to market participants as much as possible. Ultimately, it is the members who drive trade associations. More than once, I believed a staffer was moving an association in the wrong direction, but after polite, engaged conversations with the association leadership, things moved in a more positive direction.

I had the benefit of working at two major trade associations, the National Association of Home Builders and the National Association of Realtors, early in my career. That experience gave me immediate goodwill among some in the real estate industry. As importantly, it gave me an early education in the dynamics of trade associations. I understood their needs and incentives and tried to address them as much as possible without undermining the agency's statutory responsibilities.

I have long been a student of interest groups. One of my fields of study in graduate school was public choice. In graduate school and beyond, I was a regular reader of the political science literature on interest groups. I made sure I was as familiar with the work of, say, Terry Moe, as I was with that of Mancur Olson.[5] The academic literature has its limitations, but it is invaluable when engaging with stakeholders.

My most important experience in relation to stakeholders was my time on the staff of the Senate Banking Committee. While working there, I had already engaged almost all the stakeholder groups I would deal with at the FHFA. I was adamant about having an open door. As a Senate staffer, I took every meeting that was requested, if it worked with my schedule and of course with the Committee and Senate floor schedules.

Early in your career, you should develop a reputation for being accessible. It is amazing what you can achieve, even what you can get people to accept or agree to, if they are given a legitimate opportunity to make their case. Sometimes it can seem frustrating and even a waste of time, but process really does matter. Be transparent. Be accessible. Do everything by the book. It pays off.

———

A constant task during my tenure at the FHFA was challenging false beliefs. From arguing that an exit from conservatorship need not wait for Congress, to arguing that mortgage servicers did not need a government rescue, our team was always engaging with the press, Congress, and Washington stakeholders. Presenting our position with transparency, lots of data, and a firm grounding in the law allowed us to succeed where I believe others would have folded or failed. I hope that a lasting effect of my tenure at the FHFA will be a reset in much of the narrative surrounding the agency, Fannie, and Freddie. The same approach can be reproduced at any federal agency.

Chapter 14

A Day in Court

As if coping with a pandemic, working to strengthen two borderline-insolvent financial companies with trillions of dollars of obligations, and rebuilding a demoralized and directionless agency were not enough to occupy one's mind, the Supreme Court, in 2020 and 2021, was deliberating a case that could change the very nature of the Federal Housing Finance Agency (FHFA), with tremendous ramifications for our financial system. And, of course, there was the personal impact on my tenure leading the FHFA.

The case is generally referred to as *Collins* or, more formally, *Collins v. Yellen*, having begun as *Collins v. Mnuchin*. The plaintiffs—Patrick Collins, Marcus Liotta, and William Hitchcock—held shares in Fannie Mae or Freddie Mac or both. Their claim was that the Treasury Department, along with the FHFA, had essentially taken the value of their shares via the third amendment to the conservatorship, or the profit sweep.

When the companies entered conservatorship in September 2008, the Treasury Department entered an agreement with the FHFA, acting on behalf of the companies as conservator. The agreement would allow Treasury to directly purchase preferred shares in Fannie and Freddie with the intention of keeping the companies solvent. This agreement is called the preferred share purchase agreement.

Although there has been some debate over the legitimacy of the initial conservatorship decision, it has centered on whether the companies were illiquid. And while illiquidity is one reason for a conservatorship, it is not the sole reason or even a necessary one. A conservatorship is made legitimate simply by having the corporate board approve it, which was the case with Fannie and Freddie.

Some have argued that the boards were forced into agreement by the Treasury. This was a time when both the Federal Reserve and the Treasury were pressuring some firms to obtain others. We know that Bank of America was pushed to acquire Merrill Lynch. I have also been told by Bank of America executives that they were urged to purchase Countrywide. How real these pressures were is up for debate, but the existence of some pressure is indisputable.

The problem the government-sponsored enterprises (GSEs) faced was that their boards had been populated with political cronies. Fannie and Freddie had long viewed such a situation as a bonus. It strengthened the perception that the government would bail them out. Unfortunately for the companies, having a board of political appointees cuts both ways. Appointees owe their positions to politics. Their loyalty is to their government patrons, not the companies or their shareholders. That is not a recipe for having the board fight a political takeover. And fight they did not.

One of my objectives during the conservatorships was to reduce the political nature of the Fannie and Freddie boards. I inherited two corporate boards occupied mostly by large-dollar Democratic donors. My priorities were expertise and independence. I believe I am the first, for instance, to recruit former financial regulators to the boards, such as former Federal Deposit Insurance Corporation (FDIC) chair Sheila Bair or former Securities and Exchange Commission (SEC) member Kathy Casey. Such placements are critical if the companies are eventually to leave conservatorship and learn how to operate like normal large, regulated financial institutions.

———

More troubling was the fact that the authority Congress gave to the Treasury Department was meant to support the mortgage-backed securities (MBS) market by allowing Treasury to purchase the companies' debt. It was not structured, or ever intended, to be an equity injection. Then Treasury secretary Henry Paulson has admitted that he ignored congressional direction and pursued his own policy inclinations instead of those plainly expressed by Congress.[1] By law, the companies should have been placed into a receivership in 2008, in which their capital structures would have been reorganized, and the companies would have eventually exited back into the marketplace with clean balance sheets.

There had been more than a decade of litigation and uncertainty over the future of our mortgage market, not to mention massive taxpayer exposure, because of the decision by one man, Henry Paulson, to violate the law, placing his preferences ahead of those of Congress.

———

Violation of clear congressional intent should be a big deal in Washington. Sadly, it is all too common. Did Paulson at least have good reason to act as he did? I believe his objective was to protect holders of Fannie and Freddie debt. A receivership, as required by law, would have exposed debtholders to potential loss. In light of the magnitude of the losses, I do not believe they would have ever hit the MBS holders. And the unsecured debt holders would have recovered over 90 percent of their investments. With Treasury's ability to purchase agency MBS at the time, there should not have been a disruption to the MBS market, and therefore the overall mortgage market, in the event of a receivership. Since the Federal Reserve has purchased the majority of GSE MBS issued during the conservatorship, there is even less reason to believe a receivership would have disrupted the mortgage market. Congress had thought this through—a rarity, I know.

The primary reason Paulson put GSE debt holders before the law is that one of the largest debt holders was the Chinese government. At the time, Paulson was one the biggest defenders of China in Washington, having a long business history with China during his time at Goldman Sachs. Treasury's violation of clear congressional intent was in part a decision to save China from recognizing any losses on its Fannie and Freddie debt holdings.

Paulson has also claimed that Russia, another large buyer of Fannie and Freddie debt, had approached China about staging a coordinated "dumping" of Fannie and Freddie debt to disrupt the U.S. mortgage market.[2] Whether or not this is true, it certainly illustrates why the United States should not depend so heavily on foreign funding for its mortgage market. More importantly, Congress was aware of foreign holdings of GSE debt. Sen. Richard Shelby, for instance, repeatedly mentioned the need to pass a receivership provision so that we would not be forced to bail out China.

Perhaps most tragic is that China was a large buyer of Fannie and Freddie debt as part of its efforts to manipulate its currency relative to the dollar. Cycling China's excess dollar holdings into GSE debt allowed Chinese exports to gain some competitiveness relative to U.S. manufactured goods. Had China been forced to accept losses on its GSE debt holdings, it would have likely reduced its holdings of U.S. dollar assets, resulting in some appreciation of its currency. Not only did Paulson decide to put China ahead of the American taxpayer, but he also did so in a way that continued to cost American manufacturing jobs.

———

Collins, however, was not about the initial agreement, or the conservatorship itself, or even the second amendment to the agreement, which generally benefited the shareholders.

On his way out of Treasury, planning to leave after 2012 midterm elections, then secretary Tim Geithner crafted an agreement, in August 2012, with then acting FHFA director Ed DeMarco to sweep all the companies' profits in exchange for an expanded line of credit with the Treasury. This is the heart of the third amendment of the conservatorship and the heart of the *Collins* case.

As Brigham Young University law professor Aaron Nielson has observed, *Collins* really is three cases.[3] One addresses the statutory powers and responsibilities of the FHFA as a conservator. Another raises the question whether the FHFA's governance structure is constitutional. And the remaining question is how to address any harm that GSE shareholders may have suffered.

On the powers and responsibilities of a conservator, I had some sympathy for the plaintiffs. I had previously coauthored a paper on the topic with one of the world's foremost experts on bank insolvency.[4] I had no doubt that the third amendment went against the statutory framework Congress had created to address an insolvency at the GSEs. Therefore, one of my first responsibilities as director was to end the profit sweep, an action that was formalized in a September 2019 agreement with Treasury. There was essentially no profit sweep during my tenure. We were building capital at the companies, as was so clearly intended by Congress. I believe that was the single most important action I could have taken to address the illegality of the third amendment.

Building capital at the companies, with an eye toward eventual release from conservatorship, had occasionally been presented as some personal agenda of mine. It was not. It was clearly what the statute required and Congress intended.

If I had been following my own agenda, instead of the directive of Congress, I would have taken the GSEs into a receivership. That would have been the cleanest route to fixing their flawed structure. And if the circumstances ever again dictated a receivership, as they had in 2008, I had no hesitancy about following the law. In fact, during my tenure the FHFA created a resolutions team and began requiring both companies to write "living wills" in which they would pre-plan a resolution that did not depend on any assistance from the taxpayer. We engaged in several drafting exercises, working with both the Federal Reserve and the SEC, to game out a GSE receivership. Setting aside the legal requirements, whether the FHFA had the infrastructure in place to conduct a receivership in 2008 is an open question. Before my departure from the FHFA, I made sure we did have such an infrastructure in place. Any future GSE bailouts will be ones of choice, not necessity.

When I walked into Constitution Center, home of the FHFA, in April 2019, the legal conditions requiring a receivership were vague at best. The companies were earning money. There was a path to fixing the companies within the conservatorship. The explicit legal obligation was to try to do so. The primary reason in 2019 for a receivership would be to cram down the capital structure, so that the asset and liabilities sides of the balance sheets would truly be even. As I believed we then had an opportunity to work with Treasury to cooperatively achieve that restructuring, a receivership appeared unnecessary.

Since we had ended the profit sweep, the heart of the third amendment, and had no intention of ever bringing it back, I felt that the statutory issues would have little effect on the FHFA's current operation, regardless of how the case was decided. We didn't have the resources to pay any damages if they were awarded. Those would be the responsibility of the Treasury Department.

An outcome I did not expect was that the Supreme Court would read some minor cleanup language as a means of invalidating large portions of the FHFA's authorizing statute. The conservatorship powers for the FHFA are based on those of the FDIC. As one of the people who drafted them, I can attest that the Senate Banking Committee staff literally took Sections 11 and 13 of the Federal Deposit Insurance Act and modified them to suit the case of a GSE. Congress fully intended GSE conservatorship to rest on the legal processes and precedents surrounding FDIC conservatorships.

One of the responsibilities of an FDIC conservatorship is to pursue actions that benefit the FDIC, within the context of a conservatorship. We imported such language for the FHFA. That said, it is clearly labeled as an "incidental" authority. The language is meant to protect the FHFA and the FDIC from having reasonable choices that were made in their duties under a conservatorship constantly second-guessed. This authority is in no way meant to supersede those duties. *Collins* could be interpreted to mean that the FHFA, and by extension the FDIC, can do anything it pleases, whether authorized or not. Ultimately, I believe this reading is incorrect. Even if the FHFA or the FDIC can now use a conservatorship to benefit the agency, the benefit is bounded by the authorities and purposes of the agency, one of which is the purposes of a conservatorship.

Over the long term, I am deeply troubled by what the expansive reading of agency authority under *Collins* means for our economy and broader society. *Collins* reverses years of progress in limiting the discretion of government agencies. It also opens the door for financial institutions beyond the GSEs to be taken over by government and used for purely political ends. My immediate concern, of course, was about the constitutional claim against the FHFA's structure.

———

When Congress created the FHFA, it looked to the other financial regulators as a model.[5] At the time, the two most important safety and soundness regulators, beyond the Federal Reserve, were the Office of the Comptroller of the Currency (OCC) and the Office of Thrift Supervision (OTS). Both the OCC and the OTS were headed by single directors, as was the then regulator for Fannie and Freddie, the Office of Federal Housing Enterprise Oversight (OFHEO).

There are other financial regulators structured as boards. In addition to the Federal Reserve, both the FDIC and the National Credit Union Administration were framed that way. Several early drafts of what eventually became the Housing and Economic Recovery Act of 2008, which created the FHFA, also included boards.

There is no perfect framework for an agency. With boards, there can be more deliberation and moderation in outcomes. Sometimes you can also get more public transparency regarding agency decisions when they are debated at board meetings. But some boards, such as the SEC, perhaps have become too comfortable with regular party line decisions, behaving in many circumstances similarly to agencies with a single director. With one director, you can get faster action. Ultimately, an important element to consider is how much policy discretion the agency possesses.

Compared with agencies like the SEC and the Consumer Financial Protection Bureau (CFPB), the FHFA had a narrow, limited set of authorities. The swings in policy that we have seen at the FHFA mostly have not been the result of congressional delegations of decisionmaking, but rather outright violations of law. Narrowness and lack of discretion suggested a single-director model for the FHFA.

The increasing complexity of what an FHFA board would look like also became a distraction. In early drafts, Senator Shelby wanted the FHFA to mirror the FDIC, whose board consists partly of heads of other agencies. One draft had the board comprising the SEC chair, the Department of Housing and Urban Development secretary, the Treasury secretary, and the director of the FHFA. That version finally morphed into the FHFA's current oversight board. Another version had the head of the Government Accountability Office (GAO) included, until we determined that including that individual would create an issue in separation of powers, since the head of the GAO works directly for Congress.

———

A central element of the *Collins* case was the single-director structure of the FHFA. The claim focused on the removal provisions, which stated that the director could be removed only by the president "for cause." Typically, such as with Cabinet secretaries, political appointees in the executive branch serve at the pleasure of the president. That is, they can be fired at will.

Congress wanted the FHFA to be insulated from the political pressures that can come from any White House. There is always the temptation to artificially push up the housing market via credit easing before an election. If the FHFA was not independent, this pressure would result in painful housing booms and busts, with devastating long-run consequences.

An independent FHFA would also reduce the perception that Fannie and Freddie were implicitly backed by the federal government. During the debates that led to the creation of the FHFA, the George W. Bush administration argued that the FHFA should be loosely connected to the Treasury Department, along the lines of the OCC. Democrats did not trust the Bush Treasury, and Republicans were concerned that such an attachment would increase the belief that the companies were ultimately backed by the Treasury.

To a degree, many Republicans did not trust Treasury either. Despite its occasional claim of being above politics and interest group pressures, the Treasury Department, across administrations and regardless of political party, tends to reflect the positions, assumptions, and beliefs of its Wall Street partners. After all, selling Treasury debt is its primary function, so its everyday interactions are with financial companies that deal or invest in Treasuries. Many of these firms also deal and invest in Fannie and Freddie securities. Not surprisingly, the same Wall

Street firms believe that the taxpayer should be on the hook to limit any downside to them from holding Fannie and Freddie securities. Also not surprisingly, that desire has become conventional wisdom within the Treasury Department. For that reason, Republicans, such as Senator Shelby, did not trust Treasury to have influence over any new regulatory structure for Fannie and Freddie. Accordingly, Congress decided that the FHFA had to be independent.

One of the most troubling aspects of *Collins* is the Supreme Court's guessing game of what Congress would have wanted, had the supposed constitutional flaw not been included in the legislation. If a statute is unconstitutional, strike it down, unless Congress creates a separability clause or something similar. There is no such provision in the FHFA's authorizing statute. Rather than taking that route, the Supreme Court decided that Congress would have chosen to eliminate the independence of the FHFA.

Such a conclusion, however, is at odds with the legislative record. Congress obviously wanted an independent FHFA. The issue of a single director versus a board was of secondary importance. Instead of following the clear intentions of Congress, the Supreme Court substituted its own judgment.

I believe that the Supreme Court made the choice it did in the end because several members of the Court are inherently opposed to independent agencies yet lack the votes to undo independent boards such as the Federal Reserve. Even with a board like the Federal Reserve, few believe that in practice all those board members are interchangeable or equal.[6] Certainly, the chair of the Federal Reserve plays an outsize role. I see little reason to believe that constitutionally there is a great deal of difference between an independent single-director agency head and the unique outsize role of the chair of the Federal Reserve. I suspect that Justices Clarence Thomas and Samuel Alito see little difference either.

Why all the fuss about agency independence anyway? It all comes down to a few words in article II, section 3, of the U.S. Constitution. That section requires the president to "take care that the laws be faithfully executed." Yes, that's it, the entire basis for the debate. The argument is that this cannot be done unless the president can remove agency heads at will. While that argument has some logic to it, it also misses a few points. Importantly, the language does not require that the president carry out the actual execution of the law. It only requires that the president see that such actions are faithfully executed, even if they are done by others. The language does suggest that it would be unconstitutional to have an agency head that could not be removed by the president for *any* reason. Obviously, an agency head should be removable for not faithfully upholding the law.

The most bizarre aspect of *Collins* is that at-will removal allows the president to remove agency heads because they *were* faithfully executing the law. In fact, I believe that to be part of the reason for my removal by President Biden. Yes, it was mostly just politics. But the fact that I was carrying out the law was not viewed favorably by the Biden administration or by much of Wall Street. The plaintiffs may have brought forward the *Collins* case as an avenue for ending the conservatorships, but the reality is that the loss of the FHFA's independence will make an end to the conservatorships less likely, as future presidents will be tempted to use Fannie and Freddie as a means toward their own political goals.

Perhaps most unusual was that the Supreme Court never even needed to wade into the debate. The third amendment was agreed to by an acting director at the FHFA, who can be removed at will by the president. In fact, I suggest that had the FHFA been headed by an independent director in 2012, the third amendment would not have been implemented. It was undoubtedly a scheme designed by the Obama administration and agreed to by the FHFA because it lacked an independent director confirmed by the Senate.

Why would the *Collins* plaintiffs pursue a claim that was completely backward factually? It was no more than a legal strategy. Throw everything at the case and see what sticks. If anything, the companies' shareholders were better off with an independent FHFA, since an FHFA controlled by the White House would see Fannie and Freddie as political tools to be used, rather than the private companies that they legally are.

I am perhaps not the most objective person when it comes to the independence of the FHFA. As a Senate staffer, after all, I did draft the removal language that was the focus of *Collins*. I did the legal research at the time and believed that the agency structure, requiring "for cause" removal, was well within constitutional norms. And while I am not unsympathetic to the arguments for a unitary executive, I do believe that the entire constitutional case against any restrictions on a president's ability to remove independent regulators is extremely weak.

While I have been an advocate for restructuring the CFPB as a board, I find its funding mechanism and broad discretionary powers to be far more troubling than the inability to remove its director at will. I was extremely disappointed and frustrated with the decision by the Department of Justice (DOJ) to drop objections to the CFPB's funding structure.

I was even more disappointed by both the DOJ and the Supreme Court's unwillingness to allow the FHFA to present arguments in the *Collins* case. I disagreed with the DOJ on both the statutory and the constitutional issues. I was willing to leave the statutory issues to the DOJ but felt that the FHFA deserved the ability to defend its independence. The solicitor general felt differently. The DOJ's view was that the federal government speaks with one voice—the DOJ's. Since there was no one to defend the FHFA's independence, the Supreme Court appointed Nielson to argue the case. While I commend Professor Nielson for his able arguments, it still stuns me that the party most affected and most knowledgeable was not allowed to present arguments.

————

Less surprising, although still dispiriting, was how quickly some congressional defenders of FHFA independence suddenly flipped. Several senators and representatives submitted a brief in defense of the FHFA's independence when the case was heard in the Fifth Circuit U.S. Court of Appeals. The brief was drafted by the Constitutional Accountability Center and signed by, among others, Elizabeth Warren, Sherrod Brown, Chris Van Hollen, Maxine Waters, and Nancy Pelosi. It was a well-crafted, powerful brief. I found it very consistent with my views:

> In sum, OFHEO's lack of independence prevented it from robustly enforc-
> ing the law; that mistake led to billions in federal bailouts and was one
> of the market-wide failures that contributed to the near-collapse of the

American economy. In response, exercising the discretion afforded to it by the Constitution, Congress determined that a strong and independent regulator was needed to oversee Fannie Mae and Freddie Mac. As Congress recognized, it was critical that the new regulator be shielded from politically motivated pressure to weaken oversight because such pressure would undermine the agency's ability to fulfill its statutory mandate.[7]

I had heard informally that the Constitutional Accountability Center, when submitting a similar brief to the Supreme Court, approached the same members of Congress. All of a sudden, what they had believed in 2019 was not what they believed in 2020. None of the original members of Congress were willing to put their name on the same brief they had signed just a year earlier.

Worse still, some members, such as Representative Waters, called for President Biden to immediately remove me in January 2021, even though Ms. Waters had only two years earlier argued for the FHFA's independence. Then a senator, Biden had also voted to make the FHFA independent in 2008. When they had an opportunity to control the agency, their position changed. The issue had come up explicitly during my confirmation hearing when Senator Brown asked, for the record, whether I would continue to defend the independence of the FHFA. I promised him I would, and I did.

Not everyone felt the same way. While I disagreed with some Republicans, who believed that the FHFA should not be independent, I respect that I know of none who altered their position simply because of who the current director was.

———

Ultimately, the biggest impact of *Collins* will be on the growing influence of politics on the day-to-day business of financial regulation. Yes, financial regulation as a policy issue has always been political and often partisan. Yet the daily conduct of this regulation has not been so, at least not compared with other issue areas within the executive branch. Although there has long been some industry capture among financial regulators, it pales in comparison with, say, that of the Department of Agriculture or the Department of Housing and Urban Development.

The danger of daily partisan politics is also greater among financial regulators than among other executive branch agencies, since finance has historically played a role in the macroeconomy unmatched by, for example, the actions of the Department of Education or the Department of the Interior. I recall a friend who served in the Treasury Department under President Clinton describing how some within that administration wanted to lower bank capital requirements to stimulate the economy. Fortunately, such a move was not supported broadly within the Clinton administration, but more importantly, the ability to do so rested largely with independent financial regulators. I witnessed similar suggestions to reduce bank capital from within the Treasury Department during the Trump administration. Working with others in the White House, I was able to quash such proposals.

Defeating attempts to politicize financial regulation, whether at the GSEs or other financial institutions, will become ever more difficult with the loss of independence of the FHFA, the OCC, and, to a degree, the FDIC, as a result of the *Collins* case. It is imperative that Congress remedy this situation.

Chapter 15
Home, Sweet Home

June 23, 2021, began like so many recent mornings, with me grinding coffee beans while feeding my two poorly behaved cats, Charlie and Lila. After a few calls, I began an obsessive refreshing of the Supreme Court's website at 10:00 a.m., the assigned time when Court opinions were to be released. Despite being affected by the *Collins* decision, I was given no advance warning. I had to wait like everyone else.

After spending most workdays since March 2020 at my kitchen table, home had begun to feel more and more like work. By spring 2021, most of my leadership team and I were vaccinated, and a core of us started to return to the office a couple days a week. Today, I would wait to see the Court's decision before going in, as that would determine how the day would unfold.

The first case came at 10:00 a.m. sharp. Not *Collins*. The wait continued for about 15 to 20 minutes before a second case was announced. Again, not *Collins*. Maybe I would live to fight another day. Later in the hour, the final case of the morning was announced: *Collins* it was. This would be the day.

I immediately started to read the decision. The first clue was unsettling. The opinion was delivered by Justice Samuel Alito, who is well within the Court's camp for getting rid of agency independence. In fact, as I have mentioned, I suspect that Alito would vote to end the independence of the Federal Reserve, if it ever came up. This was one of those rare occasions where I was hoping for either Chief Justice John Roberts or Justice Brett Kavanaugh, as both tended toward judicial restraint.

Before I got far into the opinion, the legal team of the Federal Housing Finance Agency (FHFA) reached out. It was crystal clear that the directorship of the agency was now at will. At least it was a clean decision. I felt bound to defend the independence of the FHFA. Any ambiguous decision could have led to months, if not years, of additional litigation. I did not want to go through that, and more importantly, I did not want to see the agency continue under a cloud of uncertainty.

Just before noon, I received word from the White House that the president would like me to vacate the position by 6:00 p.m. that evening. That was fully expected; this was politics. Not to mention that I had certainly irked more than one Wall Street donor to the Biden administration.

I did find it striking that the message from the White House came from the head of presidential personnel, Cathy Russell. The remarkable part was that her husband is a former Fannie Mae lobbyist who fought hard against the creation of a strong regulator for Fannie. His wife would accomplish what he could not. Perhaps more surprising was that he now worked at BlackRock, one of the companies that had the most to gain from my departure. BlackRock is a large holder of Fannie and Freddie debt. By creating a resolution framework to transfer government-supported enterprise (GSE) losses to creditors instead of taxpayers, BlackRock would now be subject to the downside of its speculation in GSE debt.

There would still be a lot to do before 6:00 p.m. came around.

———

With a government job, my first set of responsibilities was signing my name to an endless series of forms. Some were needed to validate agency actions already taken. Some were related directly to me; for instance, would I elect to continue my current health care insurance?

And, of course, it is not government without an ethics debriefing. Going forward, what could I do or not do professionally? Oddly enough, I found this a pleasant break, partly because I generally liked and respected the agency's chief ethics counsel, Sean Dent. I had known his wife, Alane, before coming to the FHFA. She was a well-respected and successful insurance lobbyist. We might not have had the same politics, but we shared a commitment to good government.

My communications team worked out options for statements, both internal and external. The White House kept asking what we intended to say. It appeared that they wanted to hear my public take before they released theirs. It would fall to me to set the tone.

I had several friends who had been pushed out of positions immediately in January 2021. Obviously, there were positions that would turn over with any administration, but this was something different. There are a few positions in government that are intended to have set terms, regardless of administration. The Biden administration, breaking long-standing norms, worked to remove appointees holding such positions. The most high-profile was the chief counsel at the National Labor Relations Board. There were many others, including the boards of regents for the service academies, such as West Point and Annapolis.

Many appointees who were forced out made loud public statements as they left. That was their prerogative, and I certainly understood the anger. But I had worked too hard to build up the FHFA. Any statement I made had to strengthen the agency. The loss of independence would be harmful enough. My public statement would be positive and respectful. I might have disagreed with the Supreme Court's decision, but I respect their authority. The agency needed to start this new chapter on strong footing.

While the White House was most interested in my public statement, I was more concerned with my internal statement. From day one, I had seen myself as protector and defender of the FHFA's staff. By the time I left, I had exchanged words, even if briefly, with over 90 percent of the staff. I wanted them to be successful.

My message conveyed just that. My desire to express pride in having had the opportunity to lead the FHFA—and my pride in all the staff—had been accomplished. And, of course, I had expressed my view of the importance of the work ahead of FHFA, which would not end with me. I did not know what to expect in response. Most of the agency did not share my politics; many hated them. They also no longer had any incentive to hold back their thoughts. Staff could very easily tell me now what they really thought about me.

In fact, I was blown away by the response. For instance, one of the staff members within our Office on Women and Minority Inclusion wrote, "Director Calabria, I am saddened by President Biden's decision to remove you as our director. I wish you all the best and am proud to have known you. You made such a difference in this agency not only in Special Emphasis Programs but the morale at our agency improved immensely because you HONESTLY cared about your employees' well-being and success. Thank you and may God bless and keep you." Many other messages poured in.

Most heartwarming were the employees who drove in to see me off. We were still in the middle of a pandemic and in mandatory-telework mode. My core leadership team and a handful of our legal staff were in the office; otherwise, Constitution Center, where the FHFA is located, was a ghost town. The number of staff members who came in just to stop by my office and say goodbye was extremely touching. Pulling out of the garage onto D Street for one last time was bittersweet.

I was proud of what we had accomplished at the FHFA. But I also knew that the agency, along with Fannie and Freddie, had a lot of unfinished work. The supportive emails and office drop-ins took the edge off the *Collins* decision. I was leaving, but there was reason to hope that the FHFA would continue to make progress. I believe we had raised the bar on what agency staff would expect not only of themselves but also of future leadership.

———

Amid all the policy reversals and even outright failures and occasional misinformation, it is easy to forget that our federal government's response to COVID-19 and its economic impact did get some things right. I am still amazed at Operation Warp Speed and our nation's ability to develop an effective vaccine in record time. That was possible only because of the efforts of our private pharmaceutical industry.

Having witnessed up close the failures of our mortgage policy responses in the Great Recession, I was adamant that we would not repeat those. The FHFA, the Department of Housing and Urban Development, the Department of Agriculture, the Veterans Administration, and the White House, working with the mortgage industry, averted a mortgage market meltdown.

I believe what distinguished the policy successes during COVID-19 from the policy failures was whether people followed their principles or turned their back on them. Foremost, policymakers must be honest about what they do and don't know. At the FHFA, we shared what data we could, and we presented our best estimates to the public and industry stakeholders. We did not exaggerate or attempt to scare the public, Congress, or other stakeholders. When some claimed that there would be a tsunami of foreclosures and evictions, we calmly shared our estimates and made decisions based on the range of probable outcomes.

It was during my time on staff at the Senate Banking Committee that I had my first interaction with the Centers for Disease Control and Prevention (CDC). While the Banking Committee has no jurisdiction over the CDC, I did have the misfortune of being on the fifth floor of the Hart Senate Office Building (right around the corner from my office in Dirksen) when anthrax was found just down the hallway in then senator Tom Daschle's office. The CDC provided regular updates and information to the Senate in response to the anthrax attack.

I recall that the information we received from the CDC was ever-changing, though—a different story every day. Like many Senate staffers, I studied and read everything I could find on anthrax. The eroding trust and confusion could well have cost the lives of postal workers at the Brentwood facility that processed congressional mail. The whole experience left me with the distinct impression that the CDC could not always be trusted for accuracy and expertise. It was not a comforting thought. I was determined that I would not allow the FHFA to behave similarly. Lost trust can be impossible to regain.

We also stood our ground when we believed we were right. Many on Wall Street wanted me gone. They did not like my refusal to bail out servicers, or our pricing for risk, or even our strategies to cover our costs. They certainly did not like my efforts to take the taxpayer off the hook for the debts issued by Fannie and Freddie. Their allies in Congress made sure we were aware of these complaints.

I believe that once you compromise your principles in Washington, you are left defenseless. Everyone knows you will bend, and it just becomes a question of how much. Moreover, it is not just a matter of doing what's right, but also an issue of time management. Most of the requests made by industry to the FHFA during COVID-19 had little to do with directly helping families and more to do with boosting their profits. As those demands are endless, if you signal a willingness to give in, then more and more of your time is spent negotiating the terms of your surrender.

A regular temptation in Washington is to just give in, hoping you can make an issue go away, and move on. But that short-term thinking only creates more issues to deal with. I was able to focus on assisting families, while the industry quickly learned that I was not going to waste time designing bailouts and arguing over their generosity.

———

During the 2008 financial crisis, President George W. Bush proclaimed, "I've abandoned free-market principles to save the free-market system." That premise was continued under President Barack Obama. I hope to have demonstrated in these pages that Bush's decision was a tragic mistake.

Our mortgage markets and financial sector in general faced an even more daunting task in 2020. America has a long history of housing booms and busts. We know that they end, and we know how. However, COVID-19 was new territory, even keeping in mind America's experience with the Spanish flu of 1918. Many people did abandon principle. There was the occasional suggestion that I should, as well. But in truth, I kept both faith in my principles and a devotion to following the data.

Learning from the mistakes of the Great Recession allowed me to craft a mortgage response that would quickly help families and do so in a way that prioritized those most in need. We put families first. We rejected the claim that to save Main Street, you must first save Wall Street. And it all worked. Not to mention that we also designed those successful policies in such a manner that they did not cost the taxpayer a single penny. I never went to Nancy Pelosi on bended knee to beg for a blank check.

In March 2020, as the pandemic began to hit America in force, *The Atlantic* writer Derek Thompson jested, "There are no libertarians in a pandemic." Over two years later, it is hard to imagine a more inaccurate observation. The COVID-19 response was characterized by one governmental failure after another. The successes, such as the mortgage response I have described in this book, were rooted in a firm skepticism of government and informed by a sound understanding of what government can and cannot achieve. It was sticking to principles that worked.

Bailouts-or-nothing is a false choice. We have compassionate, effective, and efficient options. I believe that the FHFA, along with my friend Dr. Ben Carson and his colleagues at the Department of Housing and Urban Development, made the right choices. Let's hope that these lessons are not forgotten next time.

Acknowledgments

It really does take a village. The events described here could not have occurred without the work of my tremendous team at the Federal Housing Finance Agency (FHFA). Among the FHFA's dedicated career staff, Maria Fernandez merits special attention. Maria and her team were truly the heart of the FHFA's response to COVID-19.

While I have occasionally been critical of Fannie Mae and Freddie Mac, they deserve considerable credit for a successful response to COVID-19. Their then respective board chairs, Sheila Bair and Sara Mathew, are amazing leaders. Both stepped up during difficult times and committed themselves and their organizations to constant improvement. The companies' CEOs during 2020, Hugh Frater and David Brickman, were critical partners and outstanding leaders, despite our occasional disagreements.

John Roscoe and Adolfo Marzol provided valuable feedback on various chapters, as did Andrew Olmem, Dana Wade, and Todd Zywicki. I, of course, am solely responsible for the content. As I took no notes during the period described, the events presented are based on memory. Others will, no doubt, recall some of those events differently. Others will also interpret the importance and mechanics of those events differently. Where possible, I have relied on contemporaneous press accounts to fill in any gaps in memory.

The events described center on our work at the FHFA. That work complemented the critical efforts at the Department of Housing and Urban Development under Dr. Ben Carson, particularly the work of then Federal Housing Administration commissioner Dana Wade and HUD deputy secretary Brian Montgomery.

Cato has long been a second family to me. I could not have asked for better partners on this book than my editor, Aaron Steelman, and Cato's all-around publications genius Eleanor O'Connor. Cato's Gene Healy also provided feedback on various aspects of the project.

I would never have had the opportunity to lead the FHFA had it not been for the trust and support of Vice President Mike Pence. I do not know of a more decent, thoughtful, and public-spirited person in political life today than Mike Pence. Being part of Team Pence will always remain a highlight of my career.

It is always an honor to be nominated to serve one's country. I am deeply appreciative of the trust placed in me by President Donald Trump in nominating me to lead the FHFA. The support of Larry Kudlow, former director of the National Economic Council, was also critical in the success of the events described here.

Lastly, and most importantly, the constant support of my partner, Allison Randall, got me through both a pandemic and the process of writing my first book.

Mark Calabria
Washington, DC

Notes

INTRODUCTION

1. Kay Jowers et al., "Housing Precarity & the COVID-19 Pandemic: Impacts of Utility Disconnection and Eviction Moratoria on Infections and Deaths across US Counties," National Bureau of Economic Research Working Paper no. 28394, January 2021.

2. Miguel Faria-e-Castro and Olivia Wilkinson, "Mortgage Forbearance and Economic Recovery from the Pandemic," Federal Reserve Bank of St. Louis *Economic Synopses* 19 (2021), https://doi.org/10.20955/es.2021.19.

CHAPTER 1

1. For instance, see Talha Burki, "China's Successful Control of COVID-19," *The Lancet: Infectious Diseases* 20, no. 11 (November 1, 2020): 1240–41, www.doi.org/10.1016/S1473-3099(20)30800-8.

2. All financial market aggregate data in this chapter are from Securities Industry and Financial Markets Association (SIFMA), *Capital Markets Fact Book* (New York: SIFMA), https://www.sifma.org/resources/research/fact-book/.

3. SIFMA, U.S. Repo Statistics, https://www.sifma.org/resources/research/us-repo-statistics/.

4. SIFMA, U.S. Repo Statistics.

5. U.S. Bureau of Labor Statistics (BLS), Consumer Expenditure Surveys.

6. BLS, Consumer Expenditure Surveys.

7. Edward E. Leamer, "Housing IS the Business Cycle," National Bureau of Economic Research Working Paper no. 13428, September 2007, www.doi.org/10.3386/w13428.

8. Homeownership rates are from the U.S. Census Bureau, Housing Vacancies and Homeownership.

9. Mark Calabria, "Prepared Remarks of Dr. Mark A. Calabria, Director of FHFA, at National Association of Homebuilders International Builders' Show" (speech, Las Vegas, January 23, 2020).

10. Calabria, "Prepared Remarks."

CHAPTER 2

1. Conference of State Bank Supervisors, "Reengineering Nonbank Supervision," white paper, February 13, 2020.

2. Federal Deposit Insurance Corporation, "FDIC Statistics at a Glance."

3. National Credit Union Administration, "Quarterly Credit Union Data Summary, 2021 Q1," 2021.

4. For a general overview of the rise of nonbank servicers, see Michael Fratantoni, "Why Have Banks Stepped Back from Mortgage Servicing?," *International Banker*, September 2, 2020; and Marshall Lux and Robert Greene, "What's Behind the Non-Bank Mortgage Boom?," Harvard Kennedy School, Mossavar-Rahmani Center for Business and Government Associate Working Paper no. 42, June 2015.

5. See E. Michael Rosser and Diane M. Sanders, *A History of Mortgage Banking in the West: Financing America's Dreams* (Boulder: University Press of Colorado, 2017).

6. Subprime and Alt-A refer to the credit risk of the mortgage, more specifically the likelihood that the borrower defaults; subprime is usually in reference to the borrower's credit history. For instance, using the FICO scale of 300 to 850, subprime is generally a loan made to a borrower with a FICO of under 660. Alt-A mortgages are generally those made to prime borrowers, with FICOs over 660, but with high-risk loan characteristics, such as negative amortization or low or no documentation.

7. Lux and Greene, "What's Behind the Non-Bank Mortgage Boom?."

8. Kathryn Fritzdixon, "Bank and Nonbank Lending over the Past 70 Years," *FDIC Quarterly*, Quarterly Banking Profile 13, no. 4 (2019): 31–39.

9. Edward-Isaac Dovere, "The Battle That Changed Kamala Harris," *The Atlantic*, August 20, 2020; and David Dayen, "Kamala Harris Celebrates Her Role in the Mortgage Crisis Settlement. The Reality Is Quite Different," *The Intercept*, March 13, 2019.

10. Office of the Attorney General of California, "Attorney General Kamala D. Harris Secures $18 Billion California Commitment for Struggling Homeowners," press release, February 9, 2012.

11. Office of the Attorney General of California, "Attorney General Kamala D. Harris Secures $18 Billion."

12. Sonia Moghe, "Former New York AG Eric Schneiderman's Law License Has Been Suspended for a Year over Allegations of Abuse," CNN Politics, April 28, 2021.

13. National Mortgage Settlement, website, http://www.nationalmortgage settlement.com/about.html.

14. Mark Calabria, "Where's the Compensation for Victims in the Mortgage Settlement?," *Cato at Liberty* (blog), Cato Institute, February 10, 2012.

15. Mark Calabria, "Questions and Thoughts on the Mortgage Settlement," *Cato at Liberty* (blog), Cato Institute, February 9, 2012.

16. Barack Obama, "Remarks by President on Housing Settlement," speech, Eisenhower Executive Office Building, Room 430, February 9, 2012.

17. For greater detail on robo-signing, see David Dayen, *Chain of Title: How Three Ordinary Americans Uncovered Wall Street's Great Foreclosure Fraud* (New York: The New Press, 2016).

18. Jamie Dimon to Shareholders, letter, April 6, 2016.

19. "JPMorgan Chase Executive a Casualty of Military Scandal," *American Banker*, June 15, 2011.

20. "Stearns Lending Appoints Mortgage Industry Veteran David Lowman to Board of Managers," Business Wire, February 3, 2020.

21. Daniel Wagner, "Subprime Lending Execs Back in Business Five Years After Crash," Center for Public Integrity, September 11, 2013.

22. Brian Grow, "Executives with Criminal Records Slip through FHA Crackdown, Documents Show," Center for Public Integrity, September 10, 2010.

23. Karan Kaul and Laurie Goodman, "Nonbank Servicer Regulation: New Capital and Liquidity Requirements Don't Offer Enough Loss Protection," Urban Institute, Housing Finance Policy Center Brief, February 25, 2016.

24. Fritzdixon, "Bank and Nonbank Lending over the Past 70 Years."

25. Inspector General, U.S. Department of Housing and Urban Affairs, "Taylor, Bean & Whitaker Mortgage Corporation and Home America Mortgage, Inc., Settled Civil Claims Related to Failing to Comply with Federal Housing Administration Underwriting Requirements," Housing and FHA, 2015-CF-1806, September 9, 2015.

26. Tom Schoenberg, "Fannie Mae Officials Kept Quiet about Taylor Bean Mortgage Fraud," *Seattle Times*, July 15, 2011.

27. Mark Calabria, "Getting Government Out of the Mortgage Business, DOJ-Style," *Cato at Liberty* (blog), Cato Institute, September 19, 2014.

28. Mark Calabria, "The Mortgage Industry-Government Revolving Door," *Cato at Liberty* (blog), March 15, 2011.

29. See Section 2129 of the Housing and Economic Recovery Act of 2008.

CHAPTER 3

1. "Jack Straw," as performed by the Grateful Dead, Songwriters: Robert Hunter and Bob Weir. "Jack Straw" lyrics © Ice Nine Publishing Co., Inc.

2. See Mary Childs, *The Bond King: How One Man Made a Market, Built an Empire, and Lost It All* (New York: Flatiron Books, 2022).

3. See U.S. Securities and Exchange Commission, "U.S. Credit Markets: Interconnectedness and the Effects of the COVID-19 Economic Shock," October 2020.

4. Michael Fleming et al., "The Federal Reserve's Market Functioning Purchases," Federal Reserve Bank of New York Report no. 998, December 2021.

5. Karan Kaul and Laurie Goodman, "Nonbank Servicer Regulation: New Capital and Liquidity Requirements Don't Offer Enough Loss Protection," Urban Institute, Housing Finance Policy Center Brief, February 25, 2016.

6. Congressional Research Service, "Real Estate Investment Trusts (REITs) and the Foreign Investment in Real Property Tax Act (FIRPTA): Overview and Recent Tax Revisions," Report R44421, July 14, 2016.

7. *Morrissey v.Commissioner*, 296 U.S. 344 (1935).

8. Jiakai Chen et al., "Dealers and the Dealer of Last Resort: Evidence from MBS Markets in the COVID-19 Crisis," Federal Reserve Bank of New York Staff Report Number 93, July 2020.

9. U.S. Department of the Treasury, Financial Stability Oversight Council, 2013 Annual Report, p. 7.

10. U.S. Department of the Treasury, Financial Stability Oversight Council, 2019 Annual Report, p. 43.

11. Financial Stability Oversight Council, 2019 Annual Report, p. 88.

12. You Suk Kim et al., "Liquidity Crises in the Mortgage Market" *Brookings Papers on Economic Activity* (Spring 2018): 347-413.

13. Data as reported by primary dealers to the Federal Reserve Bank of New York. Federal Reserve Bank of New York, "Primary Dealer Statistics," January 28, 1998 to present.

14. Vikram Rao, head bond trader of Capital Group, cited in Sean Foley et al., "Contagious Margin Calls: How COVID-19 Threatened Global Stock Market Liquidity," *Journal of Financial Markets* 59, Part A (June 2022), https://doi.org/10.1016/j.finmar.2021.100689.

15. James Collin Harkrader and Michael Puglia, "Fixed Income Market Structure: Treasuries vs. Agency MBS," FEDS Notes, August 25, 2020, https://doi.org/10.17016/2380-7172.2622.

16. Rajesh Narayanan and Meredith E. Rhodes, "When Safe Became Risky: The Information Sensitivity of Subprime RMBS during the Financial Crisis of 2007-2009," SSRN, February 21, 2022, https://dx.doi.org/10.2139/ssrn.4040319.

17. Zhiguo He and Zhaogang Song, "Agency MBS as Safe Assets," National Bureau of Economic Research Working Paper no. 29899, April 2022, https://doi.org/10.3386/w29899.

18. Chase P. Ross, "Safe Asset Migration," SSRN, May 22, 2020, https://dx.doi.org/10.2139/ssrn.3549991.

19. Mark Calabria, "FHFA Director Mark Calabria's Statement at the Financial Stability Oversight Council Principals Meeting," prepared remarks, June 11, 2021.

20. Stefan Gissler, Borghan Narajabad, and Daniel K. Tarullo, "Federal Home Loan Banks and Financial Stability," Harvard Public Law Working Paper no. 22-20, June 23, 2022, http://dx.doi.org/10.2139/ssrn.4135685.

21. Financial Stability Board, "Holistic Review of the March Market Turmoil," November 17, 2020, p. 2.

CHAPTER 4

1. Whitney Airgood-Obrycki et al., "Renters' Responses to Financial Stress during the Pandemic," Harvard University, Joint Center for Housing Studies, April 8, 2021.

2. Marianne Bitler et al., "The Social Safety Net in the Wake of COVID-19," National Bureau of Economic Research Working Paper no. 27796, September 2020, https://doi.org/10.3386/w27796.

3. Kif Leswing, "New Jersey Needs Volunteers Who Know COBOL, a 60-Year-Old Programming Language," CNBC, April 6, 2020.

4. Margalit Fox, "Cushing N. Dolbeare, 78, Expert on Low-Income Housing Policy, Dies," *New York Times,* March 24, 2005.

5. The Freddie property search tool can be found at https://myhome.freddiemac.com/renting/lookup.

6. Data in this section rely on the 2018 Rental Housing Finance Survey, United States Bureau of the Census.

7. 2018 Rental Housing Finance Survey.

8. Author's estimate from 2018 Rental Housing Finance Survey.

9. Joint Center for Housing Studies of Harvard University, "America's Rental Housing 2022," p. 37.

10. Rep. Al Green, "Congressman Al Green: 'The Rent Must Be Paid, Not Delayed,'" press release, September 16, 2020.

11. Emily Benfer et al., "The COVID-19 Eviction Crisis: An Estimated 30–40 Million People in America Are at Risk," Aspen Institute, August 7, 2020.

12. Yuliya Panfil and David Spievack, "What Happened to the Eviction Tsunami?," FiveThirtyEight, January 11, 2022.

13. U.S. Census Bureau, "Household Pulse Survey Data Tables."

14. Christian Britschgi, "The Eviction Tsunami That Wasn't," *Reason,* August 10, 2021.

15. Salim Furth, "False Alarm," *The Bridge*, Mercatus Center, August 24, 2020.

CHAPTER 5

1. Bureau of Labor Statistics (BLS) Current Employment Statistics–CES (National).

2. BLS, Current Employment Statistics (National).

3. Black Knight, "Black Knight's January 2022 Mortgage Monitor," March 7, 2022.

4. Juan M. Sánchez and Olivia Wilkinson, "Forbearance during COVID-19: How Many Borrowers Used It, and for How Long?," *On the Economy* (blog), Federal Reserve Bank of St. Louis, May 31, 2022.

5. N. Edward Coulson, Thao Le, and Lily Shen, "Tenant Rights, Eviction, and Rent Affordability," SSRN, July 4, 2020, https://dx.doi.org/10.2139/ssrn.3641859.

6. Rebecca Diamond, Adam M. Guren, and Rose Tan, "The Effect of Foreclosures on Homeowners, Tenants, and Landlords," National Bureau of Economic Research Working Paper no. 27358, June 2020, https://doi.org/10.3386/w27358.

7. Emily A. Benfer et al., "Eviction, Health Inequity, and the Spread of COVID-19: Housing Policy as a Primary Pandemic Mitigation Strategy," *Journal of Urban Health* 98, no. 1 (January 7, 2021): 1–12, https://doi.org/10.1007%2Fs11524 -020-00502-1.

8. See Andrew R. Zolopa et al., "HIV and Tuberculosis Infection in San Francisco's Homeless Adults: Prevalence and Risk Factors in a Representative Sample," *JAMA* 272, no. 6 (August 10, 1994): 455-61; Andreas Pilarinos et al., "The Association between Residential Eviction and Syringe Sharing among a Prospective Cohort of Street-Involved Youth," *Harm Reduction Journal* 14, no. 1 (May 12, 2017): 1-6, https://doi.org/10.1186/s12954-017-0150-5; and Linda M. Niccolai, Kim M. Blankenship, and Danya E. Keene, "Eviction from Renter-Occupied Households and Rates of Sexually Transmitted Infections: A County-Level Ecological Analysis," *Sexually Transmitted Diseases* 46, no. 1 (January 2019): 63–68, https://doi.org/10 .1097/OLQ.0000000000000904.

9. *New Ideas for Refinancing and Restructuring Mortgage Loans, September 14, 2011, before the Housing Subcommittee, Committee on Banking, Housing and Urban Affairs,* U.S. Senate (testimony from Mark Calabria).

10. Bureau of Labor Statistic, "State Unemployment Rates in 2010," The Economics Daily, March 1, 2011.

11. See Casey B. Mulligan, "Foreclosures, Enforcement, and Collections Under the Federal Mortgage Modification Guidelines," National Bureau of Economic Research (NBER) Working Paper no. 15777, February 2010, https://doi.org/10.3386/w15777; and Casey B. Mulligan, Means-Tested Mortgage Modification: Homes Saved or Income Destroyed?," NBER Working Paper no. 15281, August 2009, https://doi.org/10.3386/w15281.

12. Kathleen C. Engel and Patricia A. McCoy, *The Subprime Virus: Reckless Credit, Regulatory Failure, and Next Steps* (Oxford: Oxford University Press, 2011), p. 131.

13. Kristopher Gerardi, Lauren Lambie-Hanson, and Paul Willen, "Lessons Learned from Mortgage-Borrower Policies and Outcomes," in *Recession Remedies: Lessons Learned from the U.S. Economic Policy Response to COVID-19*, eds. Wendy Edelberg, Louise Sheiner, and David Wessel (Washington: Brookings Institution Press, 2022), p. 186.

14. Pamela Foohey, Dalié Jiménez, and Christopher K. Odinet, "The Folly of Credit as Pandemic Relief," *UCLA Law Review Discourse* 68 (June 23, 2020): 126–145.

15. Jackson T. Anderson, David M. Harrison, and Michael J. Seiler, "Reducing Strategic Forbearance under the CARES Act: An Experimental Approach Utilizing Recourse Attestation,"*Journal of Real Estate Finance and Economics* 65, no. 2 (2022): 230-260, https://doi.org/10.1007/s11146-021-09842-4.

16. Michael J. Seiler, "The Effect of Perceived Lender Characteristics and Market Conditions on Strategic Mortgage Defaults," *Journal of Real Estate Finance and Economics* 48, no. 2 (2014): 256-70, https://doi.org/10.1007/s11146-012-9388-6.

17. JPMorgan Chase & Co. Institute, "Did Mortgage Forbearance Reach the Right Homeowners?," policy brief, December 2020.

CHAPTER 6

1. Matt Schuffham, "U.S. Mortgage Industry Braces for More Strain as Support Talks Stall," Reuters, April 10, 2020.

2. Katy O'Donnell, "Trump's Libertarian Housing Regulator Refuses to Bail Out Mortgage Firms with Public Money," *Politico,* April 16, 2020.

3. O'Donnell, "Trump's Libertarian Housing Regulator."

4. O'Donnell, "Trump's Libertarian Housing Regulator."

5. U.S. Department of the Treasury, Financial Stability Oversight Council, 2019 Annual Report, p. 122.

6. Diane Olick, "Mortgage Industry Fires Back at Regulator Who Refuses to Help Servicers Getting Slammed by Payment Delay Requests," CNBC, April 8, 2020.

7. "Nationstar Mortgage Completes Acquisition of Servicing Assets of Aurora Bank," Business Wire, June 29, 2012; and "U.S. Bankruptcy Court Approves Sale

of ResCap Mortgage Servicing and Origination Platform Assets to Ocwen and Walter Investment, and Sale of Whole Loan Portfolio to Berkshire Hathaway," *Business Wire*, November 21, 2012.

8. "FirstBank Puerto Rico Announces Acquisition of 10 Doral Bank Branches in the Island," Business Wire, February 27, 2015.

9. Federal Deposit Insurance Corporation, "Failed Bank List."

10. R. Christopher Whalen, "Calabria's FHFA Fans the Fires of Contagion," *Institutional Risk Analyst,* April 5, 2020.

11. Quicken is now known as Rocket Mortgage.

12. Federal Housing Finance Agency, "FHFA Proposes Updated Minimum Financial Eligibility Requirements for Fannie Mae and Freddie Mac Seller/Servicers," news release, January 31, 2020.

13. Laurence Platt, "Mortgage Servicers are Getting the Short End of the Stick Under the CARES Act," *HousingWire,* June 5, 2020.

14. Alan Rappeport, Matthew Goldstein, and Jeanna Smialek, "Excluded from Bailouts, Mortgage Servicers Face Cash Crunch," *New York Times,* April 20, 2020.

15. Rappeport, Goldstein, and Smialek, "Excluded from Bailouts."

16. John Dizard, "US Is on Course for a Downward Spiral of Mortgage Failures," *Financial Times,* April 10, 2020.

17. Black Knight, Mortgage Monitor, July 2020.

18. Matt Schuffham, "U.S. Treasury Panel Wants Mortgage Servicer Liquidity Support as Missed Payments Rise," Reuters, April 7, 2020.

19. Karan Kaul and Laurie Goodman, "The Price Tag for Keeping 29 Million Families in Their Homes: $162 Billion," *Urban Wire* (blog), Urban Institute, March 27, 2020.

20. Karan Kaul and Ted Tozer, "The Need for a Federal Liquidity Facility for Government Loan Servicing," Urban Institute brief, July 17, 2020.

21. U.S. Department of the Treasury, "Readout of Call of the Task Force on Nonbank Mortgage Liquidity," press release, April 1, 2020.

22. Andrew Ackerman, "Fannie, Freddie Unlikely to Aid Mortgage Companies as Payments Dry Up, FHFA Chief Says," *Wall Street Journal,* April 7, 2020.

23. Karan Kaul, "A Liquidity Vehicle for Mortgage Servicing Advances Is in Consumers' Best Interest," Policy Commons, April 9, 2020.

24. See the Ginnie Mae, "Global Market Analysis Report," December 2021.

25. Elizabeth Dexheimer, "Wall Street Puts Blame on Calabria for Blocking Mortgage Aid," Bloomberg Law, April 13, 2020.

26. Katy O'Donnell, "Trump's Libertarian Housing Regulator Refuses to Bail Out Mortgage Firms with Public Money," *Politico*, April 16, 2020.

27. Karan Kaul and Laurie Goodman, "Nonbank Servicer Regulation: New Capital and Liquidity Requirements Don't Offer Enough Loss Protection," Urban Institute brief, February 25, 2016.

CHAPTER 7

1. Walter D'Lima, Luis Arturo Lopez, and Archana Pradhan, "COVID-19 and Housing Market Effects: Evidence from U.S. Shutdown Orders," *Real Estate Economics* 50, no. 2 (Summer 2022): 303–39, https://doi.org/10.1111/1540-6229.12368.

2. Dana Anderson, "Redfin Survey: 1 in 4 Americans Want to Live Somewhere Else Due to Their Local Government's Pandemic Response," Redfin News, November 12, 2020.

3. Anderson, "Redfin Survey."

4. Lily Katz, "The Housing Market Is Hotter in Counties with Fewer Coronavirus Cases per Capita," Redfin News, December 10, 2020.

5. Dana Anderson, "Homebuyer Interest in Rural Areas Rises, with Prices Up 11% in July," Redfin News, August 17, 2020.

6. Tim Ellis, "63% of 2020 Homebuyers Made an Offer Sight Unseen, Shattering Previous Record" Redfin News, January 14, 2021.

7. Ellis, "63% of 2020 Homebuyers."

8. Patrick Gray, "The Pandemic Created a Perceived New Class Division: The Laptop Class vs. Everyone Else," TechRepublic, June 25, 2021.

9. Dana Anderson, "1 in 4 First-Time Homebuyers Are Using Stimulus Money for Down Payment: Redfin Survey," Redfin News, February 4, 2022.

10. Anderson, "1 in 4 First-Time Homebuyers."

11. Alina Ptaszynski, "Let Yourself In. Redfin Launches Self-Tour Feature for Vacant Listings," Redfin News, April 23, 2020.

12. Margo H. K. Tank et al., "Coronavirus: Federal and State Governments Work Quickly to Enable Remote Online Notarization to Meet Global Crisis," DLA Piper Financial Services Alert, August 25, 2021.

13. Dima Williams, "Real Estate as an Essential Business," *Forbes*, April 2, 2020.

14. Jason Shefferd, "Are Realtors 'Essential Business' Workers?," *Colleges of Law* (blog), April 14, 2020.

15. Will Parker, "Zillow's Shuttered Home-Flipping Business Lost $881 Million in 2021," *Wall Street Journal*, February 10, 2022.

16. Federal Housing Finance Agency, "FHFA Issues RFI on Appraisal-Related Policies, Practices, and Processes," news release, December 28, 2020.

17. See "Selling Guidance Related to COVID-19," Freddie Mac Bulletin 2020, March 31, 2020.

18. National Association of Realtors, REALTORS® Confidence Index.

19. Scholastica (Gay) Cororaton, "All-Cash Sales Are Rising Sharply amid Intense Buyer Competition," *Economist's Outlook* (blog), National Association of Realtors, May 24, 2021.

20. Rose Quint, "Some Buyers Turning to New Construction," *Eye on Housing* (blog), National Association of Home Builders, July 29, 2022.

21. U.S. Census Bureau, "New Residential Sales."

22. Lisa Johnson Mandell, "Bunkers on the Brain: 5 Homes for Sale Outfitted with Underground Shelters," Realtor.com, March 4, 2022.

23. Consumer Financial Protection Bureau, "Treatment of Certain COVID-19 Related Loss Mitigation Options under the Real Estate Settlement Procedures Act (RESPA), Regulation X; Interim Final Rule," 85 FR 39055, June 30, 2020.

24. Consumer Financial Protection Bureau, "CFPB and FHFA Announce Borrower Protection Program," press release, April 15, 2020.

25. National Association of Realtors, "NAR Commends FHFA Move Delivering Certainty to American Consumers, Homeowners," press release, May 14, 2020.

CHAPTER 8

1. National Association of Realtors, "Existing-Home Sales," press release, September 2022.

2. Freddie Mac, "Refinance Trends in 2020," research note, March 5, 2021.

3. Marcos Dinerstein, Zheli He, and Xiaoyue Sun, "Background: Marginal Propensities to Consume in the 2021 Economy," Penn Wharton Budget Model brief, February 3, 2021.

4. Dinerstein, He, and Sun, "Background."

5. Sumit Agarwal et al., "Refinancing Inequality during the COVID Pandemic," Federal Deposit Insurance Corporation (FDIC) Center for Financial Research Working Paper no. 2021-08, November 2021.

6. Ben Lane, "Fannie Mae, Freddie Mac Will Allow Borrowers Who Took Forbearance to Refinance Their Mortgage," *HousingWire,* May 19, 2020.

7. Mortgage Bankers Association "IMB Production Volumes and Profits Reach Record Highs in 2020," press release, April 13, 2021.

8. FDIC, "FDIC Quarterly Banking Profile," depository data.

9. Federal Reserve Bank of St. Louis, "Financial Statements: Federal Reserve Bank of St. Louis," March 10, 2022.

CHAPTER 9

1. David Stevens, "The Adverse Market Fee the GSEs Added to Refinance Loans Is Unwarranted," *HousingWire,* November 2, 2020.

2. U.S. House Committee on Financial Services, "Waters and Clay Slam New Adverse Market Fee That Could Cost Homeowners Thousands of Additional Dollars," press release, August 14, 2020.

3. Mortgage Bankers Association, "MBA Statement on the GSEs' Adverse Market Refinance Fee," press release, August 12, 2020.

4. Federal Housing Finance Agency, "Adverse Market Refinance Fee Implementation Now December 1," news release, August 25, 2020.

5. Benedict I. Truman, Man-Huei Chang, and Ramal Moonesinghe, "Provisional COVID-19 Age-Adjusted Death Rates, by Race and Ethnicity—United States, 2020–2021," Centers for Disease Control and Prevention Morbidity and Mortality Weekly Report 71, no 17 (April 29, 2022): 601-5, http://dx.doi.org /10.15585/mmwr.mm7117e2.

6. U.S. Department of the Treasury, "Home Affordable Modification Program (HAMP) Performance Summary," December 2021.

7. U.S. Department of the Treasury, "Special Inspector General for the Troubled Asset Relief Program Semiannual Report to Congress: April 1, 2021– September 30, 2021."

CHAPTER 10

1. Susan Wharton Gates, Days of Slaughter: Inside the Fall of Freddie Mac and Why It Could Happen Again (Baltimore: Johns Hopkins University Press, 2017).

2. Charles S. Clark, "A Tell-All about Working at Freddie Mac during the Housing Crisis," Government Executive, May 16, 2017.

3. See Section 1117 of the Housing and Economic Recovery Act of 2008, "Temporary Authority for Purchase of Obligations of Regulated Entities by Secretary of Treasury," Public Law 110–289, July 30, 2008.

CHAPTER 11

1. Oversight on the Monetary Policy Report to Congress Pursuant to the Full Employment and Balanced Growth Act of 1978, February 11, 2016, before the Committee on Banking, Housing, and Urban Affairs, 114th Cong. 40 (2016) (Federal Reserve's First Monetary Report for 2016).

2. Nominations of Bimal Patel, Todd M. Harper, Rodney Hood, and Mark Anthony Calabria, First Session, February 14, 2019, before the Committee on Banking, Housing, and Urban Affairs, 116th Cong. 25 (2019).

CHAPTER 12

1. See Ernesto Dal Bó, "Regulatory Capture: A Review," Oxford Review of Economic Policy 22, no. 2 (July 2006): 203-25, https://doi.org/10.1093/oxrep /grj013; and G. P. Manish and Colin O'Reilly, "Banking Regulation, Regulatory

Capture and Inequality," *Public Choice* 180, no. 1 (July 2019): 145–164, https://doi
.org/10.1007/s11127-018-0501-0. The foundation of modern economic literature
on regulatory captures begins with George J. Stigler and Claire Friedland, "What
Can Regulators Regulate? The Case of Electricity," *Journal of Law and Economics* 5
(October 1962): 1–16; Sam Peltzman, "Toward a More General Theory of Regulation," *Journal of Law and Economics* 19, no. 2 (August 1976): 211–40; and George
Stigler, "The Economic Theory of Regulation," *Bell Journal of Economics and Management Science* 2, no. 1 (Spring 1971): 3–21.

2. Paul Krugman, "What Happened to Asia," in *Global Competition and Inte-
gration*, eds. Ryuzo Sato, Rama V. Ramachandran, and Kazuo Mino (New York:
Springer, 1999), pp. 315–27.

CHAPTER 13

1. Robert J. Shiller, *Narrative Economics: How Stories Go Viral and Drive Major
Economic Events* (Princeton: Princeton University Press, 2019), p. 278.

2. Department of Homeland Security, "Creation of the Department of
Homeland Security."

3. Bethany McLean and Peter Elkind, *The Smartest Guys in the Room: The
Amazing Rise and Scandalous Fall of Enron* (New York: Penguin, 2013).

4. Bethany McLean, *Shaky Ground: The Strange Saga of the U.S. Mortgage Giants*
(New York: Columbia Global Reports, 2015).

5. See Terry M. Moe, *The Organization of Interests: Incentives and the Internal
Dynamics of Political Interest Groups* (Chicago: University of Chicago Press, 1980);
and Mancur Olson Jr., *The Logic of Collective Action: Public Goods and the Theory of
Groups* (Cambridge: Harvard University Press, 1965).

CHAPTER 14

1. Simon W. Bowmaker, *When the President Calls: Conversations with Economic
Policymakers* (Cambridge, MA: MIT Press, 2019), p. 484.

2. David Drezner, "Russia and the United States, Eighteen Months Later,"
Foreign Policy, February 1, 2010; and Benn Steil and Dinah Walker, "The Dangers
of Debt: Russia and China's GSE Dumping," *Geo-Graphics* (blog), Council on Foreign Relations, June 15, 2010.

3. Aaron L. Nielson, "Three Views of the Administrative State: Lessons from
Collins v. Yellen," in *Cato Supreme Court Review: 2020–2021*, ed. Trevor Burrus
(Washington: Cato Institute, 2021), p. 141–63.

4. Michael Krimminger and Mark A. Calabria, "The Conservatorships of
Fannie Mae and Freddie Mac: Actions Violate HERA and Established Insolvency
Principles," Cato Institute Working Paper no. 26, February 9, 2015.

5. For an in-depth discussion of the structure of financial regulators, see Paul Tucker, *Unelected Power: The Quest for Legitimacy in Central Banking and the Regulatory State* (Princeton: Princeton University Press, 2018).

6. Adam C. Gillette, "Form over Function: How *Collins v. Yellen* Signals a Threat to the Independence of Multimember Financial Regulatory Agencies," *North Carolina Banking Institute* 26, no. 1 (2022): 109–35.

7. Constitutional Accountability Center, "Brief of Members of Congress as *Amici Curia* in Support of Defendants-Appellees," *Collins v. Mnuchin,* no. 17-20364.

Index

Note: The letter n designates a numbered note.

About the Author

Dr. Mark A. Calabria is a senior advisor to the Cato Institute. He previously served as director of financial regulation at the Cato Institute, where he cofounded Cato's Center for Monetary and Financial Alternatives.

Calabria is the former director of the Federal Housing Finance Agency (FHFA), which regulates and supervises Fannie Mae, Freddie Mac, and the Federal Home Loan Banks. During his service at the FHFA, he led the agency's response to COVID-19 and also laid the groundwork for a removal of Fannie Mae and Freddie Mac from government conservatorship. Calabria also revitalized the FHFA as a prudential regulator, establishing the agency's new research, accounting policy, and resolution divisions.

Before he headed the FHFA, Calabria served as chief economist to Vice President Mike Pence. In that role, he led the vice president's work on taxes, trade, labor, financial services, manufacturing, and general economic issues, including serving as a key member of the team that enacted the Tax Cuts and Jobs Act of 2017, and on the team that crafted the United States-Mexico-Canada trade agreement. Calabria served as the vice president's primary representative for the U.S.-Japan Economic Dialogue. He also represented Vice President Pence on the White House Ocean Policy Committee.

Calabria served as a senior aide to the U.S. Senate Committee on Banking, Housing, and Urban Affairs under chairs Richard Shelby and Phil Gramm. During his Senate service, he acted as the primary drafter of the Housing and Economic Recovery Act of 2008, which established a stronger regulatory framework for the government-sponsored housing enterprises. He also led the banking committee's response to Hurricane Katrina, as well as its work on the Shelby-Dodd Flood Insurance Reform and Modernization Act of 2008, which served as the basis for the Biggert-Waters Flood Insurance Reform Act of 2012.

Prior to his Senate service, Calabria served as the deputy assistant secretary for regulatory affairs in the Office of Housing at the U.S. Department of Housing and Urban Development (HUD), where he supervised HUD's regulation of the mortgage and real estate market under the Real Estate Settlement Procedures Act.

Calabria has also held positions with Harvard University's Joint Center for Housing Studies, the National Association of Realtors, and the National Association of Home Builders. He holds a doctorate in economics from George Mason University.

Calabria resides in Washington, DC. He is an avid scuba diver as well as an enthusiast for rescue cats and live music. He can be followed on Twitter at the username @MarkCalabria.

About the Cato Institute

Founded in 1977, the Cato Institute is a public policy research foundation dedicated to broadening the parameters of policy debate to allow consideration of more options that are consistent with the principles of limited government, individual liberty, and peace. To that end, the Institute strives to achieve greater involvement of the intelligent, concerned lay public in questions of policy and the proper role of government.

The Institute is named for *Cato's Letters*, libertarian pamphlets that were widely read in the American Colonies in the early 18th century and played a major role in laying the philosophical foundation for the American Revolution.

Despite the achievement of the nation's Founders, today virtually no aspect of life is free from government encroachment. A pervasive intolerance for individual rights is shown by government's arbitrary intrusions into private economic transactions and its disregard for civil liberties. And while freedom around the globe has notably increased in the past several decades, many countries have moved in the opposite direction, and most governments still do not respect or safeguard the wide range of civil and economic liberties.

To address those issues, the Cato Institute undertakes an extensive publications program on the complete spectrum of policy issues. Books, monographs, and shorter studies are commissioned to examine the federal budget, Social Security, regulation, military spending, international trade, and myriad other issues.

In order to maintain its independence, the Cato Institute accepts no government funding. Contributions are received from foundations, corporations, and individuals, and other revenue is generated from the sale of publications. The Institute is a nonprofit, tax-exempt, educational foundation under Section 501(c)3 of the Internal Revenue Code.

CATO INSTITUTE
1000 Massachusetts Ave. NW
Washington, DC 20001
www.cato.org